Savannah
Guidebook

Savannah Guidebook

BY

POLLY WYLLY COOPER

&

LAURA CONNERAT LAWTON

Cherokee Publishing Company
Atlanta, Georgia
2015

Library of Congress Cataloging-in-Publication Data

Manufactured in the United States of America
First Edition

ISBN: 978-0-87797-398-0 Trade Paper
ISBN: 978-0-87797-401-7 Epub
ISBN: 978-0-87797-402-4 Mobi
20 19 18 17 16 15   10 9 8 7 6 5 4 3 2 1

Editing | Alexa Selph
Design | Pamela Buie and Kenneth W. Boyd
Front Cover Photography | Jonas N. Jordan
Inside Cover Photography | Matthew Propst, Robb Helfrick,
Polly Cooper, Jeri Nokes, and Daniel Grantham Jr.
Typeface | Electra 10.5/13
www.SavannahGuidebook.net

Cherokee Publishing Company
P. O. Box 1730, Marietta, Georgia 30061
kwbcherokee@bellsouth.net

Dedication

We salute these seven courageous women, whose inspiration in 1955 sparked the beginning of our preservation movement, making our historic district one of the loveliest in the United States today.

"The Seven" were filled with burning indignation in 1954 when our colorful City Market building was demolished for a multilevel cement parking garage.

A year later, when the historic Davenport House was scheduled to be torn down for its Savannah gray bricks, they banded together to save it just hours before the wrecking ball could get a swing at it.

So began Historic Savannah, Inc., an organization that is now a model to the world. Memories of "The Seven" have inspired us throughout the writing of this guidebook in protecting our city's heritage through advocacy, education, and community involvement.

Sitting (left to right): Lucy Barrow McIntire, Elinor Adler Dillard, Anna Colquitt Hunter
Standing (left to right): Nola McEvoy Roos, Jane Adair Wright, Dorothy Ripley Roebling, Katherine Judkins Clark

Contents

Foreword

Having grown up in Savannah, I have fond memories of this quiet, antebellum, moss-draped city. When I visit, I recall being a "stag" on the debutante scene in the 1950s, dancing to Lester Lanin's band at parties hosted by songwriter Johnny Mercer, celebrating Saint Patrick's Day with a few pints of green beer, and having private times to myself—hunting and fishing before dawn at my father's plantation in South Carolina.

The city is, indeed, a national treasure, and Savannahians are rightfully proud of their two-square-mile historic district, which is a registered National Historic District Landmark. The Historic Savannah Foundation, other organizations, and many spirited individuals deserve thunderous applause for preventing wanton destruction of classic architectural gems. Through their combined efforts, more than eleven hundred buildings have been restored.

Savannah is an ideal city for walking. James Oglethorpe, founder of the colony of Georgia, laid out the original four squares as his schematic design for the city. In successive years, this design was followed until Savannah had twenty-four squares and Forsyth Park.

Springtime finds tourists relaxing on benches in the squares and enjoying the fragrance of flowering magnolia, wisteria, tea olive, pink and white dogwoods, and azaleas. Savannah hosted the 1996 Olympic sailing events in the Wilmington River, right in the waters where I learned to sail. I competed in many regattas at the nearby Savannah Yacht Club.

This guidebook, written by my old friends Polly Wylly Cooper and Laura Connerat Lawton, will help visitors discover the same secrets and charm of this lovely city that I experienced in my youth.

—Ted Turner

A Tribute to Emmeline King Cooper

The late Emmeline Cooper coauthored the original *Visitor's Guide to Savannah* in 1995. Her research gave the book its authenticity, and her personality is reflected in many pages of this new and updated *Savannah Guidebook*.

She moved to Savannah from New York at age five and later married Robert Scotland Cooper. They had three sons. Emmeline was fluent in Italian, played the recorder, and sang harmony with Robert at gatherings with friends. Emmeline and Robert were always loved and admired by everyone privileged to know them.

Emmeline King Cooper
1929-2007

A Very Special Thank You

*to the many artists who have willingly contributed their talents
to make this the definitive guidebook on Savannah.*

Vivian Austin

Susie Chisholm, NSS

Daniel L. Grantham, Jr.

Robb Helfrick

Jonas N. Jordan

Jean Lim

Billy Nelson

Haywood Nichols

Jeri Nokes

Augusta Oelschig

Lynda Potter

Matthew Propst

Dr. Preston Russell

Charles St. Arnaud

Kitty Strozier

We especially want to thank the following artists

*whose generosity allowed us to use so many of their
beautiful works in order to fully bring this book to life:*

Jill Howell

Dan Kaufman

Pamela Lee

the late Herb Woo

Our publisher, Ken Boyd

Courtesy of the illustrator, Jill Howell

HESTER & ZIPPERER FEED & SEED   302 W. ST. JULIAN ST.   SAVANNAH, GA.

Courtesy of the Herb Woo family

Our illustrators and photographers deserve special recognition.

This page shows just a small sampling of their talent. Be on the lookout for their artwork throughout this book and in the gift shops around Savannah.

Courtesy of the artist, Pamela Lee

Courtesy of Dan Kaufman,
Studio Kaufman LLC

Courtesy of the artist, Jean Lim

Introduction

Savannah Guidebook is special. It has been written by two sixth-generation cousins who were born in Savannah, left for a spell, and years later returned to their beloved hometown. They embraced the changes and became connoisseurs of local history.

Both authors' ancestors go back to early colonial days. Their families were leaders in the struggling Georgia colony, were captured by the British in the Revolution, and stood firm through the Civil War. Later their fathers, both lawyers, shared an office building on Johnson Square. Both authors became members of the National Society of Colonial Dames of America in the State of Georgia.

As teens they wrote a column for the *Savannah Morning News* called *A Glance Askance*. Today, fifty years later, once again they have sharpened their pencils. With guidance from their publisher, Ken Boyd of Cherokee Publishing Company, who also grew up in Savannah, they have compiled *Savannah Guidebook*. Ken Boyd knows his hometown well and steered the production of this guidebook through the meticulous research, interviews, design and editing. The authors have thoroughly enjoyed working alongside him and respect his tireless determination to compile the definitive guidebook on Savannah. Through the efforts of these local authors, the result is this complete guide, written with humor, knowledge, and respect for their hometown. Jamal Touré's knowledge of African American history and the Gullah/Geechee language and culture were a valuable contribution to the African American Journey in this guidebook.

In preparing *Savannah Guidebook*, we accepted no remuneration from the institutions and establishments we have included here. Each listing was by invitation only, and the information in this guide is intended to enhance the experience of visitors to this magical city. We will continue to seek additional appropriate listings. Listings do not represent endorsements or recommendations by the authors or the publisher. All reasonable attempts have been made to ensure that the information presented was accurate and current as of the initial publication date.

Many tour companies make seasonal adjustments in their hours and days of operation. For some site locations GPS coordinates are provided. If the GPS coordinates do not place you at the front door, they will get you close enough to the location. Suggestions and corrections are welcome.

Cherokee Publishing Company, P.O. Box 1730, Marietta, GA 30061
kwbcherokee@bellsouth.net • 800-653-3952

Savannah through the Years

The year was 1732. The place was London. James Edward Oglethorpe, a distinguished soldier and prison reformer at age thirty-six, was urging King George II to sign a charter for a new colony where people "of decayed circumstances" could begin a fresh life. The colony would be called "Georgia" in honor of the king.

Oglethorpe had three strong arguments: the prospect of profits from raw materials, protection for South Carolina from the Spaniards to the south, and asylum for those fleeing religious persecution.

James Edward Oglethorpe
1696-1785
Courtesy, Oglethorpe University

Ink flowed from the royal quill on April 21, 1732, as King George II lowered his bewigged and powdered head to sign the charter for the thirteenth and last British colony in America.

"Non sibi sed aliis" (Not for self but for others) was the Latin motto chosen by Oglethorpe and the twenty other men who served as trustees for Georgia.

Next came the task of selecting settlers from the hundreds who volunteered. By early November, thirty-five families had been enrolled, and Captain John Thomas was readying the frigate *Ann* for a long sea voyage. What a change for young Oglethorpe—from a leisured life at Westbrook, his family estate in Surrey, to a leap into the unknown as leader of a shipload of men, women, and children, not to mention hogs, chickens, goats, and geese!

On November 16, 1732, the *Ann* sailed down the River Thames with the town of Gravesend at her stern and new beginnings beyond her bow.

Life Aboard the Good Ship Ann

Here are entries from a copy of the ship's log of Thomas Christie, recorded aboard the *Ann*:

> Novr. 24—Wind E.S.E. & E. by N. Moderate & fair. ¼ Hazey Wheather & fresh. ¼ No Candle to be burnt but in Lanthorn & Ordrd. Mr. Kilbury to go round Every Bodys Cradle & see all the lights put out by Eight. Mist and Lost a black lurching Bitch belong to Mr. Oglethorpe. Supposed to be flung Over board by some of the Sailors.

> Decr. 18—Wind East. Fair Whethr ¼ Mr. Oglethorpe caught a Dolphin and being Aprised of some Big-Bellyd. Women in the Ship Longing, gave it all amongst them withot. Tasting any himself.

> Decr. 20—The Long Boat was hoisted out And Mr. Oglethorpe, Dr. Herbert (ship's chaplain) Cap. Thomas, & some Others went a Dolphin fishing wth. Fishgig all round the Ship. But undr. an Unbrella, the wheather being very hot.

Oglethorpe Meets Tomochichi

Oglethorpe carried a dream in his heart and a plan in his pocket when land was sighted in February 1733. Landing at Charles Town in South Carolina, Oglethorpe proceeded with Colonel William Bull of South Carolina to Port Royal and further down the coast. Oglethorpe chose a town site on a high bluff, fifteen miles upriver from the Atlantic Ocean. Living there was a tribe of Yamacraw Indians led by the mico (chief) Tomochichi, who gave Oglethorpe permission to settle the land between the Savannah and Altamaha Rivers, plus several offshore islands.

From their first meeting, there was mutual respect between the young Englishman and the aged Indian. Oglethorpe even took Tomochichi and the chief's family back to London in 1734 to the delight of the trustees, as well as King George II and Queen Caroline.

During those first days in Georgia, Oglethorpe laid out a plan for Savannah—a gridlike pattern of streets and lanes with house lots and trust lots (areas for public buildings). Central to each of the four original wards on Yamacraw Bluff was an open space called a *square*. Oglethorpe's city plan was followed as Savannah grew from four to twenty-four squares. Two squares have been eliminated, but today we can still stroll through twenty-two of these green oases here in one of America's earliest planned cities.

Tomochichi, 1650-1739
Mico Chief of the Yamacraw

Oglethorpe's plan also provided for the Trustees' Garden near East Broad and Bay Streets, a ten-acre plot set aside to see which seeds, plants, and cuttings would thrive in Savannah's semitropical climate. It is said that the first cottonseeds were a gift to Oglethorpe from the Spanish leader Don Manuel de Montiano.

Many Countries, Many Languages

Savannah has always celebrated its ethnic diversity. Many languages were spoken in the colony, as well as various Indian dialects.

Aboard the *Ann* came Italian Paul Amatis, hired by the trustees to teach the art of sericulture, or silk production.

Later that year, the *William and Sarah* sailed into the harbor, bringing Jewish settlers. Most spoke Portuguese, and a few spoke German. On board was Dr. Diego (Samuel) Nunes Ribeiro, a physician who was invaluable to the colonists in battling yellow fever.

From Salzburg, Austria, came German-speaking Lutherans, exiled by the Roman Catholic archbishop. Oglethorpe helped them settle nearby at Ebenezer. Slavic accents, filtered through the German language, came with the hardworking, peace-loving Moravians. They arrived in 1736 on the same ship bringing the Church of England clerical brothers, John and Charles Wesley.

Also contributing to the polyglot were French Huguenots and Scottish Highlanders plus natives of Switzerland, Greece, Holland, Wales, and Ireland. When Oglethorpe's ban on slavery was lifted in 1750, slave traders brought human cargo, adding African and West Indian voices.

Georgia was, indeed, a melting pot, in terms of both its ethnic diversity and its environment, since summer temperatures in Savannah often hung (and still do!) in the upper nineties.

Bloody Fighting

The Spaniards to the south resented the growing number of colonists in Georgia. Oglethorpe's spies reported that a Spanish attack was being planned.

An early act of aggression took place on board the British ship *Rebecca* when Captain Robert Jenkins had his ear sliced off by the sword of a Spanish sailor. Captain Jenkins was earmarked for posterity when he brandished the pickled article before Prime Minister Walpole, turning stomachs and inciting warmongers. The War of Jenkins' Ear began in 1739 and lasted eight years.

One of the most strategically significant victories took place during this war at the Battle of Bloody Marsh in 1742. While the Spaniards lounged and lunched in a clearing on St. Simons Island, Oglethorpe and his troops ambushed and attacked, making the salt water run red from casualties that were mostly Spanish. The Spaniards retreated, and King George II awarded Oglethorpe the rank of brigadier general after he returned to England.

The Liberty Boys Plot Revolution

Georgia suffered a great loss when personal matters called Oglethorpe home to England in 1743. His life took a new direction when he met and married Lady Elizabeth Wright, heiress of Cranham Hall. Oglethorpe's boots never touched Georgia's sandy soil again.

Sir James Wright, 1716-1785
Royal Governor, 1760-1782

Courtesy, Georgia Department
of Archives and History

In Georgia the mood was gloomy. Malcontents met and grumbled. The population dwindled. Finally, the trustees relinquished their charter a whole year early.

From 1754 until 1776 Georgia's government was in the hands of a succession of three royal governors. But under the gas lamps at Tondee's Tavern, the Liberty Boys gathered, railing against the constrictions of Mother England. Imagine the agony of loyal-to-the-crown James Habersham when his three sons became Liberty Boys. It was young Joseph Habersham who crashed into a meeting in 1776 and put Royal Governor James Wright under house arrest.

On August 10, 1776, the words of the Declaration of Independence reverberated through the streets of Savannah. The American Revolution had begun.

Revolution, Recovery, and Prosperity

In October 1779 the American allies waged the Siege of Savannah, an unsuccessful effort to wrest the city from the British who had occupied it earlier that year. Supporting the Georgia patriots were French and Irish troops and black volunteers from Haiti, all under the command of the French count Charles-Henri d'Estaing.

Eli Whitney, 1765-1825
Courtesy, Georgia Historical Society

The Pulaski Legion was led by the gallant Polish cavalry officer Count Casimir Pulaski, who was shot from his horse and died a few days later. This was the death ground, too, of Sergeant William Jasper, whose sacrifice is commemorated by the Irish Jasper Greens militia unit and a monument in Madison Square. Nevertheless, Savannah remained in the grip of the British until the Americans finally triumphed in 1783.

The weight of Mother England had been removed, but still the colony did not prosper. When President George Washington visited in 1791, he was honored with a four-day marathon of ceremony and festivity, but the city was only a straggle of wooden houses on sandy streets.

In 1793 a young man sailed south to Savannah from New York City. His name was Eli Whitney, and his mission was to tutor the children of Catherine Littlefield Greene, widow of General Nathanael Greene. Between arithmetic and spelling lessons on Mulberry Grove Plantation, Mr. Whitney devised a machine to facilitate the process of combing seeds from cotton. This invention, the cotton gin (short for engine), speeded the production of cotton. The city's population (11,000 in 1840) doubled to 22,000 by 1860.

More people meant more houses, and many new houses were built, but of Savannah gray brick and stucco rather than flammable wood. In fact, because of disastrous fires, wooden construction was forbidden. William Jay, Charles Cluskey, John Norris, and other creative minds designed the buildings that are the architectural treasure trove of today. By 1856 all twenty-four squares were bustling, and the green expanse of Forsyth Park had been added at the city's southern border. Yes, Savannah was prosperous, but disease was on the horizon and enslaved hands were turning the wheels of progress.

Yellow Fever

Savannah's citizens endured many hardships during the nineteenth century, and the deadly viral disease yellow fever was among them. Although Georgians had dealt with yellow fever since the early days of the colony, they were hit hard by the epidemic of 1820. Already devastated by a major fire that year, they were hit again by yellow fever, which took 650 lives in a very short time.

A second epidemic took place in 1854, killing over one thousand citizens, and in 1876 an even larger number of people lost their lives to the disease. Eventually area residents and physicians realized that yellow fever was spread by mosquitoes, who made their home in the wet, swampy areas around Savannah.

Moving Toward War

As an agrarian economy grew in Savannah, so did the number of slaves—from zero in 1733 to over seven thousand in 1860.

As more land was planted in cotton, the price of slaves escalated. In 1790 a planter paid three hundred dollars for a young healthy male. By 1860 the price was as high as eighteen hundred dollars

Abolitionists called for an end to slavery, but King Cotton could not survive without slaves to plant, cultivate, and harvest. Savannah in 1860 was busy and bustling, but a terrible conflict was about to begin.

War Rips Families Apart

In November 1860 Abraham Lincoln was elected president of the United States. In December, neighboring South Carolina seceded from the Union. Here in Savannah, secession fever raged. War was coming closer.

Under orders from the governor of Georgia, Colonel Alexander Lawton, with the 1st Volunteer Regiment of the Georgia Militia, seized Fort Pulaski on January 3, 1861. The state of Georgia seceded from the Union sixteen days later.

The war that began in 1861, known both as the Civil War and the War Between the States, was one that both North and South thought would soon be over. But from Fort Sumter in 1861 until Appomattox in 1865, the struggle lasted four bloody years. More than six hundred thousand were killed, and another four hundred thousand wounded.

Here follows an oft-told story from the *Georgia History Book*, by Lawrence Hepburn:

> At the end of a hard-fought battle, after the enemy had fled, a mounted Confederate officer rode slowly over the battlefield. He came upon one of his men carefully digging a grave. Next to the shallow hole, the blue-clad body of a Union soldier was laid out.
>
> "Why are you taking such care to bury a Yank?" asked the puzzled officer.
>
> The Confederate soldier looked up with tears streaming down his boyish face, "He's my brother, sir."

Picking Up the Pieces

Progress in Savannah after the war was slow, and problems were many. King Cotton still ruled, but because there was little else on the industrial scene, the economic foundation was fragile.

The construction of the Cotton Exchange in 1886 was a testament to trust in the cotton industry, but in reality, cotton planters were losing their land as prices plummeted. A pound of cotton that brought one dollar in 1866 was sold for just seven cents in the 1890s.

In those days there was little interest in historic preservation. Many buildings were lost to demolition, decay, abuse, and neglect. Then came earthquakes, fires, and hurricanes—a string of natural disasters.

A bright spot in preservation, prior to the founding of Historic Savannah, was the enormously creative use of buildings in the Trustees' Garden area, spearheaded in the 1940s by Mary and Hansell Hillyer when Mr. Hillyer was president of the Savannah Gas Company.

For the most part, Savannah lost some of its luster in the first half of the twentieth century. Although much was lost, much still remained, and Oglethorpe's legacy— his brilliant city plan—was still in place.

Past, Present, and Future

The City Market was the throbbing pulse of downtown in 1954. The vast building teemed with buyers and sellers of everything from fresh fish, shrimp, and crabs to okra, collards, and boiled peanuts.

Could intelligent men and women demolish such a treasure and replace it with a parking garage? That's exactly what happened in spite of strong protests, thousands of signatures on petitions, and pleas from citizens to save the market. The walls came tumbling down, and a colorful slice of life became only a memory. When the Davenport House was threatened, sadness turned to fierce resolve in the hearts of the seven women to whom this book is dedicated. They banded together with others to form Historic Savannah Foundation, Inc., a powerful organization that began by saving the Davenport House. It went on to save many more buildings and neighborhoods, demonstrating time and again the economic validity of historic preservation. Since its founding in 1955, Historic Savannah has become a nationwide source of preservation information and inspiration.

Also important in the Savannah saga is the Downtown Neighborhood Association, formed in the 1960s to aid in the effort to preserve Savannah's architectural heritage. Much has been accomplished in the Historic District and in the adjoining Victorian district.

Savannah has been called the Hostess City of the South, the Most Beautiful City in North America, and one of the Top Ten Walking Cities in the United States.

Savannahians treasure these titles and work hard to ensure that they are well deserved. Welcome, and may your stay be memorable and enjoyable.

City Market (torn down in 1954)
Courtesy, Georgia Historical Society

Stop Here First:
Savannah's Visitor Centers

Savannah Visitor Center

301 Martin Luther King Jr. Blvd., 31401. 912-944-0455 or 877-728-2662.

N32° 04. 578′ W081° 05. 960′. www.visitsavannah.com.
Monday–Friday, 9:00 a.m.–5:30 p.m. daily

This is usually the first stop for information, brochures, maps, tours, reservation services, and souvenirs. Housed in what once was the Central of Georgia Railway Station, there are restrooms and plenty of parking. A twenty-minute introductory film on Savannah is shown at regular intervals. Most trolley and bus tours depart from the Visitor Center. The Savannah History Museum is also in this building.

Additional Visitor Information Services

Ellis Square Visitor Center

26 Barnard Street, 31401. 912-525-2348.

N32° 04. 848′ W081° 05. 647′.
Open daily, generally 10:00 a.m.–9:00 p.m. *(closing times vary)*

Forsyth Park (The Fort) Visitor Center

Located in the park's café. 912-238-7848.

N32° 04. 091′ W081° 05. 726′.
Open daily, 8:00 a.m.–7:00 p.m. No attendant.

Georgia Visitor Center

I-95 South (near the South Carolina state line)
P.O. Box 7208, Garden City, GA 31418. 912-963-2546.

N32° 12. 993´ W81° 10. 453´.

Open daily, 8:30 a.m.–5:30 p.m.

Pooler Chamber of Commerce Visitors Bureau

(inside the National Museum of the Mighty Eighth Air Force)

175 Bourne Avenue, Pooler, GA 31322. 912-748-0110.

N32° 06. 919´ W081° 14. 149´. www.visitpooler.com.

Monday–Thursday, 9:00 a.m.–4:00 p.m.
Friday, 9:00 a.m.–1:00 p.m.

River Street Visitor Center

1 West River Street (behind Savannah City Hall), 31401. 912-651-6662.

N32° 04. 890´ W081° 05. 454´.

Open daily, 9:00 a.m.–8:00 p.m. February through November.
Open daily, 9:00 a.m.–6:00 p.m. December and January.

Savannah Convention and Visitors Bureau

101 East Bay Street, 31401. 912-644-6401 or 877-728-2662.

N32° 04. 820´ W081° 05. 394´.

Monday–Friday, 8:30 a.m.–5:00 p.m.

Savannah–Hilton Head International Airport Visitor Center

400 Airways Avenue, 31408. 912-966-3743.

N32° 08. 125´ W081° 12. 620´.

Open daily, 9:00 a.m.–10:00 p.m.

Tybee Island Visitor Center

802 First Street at Campbell Avenue, Tybee Island, GA 31328.
912-786-5444 or 800-868-2322.

N32° 00. 980´ W081° 50. 939´. www.tybeevisit.com.

Open daily, 9:00 a.m.–5:30 p.m.

Inquire Here First

Visit Savannah

Savannah Convention and Visitors Bureau
101 East Bay Street, 31401. 912-644-6401, 877-728-2662.

Monday–Friday, 8:30 a.m.–5:00 p.m.

www.visitsavannah.com

Visit Savannah serves as the primary destination marketing organization for the Savannah-area tourism industry.

Savannah, established 1733, entertains and captivates visitors with her gracious hospitality and charming eccentricities. With surprises around every corner, the city intrigues guests with an eclectic blend of the old and new, both hip and historic, as you explore Savannah's countless sights and sounds.

Visit the website for basic information, up-to-date details on what's happening in Savannah, special offers, and upcoming seasonal events.

Savannah Waterfront Association

310 East Lower Factors Walk, 31401. 912-234-0295.

www.riverstreetsavannah.com and info@riverstreetsavannah.com

The Savannah Waterfront Association is a 501 (c) (3) organization responsible for providing free festivals and events for the public in the River Street area. Festivals include:

          ❧ First Friday & Saturday Festivals (March-December),

          ❧ St. Patrick's Day Celebration on the River,

          ❧ River Street Fourth of July Celebration, and

          ❧ River Street's Up the Cup New Year's Eve Celebration

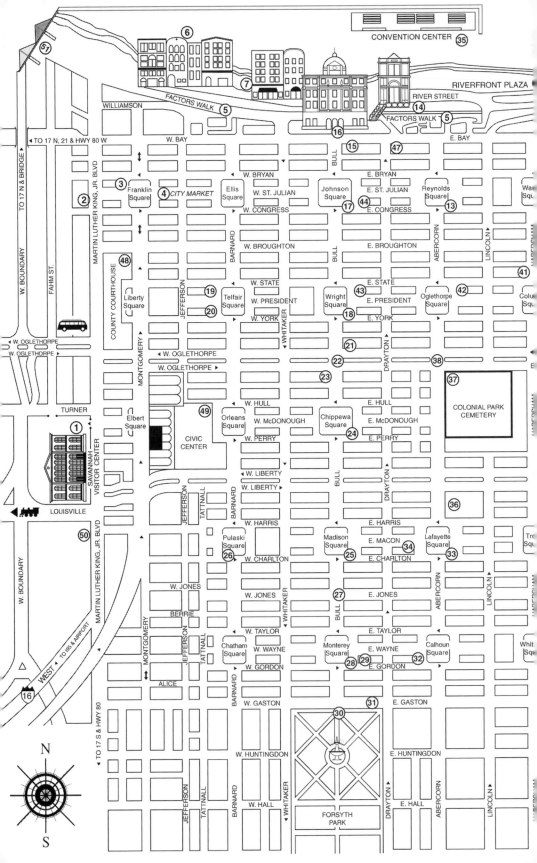

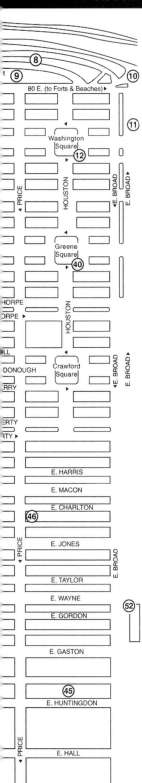

1. Savannah Visitor Center
2. Ships of the Sea Museum
3. First African Baptist Church
4. City Market
5. Factors' Walk
6. West End of River Street
7. Riverfront Plaza/River Street
8. Waving Girl Monument/ 1996 Olympic Torch
9. Emmet Park
10. Fort Wayne
11. Trustees' Garden Village
12. Washington Square
13. Reynolds Square
14. Cotton Exchange
15. U.S. Custom House
16. City Hall
17. Johnson Square
18. Wright Square
19. Telfair Museum of Art
20. Trinity United Methodist Church
21. Juliette Gordon Low Birthplace
22. Oglethorpe Avenue
23. Independent Presbyterian Church
24. Chippewa Square
25. Madison Square
26. Pulaski Square
27. Jones Street
28. Monterey Square
29. Temple Mickve Israel
30. Forsyth Park
31. Gaston Street
32. Wesley Monumental United Methodist Church
33. Whitefield, Troup, and Lafayette Squares
34. Andrew Low House
35. Savannah Int'l Trade & Convention Center
36. Cathedral of St John the Baptist
37. Colonial Park Cemetery
38. Oglethorpe Avenue
39. Columbia Square
40. Greene Square
41. Davenport House
42. Owens-Thomas House
43. Lutheran Church of the Ascension
44. Christ Church Episcopal
45. King-Tisdell Foundation and Cottage
46. Beach Institute
47. Savannah Area Chamber of Commerce
48. Chatham County Courthouse
49. Savannah Civic Center
50. Historic Railroad Shops
51. Talmadge Memorial Bridge
52. Mother Mathilda (Matilda) Beasley Park

AREAS O

HISTORIC DISTRICT, ISLANDS/BEAC

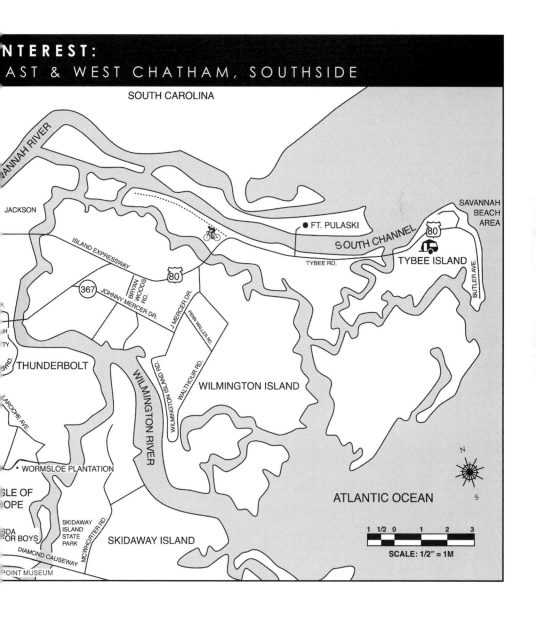

NTEREST:
AST & WEST CHATHAM, SOUTHSIDE

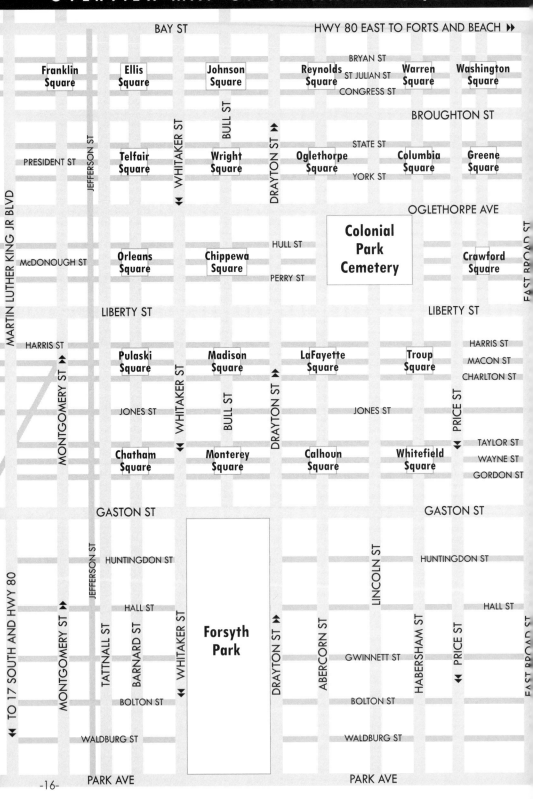

Getting Around in
the Historic District

Getting around downtown is easy and costs nothing, thanks to the dot (Downtown Transportation) fare-free transportation system. Parking your car downtown, however, can be a problem, although visitors may purchase a one- or two-day parking pass at the Mobility and Parking Services Office at 100 East Bryan Street (912-651-6470) or at the Visitor Center. The pass can be used at the parking meters or in any of the city's downtown parking garages. Parking meters and time limits are strictly enforced Monday through Friday, 8:00 a.m.–5:00 p.m.

The three-part fare-free transportation system consists of the dot Express Shuttle, the dot River Street Streetcar, and the dot Savannah Belles Ferry. Pick up a brochure with a map of the dot system routes at any visitor center.

The dot Express Shuttle winds through the historic district, passing museums, historic sites, shops, restaurants, hotels, visitor centers, and parking facilities. The shuttle runs daily at twenty-minute intervals between 7:00 a.m. and 9:00 p.m. (11:00 a.m. to 9:00 p.m. on Sundays). Look for it at any of the twelve shuttle stops. It connects with the dot Savannah Belles Ferry and the dot River Street Streetcar at City Hall Landing on River Street.

The dot River Street Streetcar shuttles between six stops along River Street next to the Savannah River. It's called "Dottie." The car starts on Montgomery Street, traveling along River Street, making a stop at Barnard Street and then at the Transit Terminal at City Hall. Here the connection can be made to city buses, the dot Express Shuttle, and the dot Savannah Belles Ferry to Hutchinson Island. Continuing along the old abandoned tracks in the cobblestones, the streetcar stops at Abercorn and Habersham before its final stop at the Waving Girl landing. The streetcar runs Thursday through Sunday, noon to 9:00 p.m. It is an authentic refurbished 1930s streetcar with environmentally friendly green technology. It is the first biodiesel-fueled hybrid streetcar in America. In the future, if more tracks are put down, the River Street Line could be extended to the Tricentennial Park, home to the Savannah History Museum, the Battlefield Memorial Park, the Georgia State Railroad Musuem, the Savannah Children's Museum, and the Visitor Center.

The dot Savannah Belles Ferry crosses the Savannah River every few minutes on a ten-minute trip, connecting River Street with the International Trade Center and the Westin Hotel on Hutchinson Island. The ferry runs daily from 7:00 a.m. until midnight from two landings on River Street. The Savannah Belles are named *Juliette Gordon Low, Susie King Taylor, Florence Martus,* and *Mary Musgrove,* four women of note in Savannah's history.

Savannah's CAT (Chatham Area Transit) provides bus service beyond the historic district for a fare. There is one fare-free route in the Historic District. Buses "lean down" to allow wheelchair access, and racks are provided to carry bikes on the fronts of the buses. CAT's headquarters are located at the Greyhound bus station on Oglethorpe Avenue, at the site of the new downtown transit center. Beneath soaring metal canopies the new center offers monitors that provide regularly updated arrival and departure times. Another feature will be a pilot bike-share program that allows customers to rent bicycles from a solar-powered kiosk. Bike stations have been set up at CAT's transit center on Oglethorpe Avenue and in Ellis Square. Each location has eight bicycles available for rent. The cost ranges from $2.00 per half hour to membership fees of $20.00 for a seven-day pass and $60.00 for an annual pass. Riders may return bicycles to either of the two locations. The program operates daily between 5:30 a.m. and 11:00 p.m.

Public transportation began in Savannah in 1869 with the first streetcar to Isle of Hope, Skidaway Island, Thunderbolt, Montgomery, and White Bluff. The first cars were drawn by one horse or mule and had room for twelve seated passengers. The cars were heated by woodstoves and lighted by kerosene lamps, and the horses wore bells to alert pedestrians of their approach.

In 1890 the first electric streetcars ran along rails in the center of the street. The streetcar barn was located at Gwinnett Street and Harmon Street, at the site of the present Chatham Area Transit Authority. The early streetcars were staffed by a motorman who stood on an open platform. He wore a heavy wool blue coat and trousers year-round. There was no heat on board, and in winter the motorman would stand in a cardboard box with rags wrapped around his feet to stay warm. Passengers shivered and snuggled to keep warm.

In 1946 the Savannah Electric Company sold its holdings to the Savannah Transit Company, and streetcars were replaced by buses. On August 26, 1946, the last streetcar operated in Savannah. The father of one of the authors made the final sentimental trip to Isle of Hope, telling his five-year-old daughter Laura about it.

In 1987 the Savannah Transit Authority was replaced by the Chatham Area Transit Authority with a forward-thinking board committed to public service. Five new bus routes were added, and service levels were improved on existing routes. CAT reinstated both night and Sunday service. The CAT board invested in extensive marketing, and a new logo and color scheme were implemented. Elaine Longwater and Kitty Strozier were recognized for the slinky CAT appearing on the sides of buses and the trendy slogan "Catch a Cat."

In 1989 the CAT board approved the Teleride van service for citizens with disabilities who were unable to use the CAT fixed-route bus service. In that same year CAT installed thirty-one new bus shelters and over ninety new passenger benches.

In 1994 the electric-powered dot Express Shuttle began to circulate in the historic district. The shuttle is free to locals and tourists who want easy transportation to anyplace downtown. At this time the first lift-equipped buses arrived, expanding transportation options for people with disabilities.

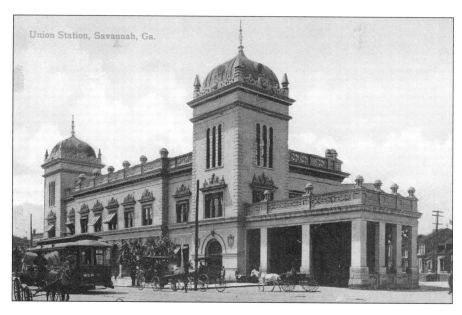

Union Station, Savannah, Ga.

Savannah's magnificent Union Railway Station, built in 1902, was brutally demolished in 1963 to allow I-16 to enter the city.

Savannah Tour Companies

Explore the historic and Victorian districts, as well as the forts, islands, museums, haunts, cemeteries, gardens, rivers, and marshes in the many ways listed here.

Try some of the specialty tours—focusing on history, architecture, treasure hunts, African American culture, movie sites, photography, gardens, nature, fishing, and dolphin watching.

Trolley Tours

Oglethorpe Trolley Tours *– 7 Rathborne Road, 31415. 912-233-8380 or 866-374-8687.* www.oglethorpetours.com.

Offers a 90-minute narrated history tour of the Historic District with on-and-off privileges. Also a haunted tour. Departs from the Visitor Center. Free parking. Credit cards. Children's fares.

჋

Old Savannah Tours *– 250 Martin Luther King Jr. Blvd., 31401. 912-234-8128 or 800-517-9007.* www.oldsavannahtours.com.

Offers a 90-minute narrated history tour of the Historic District with on and off boarding privileges. Other tours: the Paula Deen tour, the Victorian District, Beach Institute area, and a haunted tour with supper at the Pirates' House and a stop at the Sorrel-Weed House. Departs from the Visitor Center. Free parking. Credit cards. Children's fares.

Old Town Trolley Tours – *1115 Louisville Road, 31415. 912-233-0083.* www.trolleytours.com.

Offers a 90-minute tour of the Historic District, the colonial district, and the Victorian district with on-and-off boarding privileges. Other tours: Ghosts and Gravestones, Paula Deen Tour, and Holiday Tour. Look for the orange trolleys. Departs from the Visitor Center. Free parking. Credit cards. Children's fares.

ଋ

Fare-free dot (Downtown Transportation) Express Shuttle, the River Street Streetcar, and the Savannah Belles Ferry – *912-447-4026.* www.connectonthedot.com

Tour on your own on the Express Shuttle, the Savannah Belles Ferry, and the River Street Streetcar—all free! The shuttle loops through the Historic District, connects with the Visitor Centers, historic sites, shops, and restaurants. Eleven stops daily, 11:00 a.m. to 9:00 p.m., connects with the River Street streetcar that runs back and forth along the waterfront Thursday–Sunday, noon to 9:00 p.m., as well as the ferry that crosses the Savannah River to Hutchinson Island.

Carriage Tours

Carriage Tours of Savannah – *912-236-6756.* www.carriagetoursofsavannah.com.

A 50-minute narrated clip-clop through the Historic District. Follow the horse's switching tail and the guide's bewitching tale. Board at City Market. Also ghost and private tours. Reservations. Credit cards. Children's fares.

ଋ

Historic Savannah Carriage Tours – *100 Aberdeen Street, 31401. 912-443-9333 or 888-837-1011.* www.savannahcarriage.com.

A 50-minute history tour covers the major landmarks in the Historic District. They also offer *A Taste of Savannah* tour and *Magic in the Moonlight* tour. Board near the Hyatt Regency and Ellis Square. Private pickup offered. Reservations. Credit cards. Children's fares.

ct

Madison Tour Company – *31 Barnard Street, 31401. 912-658-1364.* www.madisontourcompany.com.

Experience the colonial history of this southern city with a 50-minute ride narrated by a licensed guide that leaves from Ellis Square. Also private tours, Paula Deen tours, wedding and elopement tours, special events, and birthday party tours. Reservations. Credit cards. Children's fares.

ct

Plantation Carriage Company – *88 Randolph Street, 31401. 912-201-9900.* www.plantationcarriage.com.

60-minute rides in the Historic District leave from Ellis Square with licensed guides at the reins. You will enjoy seeing old houses, churches, and gardens in thirty blocks of the heart of the Historic District. Reservations. Credit cards. Children's fares.

Riverboat Cruises

River Street Riverboat Company – *9 East River Street, 31401. 912-232-6404 or 800-786-6404.* www.savannahriverboat.com.

The captain narrates intriguing tales about the port and visiting ships from all over the world. Bring your camera. Also offers dinner with entertainment cruises, gospel dinner cruises, journey-to-freedom dinner performances, Saturday luncheon, Sunday brunch, moonlight and music, plus murder mystery cruises. Reservations. Credit cards. Children's fares. The *Georgia Queen* and the *Savannah River Queen* cast off from docks behind City Hall.

Walking Tours

A Walk through Savannah – *912-921-4455.* www.awalkthroughsavannah. bravehost.com.

Ted takes small groups on individualized walking tours for one to three hours. You can choose among tours focusing on the Civil War, architecture, houses of worship, Johnny Mercer, *Midnight in the Garden of Good and Evil*, or a combination of these. Children's tour or a ghost tour. Reservations. Cash only. Children's fares. Ted's tours start at Johnson Square, or he will meet you at your downtown hotel.

Adventures in Savannah – *912-356-9188.* www.adventuresinsavannah.com.

Tours on Savannah history, African American history, architecture, movie sites, *Midnight in the Garden of Good and Evil,* Paula Deen, ghost tours, and Girl Scout Discovery Badge tours, including the Savannah Safari Walking Adventure. Takes groups to Charleston and Beaufort, SC, and St. Simons, Jekyll Island, and Okefenokee Swamp in Georgia. Reservations. Cash or checks. Children's fares.

ȸ

Cool Savannah Tours – *42 East Bay Street, 31401. 912-233-3667.* www.circasavannah.com.

Leave from 42 East Bay Street for a 90-minute overview of Savannah's history. They also offer ghost walks and a haunted pubs tour. Gift shop. Reservations. Credit cards. Children's fares.

ȸ

Free Savannah Walking Tours – www.freesavannahtours.com.

No reservations, no cost. Tips accepted if you like the tour. Depart Monday–Saturday, 11:00 a.m. and 2:30 p.m. from Johnson Square for a 90-minute overview of Savannah's history.

ȸ

Grits and Magnolias – *912-238-1151.*

Led by a licensed guide, this 90-minute tour is an overview of Savannah's founding up to today. Leaves from 1 Broughton Street. Reservations. Cash only.

ȸ

Let's See Savannah – *912-414-1357.* www.letsseesavannah.com.

A local Savannahian tells groups about the history and culture of our city. Gather in Lafayette Square. Call for times. Reservations. Credit cards. Children's fares.

ȸ

Noble Jones Tours – *912-660-6468.* www.noblejonestours.com.

Led by a local Savannahian, the tour leads you through the Historic District. Tour themes include Civil War, "The Book," Hidden Gardens, and Murder and Mayhem. Leave from Reynolds Square Monday-Friday 9:30 a.m. Reservations. Credit cards. Children's fares. Leashed doggies free.

Old City Walks – *912-358-0700.* www.oldcitywalks.com.

Take a walking tour with accomplished photographer, Phil Sellers, who will show you architectural elements, share some back stories, and other lesser-known historical facts. Ten different tours. Reservations required.

&

Orlando Montoya Tour – *912-308-2952.*

You've heard him giving the news on Georgia Public Radio, but Orlando Montoya leads a personalized walking tour as well. Expect the same in-depth coverage and interesting information that we're used to hearing from him.

&

Savannah Belle Walking Tours – *912-655-9896.* www.savannahbelletours.com.

Two 90-minute tours depart daily from Reynolds Square. Every tour includes historic homes, Civil War and Colonial history, and architecture. Each square has a story to be told. Reservations. Cash only. Children's fares.

&

Savannah by Foot Historic Tour – *912-238-3843.* www.savannahtours.com.

Learn Savannah's fascinating history. Stroll through scenic squares with important monuments with a licensed guide. Creepy Stroll Family Tour and Creepy Crawl Haunted Pub Tour. Reservations. Credit cards. Children's fares.

&

Savannah Dan Walking Tours – *912-398-3777.* www.savannahdan.com.

Stroll through the squares. Visit movie sites—see where Forrest Gump sat on his bench. Two walks daily from Johnson Square. Reservations. Cash only.

&

Savannah Heritage Tours – *912-224-8365.* www.savannahheritagetour.com.

A two-hour history of Georgia's first city leaves from the Visitor Center or will pick up. Enjoy Savannah's architecture, hidden gardens, intricate ironwork and landscaped squares. Other tours: Daisy Girl Scouts, haunted tour, "The Book" tour, cemetery tour. Reservations. No credit cards. Children's fares.

Savannah Safari Walking Adventure (for youngsters) – 912-353-9999. www.savannahsafari.com.

An official badge-earning program of the Girl Scouts of America. Hunt for dolphin downspouts, terra-cotta lions, wrought-iron eagles on walls, in gardens, or on porches in the artistic jungle of this walking town. Fill in the blanks in poems at each animal. Safari books are sold at the Visitor Center, Girl Scout Birthplace or Girl Scout First Headquarters. Walk it yourself or hire a guide. Excellent for groups, birthday parties, or families. Allow an hour and a half.

ॐ

Savannah – The Walking City Tour – 912-272-2513. www.walkingsavannah.com.

A two-hour stroll of squares takes you through mansions, monuments, and houses of worship. Leave from Wright Square. Also offers a Civil War tour. Reservations. Cash only.

ॐ

Savvy Savannah Tours – 912-663-4400. www.savvysavannahtours.com.

Offers *Scenes of Savannah Past*—a 90-minute narration of the Historic District. Departs from the Pirates' House at 3:00 p.m. daily. Other tours are the cinema tour, the spiritual tour, the suds tour, and Spectres of Savannah. Credit cards. Reservations. Children's fares.

ॐ

See Savannah Walking Saunter – 912-441-9277.

A 90-minute narration of the Historic District with a focus on architecture, the Civil War, and gardens. The guide will share a notebook with architectural images, maps, photographs of historical personalities, and original interiors and exteriors of homes. Departs from Tomochichi's boulder in Wright Square. Call for times. Cash only.

ॐ

Students See Savannah – 912-236-8730.

Let Ann Tatum plan your trip with your students, from room reservations to meals and sightseeing. She's been making history come alive for twenty-five years, and she will tailor her itinerary to meet the special needs of your group.

Travel thru Time Tours – *912-335-8496.* www.travelthrutimetours.com.

Walk with your guide through a city that has captured the dreams of many and survived the struggles of a new colony. Learn the stories of James Oglethorpe, George Washington, Marquis de Lafayette, and others whose lives are intertwined with Savannah's history. Tours begin at 10:30 a.m. and 1:30 p.m. and last an hour and a half. The Historic Savannah Tour meets in Reynolds Square, and the Colorful Characters Tour and the Eye Spy Tour meet in Columbia Square. Special rates for private, personalized, or group tours. Reservations required. Credit cards. Children's fares.

&

Victorian Lady Tours – *912-232-7708.*

Walk through the Historic District with a Victorian Lady in costume who is an expert on the history and architecture of old Savannah. Call for times. Cash only.

Self-driving CD Tour

The Savannah Story – Put the CD in your player in your car, and take a tour written by two sisters and a brother who know Savannah history. They'll tell you where to stop and get out, and which places just to drive by. Proceed at your own pace. Available at the Visitor Center, Books on Bay, the Davenport House Museum Shop, E. Shaver Bookseller, or at the website: www.thesavannahstory.com.

Pedicab Tours

Royal Bike Taxi – *10 West Jones Street, 31401. 912-341-3944.* www.royalbiketaxi.com.

Open-air, three-passenger pedicabs. Flag it down or phone ahead. Not a structured tour, but the drivers are informative. Credit cards.

&

Savannah Pedicab – *635 East Broughton Street, 31401. 912-232-7900.* www.savannahpedicab.com. Same as above. Cash only.

Segway PT Tours

Segway Tours of Savannah – *234 Martin Luther King Jr. Blvd., 31401. 912-233-3554. www.segwayofsavannah.com.*

Arrive 45 minutes early for helmet fitting and training. Licensed guides lead 90-minute historic tours. 10:00 a.m., noon, and 2:00 p.m. Bonaventure Cemetery tour 1:00 p.m. Reservations. Credit cards.

Scooter Tours

Motorini Scooter Tours – *236 Drayton Street, 31401. 912-201-1899. www.vespasavannah.com.*

Tours led by licensed guides on Saturdays 11:00 a.m., 1:00 p.m., and 3:00 p.m. from Motorini's. Only twelve scooters per tour. Short orientation and training required. Will customize your tour. Reservations. Credit cards.

Bicycle Tours

Pedals Eco Entertainment Tours – *526 Turner Blvd., 31401. 912-508-5080. www.savannahpedals.com.*

Pedal a fifteen-seat modern bicycle on the two-hour tour with guide and driver. Popular Pub Crawl as well as scenic and historic tours. Reservations. Credit cards.

ॐ

Savannah Bike Tours – *912-704-4043. www.savannahbiketours.com.*

Pedal through the Historic District, stopping for photo opportunities and to admire significant landmarks. Two-hour tours offered daily. Reservations. Cash only.

ॐ

Savannah Slow Ride Stories of the South Tour – *912-414-5634. www.savannahslowride.com.*

Laugh and pedal together with fourteen others as a guide narrates. You will dismount three or four times. Reservations. Credit cards.

Aerial Tours

Savannah Aviation Aerial Tours – *34 Hangar Road, 31408. 912-964-1022. www.savannahaviation.com.*

Soar on a 45-minute narrated flight over Savannah and nearby islands. Double occupancy required. Reservations. Credit cards. Free parking. Children eight and under are free.

For visitors with specific areas of interest, take a look at these unique tours.

African American History Tours

Day Clean Journeys – 912-220-5966. www.daycleansoul.com. www.geecheekunda.com.

Board the bus or van to see underground railroad sites, ports of entry for slaves, the Civil Rights Museum, monuments and markers, the Beach Institute, and slave burial grounds. Reservations. Credit cards. Jamal Touré will be your guide.

 &

Footprints of Savannah – 912-695-3872. www.footprintsofsavannah.com.

Join Vaughnette Goode-Walker at Wright Square for a walking tour and the complete story of Savannah's antebellum years. Learn how intricately the city and its citizens were involved in the institution of slavery. Reservations. No credit cards.

&

Freedom Trail Tours – 912-398-2785. freedomtrailtour@bellsouth.net.

Board the bus or van to see many African American historical sites, monuments, buildings, and burial grounds. Reservations. Credit cards. Children's fares.

&

Journey to Freedom Dinner Cruise – *9 East River Street, 31401. 912-232-6404 or 800-786-6404.* www.savannahriverboat.com.

Songs, stories, and dancing by the Gullah Geechee people. Authentic southern buffet. Thursday nights, April–August. Reservations. Credit cards. Children's fares.

&

Gospel Dinner Entertainment Cruise – *9 East River Street, 31401. 912-232-6404 or 800-786-6404.* www.savannahriverboat.com.

Gospel singing. A cultural and culinary event. Monday nights, April–October. Reservations. Credit cards. Children's fares.

Architectural Tours

Walk past the oldest and newest of the city's buildings. Of special interest are the old churches, Savannah architects, the unique town plan, and restored houses and buildings. Most tours last 1.5 to 2 hours.

A Walk through Savannah – *912-921-4455.* www.awalkthroughsavannah. bravehost.com.

Walk with Ted through the Historic District to view the decorative and functional ironwork, including unique cast downspouts and piazza rails. Stroll by homes and churches, from Federal to neo-Gothic, Italianate to English Regency. Reservations. No credit cards. Children's fares.

ॡ

Architectural Tours of Savannah – *912-604-6354.* www.architecturalsavannah.com.

Tours are led by Jonathan Stalcup, a graduate of the Savannah College of Art and Design. Several different tours are offered. Reservations. No credit cards.

ॡ

Historic Savannah Architecture – *912-659-1487.* www.savannaharchitours.com.

Follow an expert, Beth Reiter, Savannah's past director of historic preservation, discussing the town plan, architecture, and historic preservation. Four different walking tours. Reservations. Cash or check only. Children's fares.

ॡ

Savannah Rambles: Architectural Walking Tour – *912-704-8170.* www.savannahrambles.com.

Architect Dirk Hardison knows the Historic District well. Reservations. Cash or checks. Children's fares.

Bonaventure Cemetery Tours

*330 Bonaventure Road, 31404. 912-651-6843. www.bonaventurehistorical.org.
Open daily 8:00 a.m.–5:00 p.m. N32° 02. 707´ W081° 03. 039´.*

Bonaventure Cemetery is one of the loveliest cemeteries in America. It was a land grant from King George II and was purchased by the city in 1907, after many years as the colonial plantation of the Tatnall family. In a recent Yahoo Travel article, "12 Cemeteries to See Before You Die," Matt Bell lists Bonaventure in the seventh position. It is one of only two U.S. cemeteries included on the list.

Take a Walk Back in Time – 912-412-4687. www.bonaventurehistorical.org.

Free walking tours led by Bonaventure Historical Society volunteers are given year-round on the second Saturday and Sunday of each month. Gather at the intersection of Mullryne and Wiltberger Ways at 2:00 p.m. on Saturday, or 2:00, 2:30, or 3:00 p.m. on Sunday. Walk for one to two hours. Wear comfortable shoes. Bring water. Donations go to cemetery restoration. Visitor Center open 10:00 a.m.–4:00 p.m. each Saturday and Sunday.

ൠ

Bonaventure Cemetery Tours – 912-292-0960 or 866-666-3323. www.bonaventurecemetery.tours.com.

Two tours daily. Reservations. Credit cards. Children's fares.

ൠ

Bonaventure Journeys – 912-604-4423 or 877-662-2662. www.bonaventurecemetery.com.

Shannon Scott leads day walks and evening and after-dark tours. Reservations. Credit cards. Children's fares.

ൠ

Savannah Heritage Tours – 912-224-8365. www.savannahheritagetour.com.

A 90-minute tour. Reservations. Cash only. Children's fares.

Tour Bonaventure – 912-665-4258. www.tourbonaventure.com.

Three tours leave daily from the Visitor Center on an air-conditioned bus. Reservations. Credit cards.

ൠ

Segway Bonaventure Cemetery Tour – 912-233-3554. www.segwayofsavannah.com.

A 90-minute tour Monday-Saturday at 1:00 p.m. Reservations 24 hours in advance. Credit cards.

Midnight in the Garden of Good and Evil Tours

Author John Berendt published his first book, Midnight in the Garden of Good and Evil, *in 1994, and it became an international best seller. Tourists came from all over the world to see this charming southern city whose secrets had been revealed by an annoying outsider. Most Savannah businesses were thrilled with the increased tourism. Old Savannah families ignored the whole thing.*

Oglethorpe Trolley Tours – *7 Rathborne Road, 31415. 912-233-8380 or 866-374-8687.* www.oglethorpetours.com.

Reservations. Credit cards. Children's fares.

&

Savannah Heritage Tours – *912-224-8365.* www.savannahheritagetour.com. Reservations. Cash only. Children's fares.

&

A Walk Through Savannah – *912-921-4455.* www.awalkthroughsavannah. bravehost.com.

Reservations. Cash or checks only. Children's fares.

&

Noble Jones Tours – *912-660-6468.* www.noblejonestours.com.

Hear about the trials, tribulations, and manipulations of the characters in "The Book." Two-hour tours Monday–Saturday from Reynolds Square. Reservations. Credit cards. Children's fares. Dogs welcomed.

Movie Tours

As mayor of Savannah in the 1970s, John Rousakis got the idea that Savannah would be a great place to make movies. He knew what a boost it would be to the local economy, and he didn't mind when he was given a role in some of them, which he performed as a professional. That began a trend of making films in Savannah, which continues to the present.

Savannah Movie Tours – 912-234-3440. www.savannahmovietours.com.

See filming sites. View movie clips in the bus on this 90-minute tour. Reservations. Credit cards. Children's fares.

ॐ

Savvy Savannah Tours – 912-663-4400. www.savannahtours.com.

See sites from movies filmed here. Two 90-minute tours daily. Reservations. Credit cards.

Civil War Tours

Savannah was occupied by the Yankees during the Civil War, after Sherman's famous March to the Sea from Atlanta to Savannah in 1864. Civil War tours take you to significant sites and tell about this part of Savannah's history.

Footprints of Savannah – 912-695-3872.

A walking tour with emphasis on the historical sites of special interest to African Americans. Tours are led by a knowledgeable African American historian and begin in Madison Square. Reservations required. Credit cards accepted, cash preferred. Children's and senior citizens' fares.

ॐ

Noble Jones Tours – 912-660-6468. www.noblejonestours.com.

An in-depth and entertaining tour of Savannah before, during, and after the Civil War. A two-hour tour is offered twice daily and leaves from Reynolds Square. Reservations. Children's fares. Credit cards. Dogs welcome.

Savannah the Walking City – *912-272-2513.* www.walkingsavannah.com.

The stories of the men and women who fought, worked, and died during the Civil War take on real life meaning during this tour. Reservations. No credit cards. Student fares.

ক

See Savannah Walking Tours – *912-441-9277.* www.seesavannah.com.

The Homemade Thunder Civil War Tour tells the story in the words of the city's residents who witnessed the conflict. One tour daily leaves from Tomochichi's rock in Wright Square. Reservations not required. Credit cards. Children's fares.

ক

A Walk Through Savannah – *912-921-4455.* www.awalkthroughsavannah. bravehost.com.

Ted Eldridge and his dog Molly will lead you through downtown Savannah's Civil War sites, including Christ Church, where before the war Bishop Elliott preached to his congregation trying to avoid war. During the war Bishop Elliott preached about the noble and valiant young men who were willing to die for their cause, expressing great love and sympathy for their families. Ted is the only tour guide with a key to the church. Reservations. Check or cash only. Children's fares.

Gardens, Gates, and Ironwork Tours

Noble Jones Tours – *912-660-6468.* www.noblejonestours.com.

Once a day, Monday–Saturday, February–October. 1.75 hours. Departs from Madison Square. Reservations. Credit cards. Children's fares.

ক

See Savannah Walking Tours – *912-441-9277.* www.seesavannah.com.

Once a day this tour leaves from Tomochichi's Rock in Wright Square. Reservations not needed. Credit cards. Children's fares.

ক

A Walk Through Savannah – *912-921-4455.* www.awalkthroughsavannah. bravehost.com.

Ted knows the names of most of the trees and plants as well as most of the garden owners. Reservations. Cash or checks. Children's fares.

Paula Deen Tours

Visit places with significance in Paula's life, plus a few surprises. Have lunch at her restaurant, The Lady and Sons, and perhaps receive some special gifts.

Madison Tour Company – *912-658-1364.* www.madisontourcompany.com. Offers a horse-drawn carriage ride including lunch. Reservations. Credit cards.

ℰ

Old Savannah Tours – *912-234-8128 or 800-517-9007.* www.oldsavannahtours.com.

Reservations. Credit cards. Children's fares.

ℰ

Old Town Trolley Tours – *912-233-0083.* www.trolleytours.com.

Reservations. Credit cards. Children's fares.

Food Tours

Eat It and Like It Gourmet Foodie Tour – *912-233-0083.* www.eatitandlikeit.com.

Hop on the Old Town Trolley (the orange one) and enjoy five small plates, five wine pairings, and an air-conditioned tour bus that stops at five of Savannah's finest restaurants. Reservations. Credit cards.

ℰ

Foody Tour by Bus – *912-234-3440.* www.savannahmovietours.com.

Eat with locals. Discover well-kept food secrets at six stops. Departs from the Visitor Center and lasts 2 hours, 45 minutes. Reservations. Credit cards. Children's fares.

ℰ

Walking Foody Tour – *912-234-3440.* www.savannahmovietours.com.

Leave from Wright Square Café, 21 West York Street, for a 2 hour and 15 minute stroll, stopping in various cafés and restaurants for samples. Reservations. Credit cards. Children's fares.

Savannah Taste Experience – *118 Barnard Street, 31401. 912-388-0004 or 800-979-3370.* www.savannahtasteexperience.com.

A three-hour walking and tasting tour through Savannah's squares, where you will sample delicacies from seven different restaurants and specialty food stores. Reservations. Credit cards. No cash.

First Squares Food Tour – (part of the Savannah Taste Experience) *800-979-3370.*

Taste your way from the savory Riverfront through some delicious bites on the original squares of historic downtown Savannah. Reservations. Credit cards.

ȼt

Famous and Secret East Side Food Tour – (part of the Savannah Taste Experience) *912-388-0004 or 800-979-3370.*

Start at the Pirates' House for a gourmet tour of six nearby Savannah restaurants. Reservations. Credit cards.

Photographic Tours

Capturing Savannah Photographic Tours – *832-524-4624.* pabloandbritt@capturingsavannah.com.

This company offers two photographic tours of Savannah: The Luxurious Squares and Forsyth Park Tour is a 90-minute walking tour of many of Savannah's most photogenic sites. The Family Portrait Tour is a two-hour tour of the best sites for a family portrait. Reservations. Major credit cards.

ȼt

Photographic Walking Tours of Savannah – *912-414-6699.* www.photographicwalkingtoursofsavannah.com.

Learn the history of Savannah while picking up photographic tips and tricks that will lead to that perfect image. Two-hour tours depart daily from Madison Square at 11:00 a.m. and 5:00 p.m. Bring your camera or rent one from us. Reservations. Credit cards. Children's fares.

Port Wentworth Driving Tour

Port Wentworth Driving Tour – *1732 GA Highway 21, 31407. 912-965-1999.*

The nearby town of Port Wentworth, GA, stands on the site of several early Georgia colonial plantations, including Mulberry Grove, where Eli Whitney invented the cotton gin in 1793. Whitney's invention revolutionized agriculture and the economy of the South. The Port Wentworth Chamber of Commerce provides a map with GPS coordinates for sixteen points of interest.

Ghost and Haunted Tours

Ghost, haunted, and creepy tours plus tales of the paranormal, pirates, murderers, angels, and outlaws and lost cemeteries with voodoo! These dark stories may have begun with the reputed Pirates' House tunnel to the river used to shanghai drunken sailors onto waiting ships in the harbor. As evening falls, many feel the tingle of restless spirits in lanes, pubs, and squares. Hear stories of treasure, swashbucklers, buccaneers, and voodoo. Creep through shadows to hear about house hauntings, local legends, lost cemeteries and ritual homicides. Savor the dark side of America's most haunted city. If you dare!

A Walk through Savannah – 912-921-4455. www.awalkthroughsavannah. bravehost.com.

Ted knows all the stories about ghosts and creepy things in Savannah. Join Ted after dark for a tour by lantern light. Reservations. No credit cards. Children's fares.

 c‌t

Afterlife Tours – 912-398-7820. www.afterlifetours.net.

Hear and see evidence of the paranormal at each researched stop. Two tours of 90 minutes, Thursday, Friday, Saturday. Reservations. Credit cards. Children's fares.

c‌t

America's Most Haunted City Tour (6th Sense Savannah) – 912-292-0960 *or* 866-666-3328. www.6thsenseworld.com.

A ghost history from the precolonial era to the twenty-first century. Learn why Savannah is called America's most haunted city. Allow 90 minutes. Departs from Starbucks, 1 East Broughton Street. The 7:00 p.m. tour is family-friendly. The 9:00 p.m. tour is for adults only. Reservations. Credit cards. Children's fares.

Angels, Outlaws, and Sinners (6th Sense Savannah) – *912-292-0960 or 866-666-3328.* www.6thsenseworld.com.

Stories of illustrious criminals of the 1920s, prohibition's speakeasy culture, women of the night, and Kickapoo Joy Juice. Tales of the late Bo Peep, owner of Savannah's favorite watering hole. A 90-minute tour. Leave from the parking lot across Congress Street from Christ Church, 28 Bull Street. Reservations. Credit cards.

ॐ

Carriage Tours of Savannah – *912-236-6756.* www.carriagetoursofsavannah.com.

Ghost stories of Savannah. Reservations. Credit cards. Children's fares.

ॐ

City of the Dead – *912-344-0864 or 855-258-3672.* www.blueorbtours.com.

Called the city of lost cemeteries and the city built on its dead, there are many unmarked graves in the Historic District. Take the 90-minute walk and learn why this is America's most haunted city. One tour daily departs from Chippewa Square at 9:00 p.m. Reservations. Credit cards.

ॐ

Creepy Stroll Ghost Tour (Savannah by Foot) – *912-238-3843.* www.savannahtours.com.

A night of family-friendly stories and chilling fun-filled adventure. On the 90-minute stroll, hear creepy tales of ghostly manifestations and local legends. Reservations. Credit cards. Children's fares.

ॐ

Ghost Hunters Paranormal Tours – *912-257-2223.* www.savannahtours.net.

Visit the haunted Sorrel-Weed House and carriage house. Visit Colonial Park Cemetery. 90-minute walks start after 6:00 p.m. at 6 West Harris Street. Reservations. Credit cards. Children's fares.

ॐ

Ghost Talk Ghost Walk – *912-233-3896.* www.ghosttalkghostwalk.com.

The guide shares stories from Margaret DeBolt's book *Savannah Spectres and Other Strange Tales.* Tours leave Reynolds Square. Reservations. Cash or checks. Children's fares.

Ghosts and Hauntings (See Savannah) – *912-234-3571.* www.seesavannah.com.

Guides give two nightly 90-minute tours from Wright Square. Reservations. Cash only. Children's fares.

 et

Gribble House Paranormal Experience – *234 Martin Luther King Jr. Blvd., 31401. 912-856-4316.* www.gribblehouse.com.

In 1909 a triple murder shocked locals. The house was demolished, but spirits of the victims hang around. Investigate the building site and communicate with those beyond the grave with state-of-the-art equipment. Adults 18 and older only. Reservations. Credit cards.

et

Haunted History – *912-604-3007.* www.ghostsavannah.com.

A 90-minute walk through the historic squares. Hear chilling stories of ghosts. A guide in costume tells legendary tales of tragedy and romance. Two tours nightly leave from the main gate of Colonial Park Cemetery. Reservations. Cash or travelers' checks. Children's fares.

et

Haunting Good Time Ghost Tour – *912-233-3667.* www.csavannah.com.

Tour departs from 42 East Bay Street. Explore the deep and dark history of America's most haunted city. Reservations. Credit cards. Children's fares.

et

Hearse Ghost Ride – *912-695-1578.* www.hearseghosttours.com.

Go through cemeteries and the Victorian and the Historic Districts for a 75-minute drive searching for lurking spirits. The hearse seats up to eight victims. Reservations. Credit cards. Children's fares.

et

Historic Savannah Carriage Tours – *912-443-9333.* www.savannahcarriage.com.

The Savannah Spirits and Spectres tour features chilling ghost stories, folklore, and legends while clip-clopping along eerie moss-canopied streets. Reservations. Credit cards. Children's fares.

Midnight Haunted Tour (6th Sense Savannah) – *912-292-0960 or 866-666-3328.* www.6thsenseworld.com.

Tales of human possession, spirit photography, exorcism, voodoo, occultism, vampires, and morgue tunnels. Allow ninety minutes. Leave from Clary's Café, 404 Abercorn Street. Adults only. Reservations. Credit cards.

ct

Midnight Voodoo – *912-349-4451.* www.hauntedsavannahtours.com.

Hear stories of cannibalism and voodoo. Adults 18 and older only. Allow two hours. Depart at 10:00 p.m. from Lafayette Square. Reservations. Credit cards.

ct

Murder and Mayhem (Noble Jones Tours) – *912-660-6468.* www.noblejonestours.com.

Murder, scandal, lies, and gossip about Alice Riley, our first murderer, to Danny Hansford, our most infamous victim. Ninety-minute walks depart from Chippewa Square on Monday, Thursday, Friday, and Saturday at 5:00 and 7:00 p.m. Reservations. Credit cards. Children's fares.

ct

Oglethorpe Trolley Tours – *912-233-8380 or 866-374-8687.* www.oglethorpetours.com.

The evening ghost tour is a narrated 90-minute ride through the Historic District. Reservations. Credit cards. Children's fares.

ct

Old Savannah Tours – *912-234-8128 or 800-517-9007.* www.oldsavannahtours.com.

Trolley Tales of Historic Haunts gives a spooky overview through special arrangements with the Pirates' House and the Sorrel-Weed House. Reservations. Credit cards. Children's fares.

ct

Old Town Trolley Tours – *912-233-0083.* www.ghostsandgravestones.com.

The Ghosts and Gravestones tour is a 90-minute exploration of the dark side with the town's gravedigger on an evening of ghostly tales. Reservations. Credit cards. Children's fares.

Original Haunted Savannah Tours – *912-349-4451.* www.hauntedsavannahtours.com.

Discover ghosts, ghouls, and legends. Hear about the dark history of Savannah. Allow 90 minutes. Departs nightly at 8:00 p.m. from Lafayette Square. Reservations. Credit cards. Children's fares.

ঐ

Original Hauntings Tours – *912-441-9277.* www.seesavannah.com.

Prepare to be scared. Allow 90 minutes. Leaves nightly at 9:00 p.m. from Tomochichi's boulder in Wright Square. Reservations not necessary. Cash or checks preferred. Children's fares.

ঐ

Savannah Hauntings Tour (Savannah Heritage Tours) – *912-224-8365.* www.savannahheritagetour.com.

Hear about infamous spirits Alice Riley, Anna, Gracie, and the pirate Captain Flint. Allow two hours. Reservations. Credit cards not accepted. Children's fares.

ঐ

Scary Ghost Tours – *912-234-3440.* www.savannahmovietours.com.

Hear tales of famous ghosts and murderers. Stop at two haunted locations. The 90-minute tour departs from the Pirates' House, 20 East Broad Street. Reservations. Credit cards. Children's fares.

ঐ

Sixth Sense Savannah Tour – *912-292-0960 or 866-666-3323.* www.6thsenseworld.com.

Hear about poltergeists, hags, exorcism, missing cemeteries, and disembodied spirits. Allow 90 minutes. Depart from Clary's Café, 404 Abercorn Street at 7:00 p.m. The 9:00 p.m. tour is for adults. Reservations. Credit cards. Children's fares.

ঐ

Spectres of Savannah (Savvy Savannah Tours) – *912-663-4400.* www.savvysavannahtours.com.

Ghost stories about the Pirates' House's rum cellar tunnel and the Marshall House once occupied by General Sherman as a hospital for soldiers during the Civil War. Allow 90 minutes. Depart from the Pirates' House at 8:00 p.m. and 10:00 p.m. daily. Reservations, credit cards.

Uncensored Zombies (Blue Orb Tours) – *912-344-0864 or 855-258-3672.* www.blueorbtours.com.

Uncensored with adult content. Must be 18 or older. Allow two hours. Leave Chippewa Square at 10:00 p.m. Reservations. Credit cards.

Pubs and Taverns Tours

If you choose to take a tour where you are led in and out of Savannah's pubs and taverns, you will be beguiled with lurid tales of the city's most notorious characters, some real and some fictional. Each tour will introduce you to scoundrels and pirates, as well as to unique individuals you might actually find sitting next to you at one of these bars in the Historic District. Reservations required. Major credit cards. You must be 21 or older to take these tours.

The Martini Tour – *912-234-3440.* www.savannahmovietours.net.

This tour takes you to four of Savannah's downtown pubs and lasts two hours.

ৎ

Savannah Pub and Tavern Tour – *912-661-1880.* www.cobblestoneconnections.com.

Venture into three of Savannah's most distinctive pubs over a two-hour period.

ৎ

Savvy Savannah Tours – *912-663-4400.* www.savvysavannahtours.com.

Two tours: The **Savannah Shaken Tour** toasts your way through Savannah with four martinis within 90 minutes. The **Savannah Suds Tour** reveals the history of craft beer while you enjoy brews from four different pubs.

ৎ

Savannah Slow Ride – *912-414-5634.* www.savannahslowride.com.

Climb on a fifteen-person bicycle for a slow ride through Savannah's pubs. Reservations. Major credit cards.

ৎ

Pedals Eco-Entertainment – *526 Turner Blvd., 31401. 912-508-5080.* www.savannahpedals.com.

Take a pub crawl on a fifteen-seat bicycle with a driver. Reservations. Major credit cards.

Haunted Pub Tours

A ghostly adventure awaits you if you take a haunted pub tour through Savannah's historic pubs. You must be at least 21 years old to participate.

C Savannah Tours – *42 East Bay Street, 31401. 912-233-3667.* www.csavannah.com.

Reservations. Major credit cards.

ଶ

Creepy Crawl Haunted Pub Tours – *912-238-3843. www.savannahtours.com.*

This tour has been operating for nineteen years, and the two-an-a-half-hour tour visits five or six pubs each night. Reservations. Major credit cards.

ଶ

Cobblestone Tours – *912-604-3007. www.ghostsavannah.com.*

Take a two-hour walking tour of the haunted pubs with your guide in period costume. Alcohol is not required or provided, but definitely encouraged. Reservations. Major credit cards.

ଶ

Enjoy a Few Spirits with Your Meal Tour – *912-856-4316.* www.gribblehouse.com/tondees.

Delve into Savannah's dark and secret past as you dine in one of the city's most haunted locations—Tondee's Tavern, 7 East Bay Street. Ghostly stories will be told that define Savannah as America's most haunted city. After dinner you will have exclusive access to explore the basement of Tondee's Tavern with the ghost-hunting equipment provided. Minimum age is 14. Reservations. Credit cards.

Nature and Charter Tours

Alligators Galore – *912-695-2305. www.alligatorsgalore.com.*

Explore secluded beaches. See alligators and dolphins. Design your personalized trip with local naturalists. Transportation not provided. The guide will ride in your car, or you can follow the guide for bird and alligator tours. Kayak tours depart from several locations. Daily paddles are two to six hours. Reservations. Cash only. Children's fares.

ঞ

Bull River Marina Eco/Dolphin Tours – *8005 Old Tybee Road (U.S. Hwy 80 East)*. *912-897-7300 or 877-898-7300*. www.bullrivermarina.com.

Dolphin tours, shark fishing, and deep sea charters (bait and tackle provided), boat rentals, guided kayak nature tours, and sunset cruises. Enjoy Mother Nature on the 90-minute ride in a 40-foot pontoon boat. Also daily water taxi and sightseeing rides to Daufuskie, Hilton Head, Wassaw, Williamson Island, Beach Hammock, Little Tybee, and the old Tybee lighthouse. Reservations. Credit cards.

ঞ

Captain David Newlin Fishing Charters – *912-756-4573*. www.captaindn.com.

Catch redfish, trout, tarpon, shark, kings, cobia, barracuda, sea bass, sheepshead, or striped bass. One to six fishermen for four- to ten-hour trips. License and tackle on board. Depart from either of two southside locations. Also boat rides to explore scenic coastal waters. See dolphin, sea turtles, eagles, alligators, and shore birds. Reservations. Credit cards.

ঞ

Captain Jack McGowan's Coastal River Charters – *912-441-9930*. www.coastalrivercharters.com.

Fish for red drum, spotted sea trout, tarpon, shark, flounder, and stripes. Tackle, ice, and photo included. Leave from Thunderbolt. Reservations. Cash or checks preferred. Family rates.

ঞ

Compass Sailing – *912-441-3265*. www.compasssailing.com.

Half- and full-day charters on a 38-foot Morgan sailboat. See egrets and dolphins. May include ocean sailing depending on the weather and guests' preferences. Sailing lessons available. Leave from Bull River Marina on U.S. Highway 80 East, 31410. Reservations. Credit cards.

ঞ

Dolphin Magic – *912-897-4990 or 800-721-1240*. www.dolphin-magic.com.

Two hours of narrated history of the historic waterways while cruising scenic marshes and barrier islands. See Fort Jackson, Fort Pulaski, Elba and Cockspur

Islands and lighthouse, and Tybee Island and lighthouse aboard a 41-foot vessel seating forty-eight passengers. Departs from 312 East River Street. Reservations. Credit cards. Children's fares.

ↄt

East Coast Paddleboarding – *912-484-3200.* www.eastcoastpaddleboarding.com.

Choose from a variety of boards accommodating all styles of paddling and all sizes of paddlers, including both children and adults. Nationally certified instructors will guide you in waves or for flat water paddling. Rentals, lessons, sales and tours. Reservations. Credit cards. Children's fares.

ↄt

Eco Boat Tours – *912-898-1800.* www.savannahnature.com.

Takes groups of two to sixty. Explore the Savannah River, barrier islands, Skidaway Island State Park waters, Wormsloe Historic Site waters, and Thunderbolt and Wassaw Island. Depart from Hogan's Marina, 36 Wilmington Island Road, 31410. 912-897-3474. Reservations. Credit cards.

ↄt

Good Times Charters – *912-335-2545.* www.savannahgoodtimes.com.

Historic maritime tours are given daily and for private groups of ten to forty-five people. Sunset cruise once a week. Learn the importance of the river in the development of Savannah. Hear about natives and pirates that sailed these waters and ships that made maritime history. See forts that played major roles in the formation of the nation. Departs from 502 East River Street, 31401. Reservations. Credit cards.

ↄt

Moon River Kayak Rentals – *912-344-1310.* www.savannahnature.com.

Explore estuaries, marshes, and rivers on your own, or with a guide. Depart from Hogan's Marina, 36 Wilmington Island Road, 31410. 912-897-3474. Reservations. Credit cards.

ↄt

Moon River Kayak Tours – *912-344-1310.* www.moonriverkayak.com.

Paddle historic and scenic Moon River and the Skidaway Narrows for a 2½-hour tour led by a local naturalist. Departs from Hall Boat Ramp (Butterbean Beach) on Diamond Causeway at the bridge leading to Skidaway Island. Reservations. Credit cards.

Rusty Anchor Island Hoppers – *912-349-4290.* www.youngsmarina.com.

Create memories with a personally designed tour led by a licensed captain. Groups of from two to six for four- to eight-hour trips. Departs from Young's Marina, 218B Wilmington Island Road, 31410. Reservations. Credit cards.

ct

Savannah Canoe and Kayak – *912-341-9502.* www.savannahcanoeandkayak.com.

Explore scenic beaches and tidal salt marshes. Instruction classes offered. Three-hour and full-day trips, plus multiday camping. Retail store for paddlers, 414 Bonaventure Road, 31404. Reservations. Credit cards. Children's fares.

ct

Wilderness Southeast – *912-236-8115.* www.wilderness-southeast.org.

Nature and wildlife tours led by experienced guides. Ask about the Blackwater River Paddle on a mirror of clear black water with flora and turtles. On the Wild Island and Estuary Exploration you'll see dolphins and osprey as the motorboat winds among marsh grass. Enjoy beachcombing and birding. Reservations. Credit cards. Children's fares.

Savannah Panorama

A Driving Overview of the Famous Squares in the Historic District

Driving time: approximately two hours

Leave the Visitor Center through the back gate. Take the first right for two blocks to Oglethorpe Avenue. Turn right and go through two lights, then two blocks to Barnard Street and turn right. Now you are in the quiet part of town and ready to drive around Savannah's lovely squares. The first one is …

Orleans Square

This square was named for the 1815 victory of General Andrew "Old Hickory" Jackson in the Battle of New Orleans during the War of 1812. The fountain was given in 1989 by Savannah's German heritage organizations. Orleans Square was added to the city plan in 1815.

❶ Savannah Civic Center

❷ Champion-McAlpin-Harper-Fowlkes House

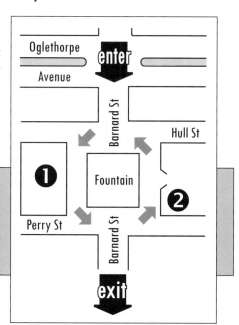

Points of interest:

❶ Savannah Civic Center (1971) – *301 West Oglethorpe Avenue, 912-651-6550.*

This is a facility for symphony concerts, circus performances, art shows, and tractor pulls. The Johnny Mercer Auditorium is named for songwriter Johnny Mercer, who wrote the lyrics for *Moon River, The Days of Wine and Roses, You Must've Been a Beautiful Baby, I Left My Sugar in Salt Lake City*, and over fifteen hundred other songs.

It was built on the site of the Bulloch-Habersham House, designed by William Jay (c. 1820) and torn down in 1914, before historic preservation became a priority.

Champion-McAlpin-Harper-Fowlkes House

❷ Champion-McAlpin-Harper-Fowlkes House (1842) – *230 Barnard Street, 912-234-2180.*

Charles Cluskey, an Irish architect, designed this mansion of scored stucco over Savannah gray bricks, with two-story Corinthian columns on a masterpiece of Greek revival architecture. Note the graceful curves of the sandstone stairs.

First to live here was banker Aaron Champion, who bequeathed it to his only daughter, Mrs. James McAlpin. She also inherited Hermitage Plantation from her father. Savannah gray bricks were handmade at the Hermitage. In 1939 Mrs. Hunter McGuire Fowlkes (Alida Harper) acquired this house. Today it belongs to the Georgia Chapter of the Society of the Cincinnati. It is assumed to be the house in the book *The Damned Don't Cry* by Harry Hervey. Visitors welcome.

 Continue around the square and exit south on Barnard Street for two blocks to …

Pulaski Square

Named for Polish Count Casimir Pulaski, hero of the Revolutionary War, this square was laid out in 1837 and is shaded by nineteen majestic oak trees. Count Pulaski fought with the patriots in the War for American Independence. On October 12, 1779, he was wounded during the Siege of Savannah and died a few days later. A monument to Count Pulaski stands in Monterey Square. He was also honored in the naming of Fort Pulaski.

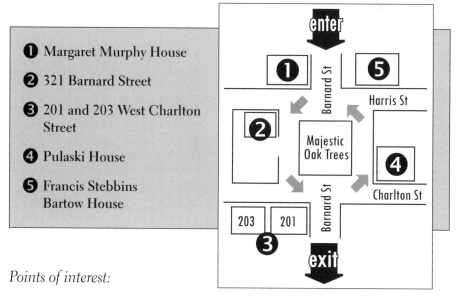

❶ Margaret Murphy House

❷ 321 Barnard Street

❸ 201 and 203 West Charlton Street

❹ Pulaski House

❺ Francis Stebbins Bartow House

Points of interest:

❶ **Margaret Murphy House** (1992) – *200 West Harris Street.*

The handsome blue corner building, an example of compatible new construction in the Historic District. Built in Savannah's favorite "high stoop" design, it refers to Margaret Murphy Green, a longtime friend to the neighborhood.

❷ **321 Barnard Street.**

Built in 1845 for butcher Bernard Constantine from Philadelphia, Mills Lane IV, philanthropist and preservationist, restored and lived in this house until 2001. He founded the Beehive Press and published a classic series of books on southern architecture and firsthand stories of life in early Georgia.

❸ 201 and 203 West Charlton Street *(Charlton Hall and Solomons' House).*

#203 was built in 1853 for Cecilia Solomons and her husband A. A. Solomons, a druggist. An ad in 1859 promoted perfumery, paints and oils, surgeons' instruments, and garden seeds at A. A. Solomons Drug Store in Market (Ellis) Square.

#201, Charlton Hall, is an administration building for Savannah College of Art and Design (SCAD).

❹ Pulaski House (1915) – *328 Barnard Street.*

A massive red brick structure with green awnings. The original building was torn down in 1914. This one once housed the Jewish Educational Alliance and later the Salvation Army. Now it is a dormitory for SCAD students.

❺ Bartow House (c. 1850) – *128 West Harris Street.*

The corner clapboard house with side porches. This house was built for Civil War hero Francis Stebbins Bartow, who died in 1861 in the first Battle of Bull Run, after leading Savannah's Oglethorpe Light Infantry to Richmond. The rank of brigadier general was awarded posthumously. Busts of General Bartow and General Lafayette McLaws, also a Confederate hero, flank the Confederate Monument in Forsyth Park.

 Continue around the square and south on Barnard Street to ...

Chatham Square

Chatham Square honors William Pitt, Earl of Chatham. As Savannah grew southward, this square was added in 1847. Its namesake was a stalwart ally of the colonists in the English Parliament.

Points of interest:

❶ Pepe Hall – *212 West Taylor Street.*

Handsome Ludowici-barrel-tiles roof. These clay tiles were made in the town of Ludowici, Georgia, in the twentieth century. SCAD now uses this former school building for fiber instruction. The original Barnard Street School of 1854 was used by General Sherman's Union Army as a hospital during the Civil War. The present building was erected in 1906 in Mediterranean Revival style, with battered brick basement and bell tower.

❷ Double Houses – *421 and 423 Barnard Street.*

Built for William Kine in 1854. Mr. Kine was a dry goods merchant who worked at J. Sherlock and Co. on Broughton Street.

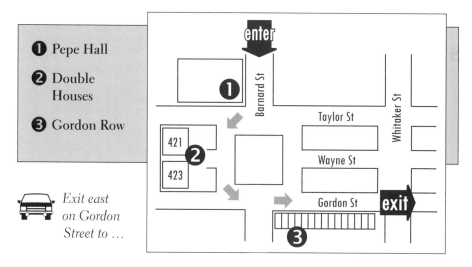

❶ Pepe Hall

❷ Double Houses

❸ Gordon Row

Exit east on Gordon Street to ...

❸ Gordon Row — *Gordon Street between Whitaker and Barnard Streets.*

Fifteen identical brick houses built in 1854. Each one has three stories on a street-level basement and a backyard for shrimp boils or sunning. Many local citizens still moan over missed opportunities to buy one in the 1950s for fifteen hundred dollars.

Georgia Historical Society
Courtesy, Dan Kaufman/Studio Kaufman, LLC

At the corner turn right onto Whitaker Street, approach the light at Gaston Street. On the right across Gaston Street is …

The Georgia Historical Society – *501 Whitaker Street. 912-651-2125.*

Founded in 1839, the Georgia Historical Society is the oldest cultural institution in the state and one of the oldest historical organizations in the United States. It is responsible for collecting, examining, and teaching Georgia history. The building was built in 1876 and named for William Brown Hodgson, American diplomat, Savannah native, and curator of the Historical Society for twenty-five years. The building features high vaulted ceilings and decorative ironwork and is listed on the National Register of Historic Places. In 2011 the Society purchased the building across Gaston Street and expanded into the Jepson House Educational Center, named for philanthropists Robert S. and Alice Jepson.

 Continue down Whitaker Street to the end of the park. Turn left on Park Avenue to circle …

Forsyth Park

These acres are for walking, jogging, tennis, frisbee, soccer, football, and pigeon feeding. A vision conceived by William Brown Hodgson, the park dates from 1851. The name honors John Forsyth, American statesman and governor of Georgia in 1828.

The park was designed by Frederick Law Olmsted, who also designed Central Park in New York City. The wooded section at the north end is the Forsyth Park Arboretum, twelve acres, including fifty species of native and adaptive exotic species of trees. Under the halo of mist in the center of the park is a white, cast-iron fountain with spouting tritons, similar to the fountain in Place de la Concorde, Paris, and the twin of one in Cuzco, Peru.

In the center of the promenade is the monument to Confederate Dead in the Civil War. The gift of G. W. J. DeRenne, this monument by British sculptor David Richards was installed in 1879. It bears these poignant words: *Come from the four winds, O Breath, and breathe upon these slain that they may live.*

At the south end of the arboretum is the Fragrant Garden for the Blind. The garden has been given a facelift by the Trustees Garden Club and is open most mornings. Bronze plaques provide the names of the plants in English and Braille as well as their Latin names.

There is a mini-visitor center in the nearby restaurant, the Fort Café, that offers restrooms and lunch with indoor or outdoor seating.

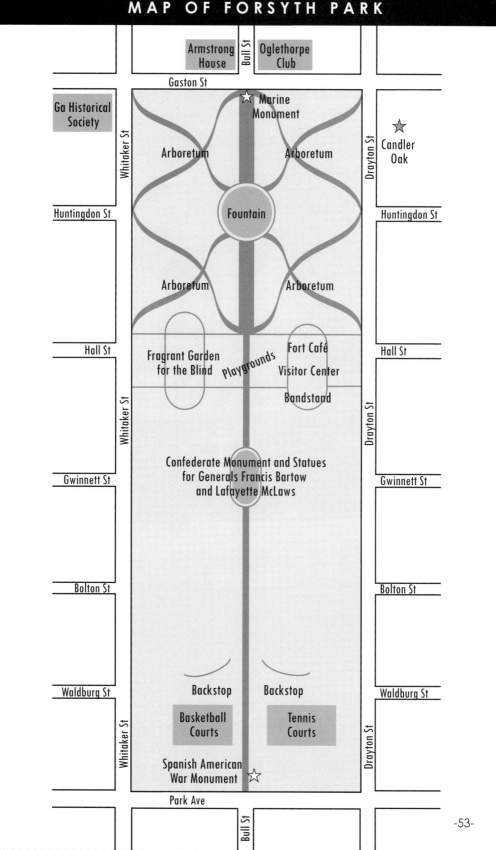

Forsyth Park Fountain

Courtesy of the artist, Pamela Lee

After circling two sides of the park, turn left onto Drayton Street. As you approach the light at Gaston Street, notice on your right …

Candler Oak – *Drayton and Gaston Streets.*

A giant live oak tree 270 years old. This tree stood tall when General Sherman camped his soldiers under it during the Civil War, but in recent years it had begun to decline. In 1982 the Savannah Tree Foundation saved this historic tree. In 1985 they had the surrounding asphalt removed, and they continue to water, mulch, and fertilize the tree.

 At Gaston Street turn left for one block. Turn right onto Bull Street. On your left is …

The George Ferguson Armstrong House – *447 Bull Street.*

A white brick mansion, built for a shipping executive who served in the Spanish-American War. George Armstrong served with the Chatham Artillery. He built this house in 1920 (Henrik Wallin, architect) of brick and snowy glaze. The design is Ecole des Beaux Arts, reminiscent of buildings in Paris. Armstrong Atlantic State University, now south of the city, began here in 1935. Now the house is home to a well-respected law firm. You might see attorney Sonny Seiler walking his bulldog, Uga, the mascot of University of Georgia's football team.

George Ferguson Armstrong House

 Look to your right at the stately brick mansion …

The Oglethorpe Club – *450 Bull Street.*

The oldest private men's club in Georgia. Built in 1857, this was the home of Edmund Molyneux, British consul in Savannah. Union General Oliver Howard used the mansion during General Sherman's occupation of the city during the Civil War.

In 1885 it was sold to Confederate General Henry R. Jackson—lawyer, soldier, diplomat, and poet. He was judge of the Eastern Circuit of Georgia and prosecutor for the United States in the famous case of the slave ship *The Wanderer*. He was president of the Georgia Historical Society.

 Continue north on Bull Street to …

Monterey Square

This square, laid out in 1847, commemorates the capture of Monterrey, Mexico, by General Zachary Taylor in 1846. Here stands the monument to the Polish officer Casimir Pulaski. The sculptor was Robert Launitz.

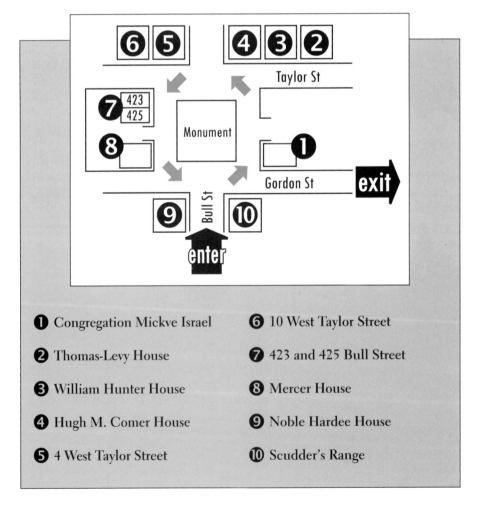

❶ Congregation Mickve Israel

❷ Thomas-Levy House

❸ William Hunter House

❹ Hugh M. Comer House

❺ 4 West Taylor Street

❻ 10 West Taylor Street

❼ 423 and 425 Bull Street

❽ Mercer House

❾ Noble Hardee House

❿ Scudder's Range

Points of interest:

❶ Congregation Mickve Israel
– 20 East Gordon Street, 912-233-1547.

A historic synagogue with Gothic architecture. Dating from 1733, it is the oldest Jewish congregation in the South and the third-oldest in the nation. Its first members included Sephardic and Ashkenazic Jewish settlers who came to Georgia aboard the ship *William and Sarah* in 1733. Mickve Israel received a perpetual charter from Governor Edward Telfair in 1790. Gothic in design, this building was consecrated in 1878. Of special interest is the fifteenth-century Torah brought to this country by early settlers.

❷ Thomas-Levy House
– 12 East Taylor Street, 912-232-0338.

Congregation Mickve Israel

Courtesy, Dan Kaufman/Studio Kaufman LLC

A Second Empire Baroque-style residence with curved windows above the entrance. Virginia and John Duncan operate their antiquarian bookstore downstairs. Do visit V & J Duncan Antique Maps, Prints, and Books. Built in 1869, this house was remodeled in 1897 as a wedding-cake-style townhouse with Georgia marble steps. It was featured in a 1979 movie, *Orphan Train*. (Photo on next page.)

❸ William Hunter House (c. 1872) *– 10 East Taylor Street.*

Side galleries on two stories, golden yellow stucco. Cast-iron exterior "eyebrows" accent the windows of this restored four-story house.

❹ Hugh M. Comer House (1880) *– 2 East Taylor Street.*

An Italianate mansion with a pair of palm trees out front. This mansion of stucco-over-brick is handsome and historic. It was built for Hugh Comer, president of the Central of Georgia Railway Company. Jefferson Davis and his daughter, Winnie, visited the Comers here in 1886.

❺ 4 West Taylor Street (1852)

Two iron cranes keep watch at the stairs. The story goes that guardian cranes, symbols of vigilance, stand on one foot clasping a stone in the raised foot. Should either bird begin to snooze, the stone falls onto his standing foot, jolting him awake.

Thomas-Levy House

❻ 10 West Taylor Street (1852) – *912-234-5520.*

Sunset-pink stucco with cast-iron entrance stairs. The original two-story brick house was embellished in the early 1900s with cast-iron balconies, a Ludowici tile roof, and a Dutch Colonial third floor, creating a mid-nineteenth-century house with a New Orleans accent. The antiques shop on the street level is open by appointment.

❼ 423 and 425 Bull Street (1858).

Exquisite ironwork, reminiscent of Gramercy Park in New York. This pre–Civil War pair of houses was built of scored stucco over brick. Its first owner was Presbyterian minister Dr. Charles Rogers. Unusual details are cast-iron porticoes and covered balconies.

❽ Mercer House (1860–1871) – *429 Bull Street, 912-238-0208.*

Red brick, framed by a handsome iron fence. This Italianate-style house was designed by architect John Norris for General Hugh Weedon Mercer prior to the Civil War. The story of Jim Williams, the well-known antiques dealer who restored the house, is told in John Berendt's book *Midnight in the Garden of Good and Evil*. A descendant of General Mercer's was Savannah's own lyricist, Johnny Mercer. Open for tours. Gift Shop.

Mercer House (1860–1871)

Courtesy of the artist, Pamela Lee

❾ Noble Hardee House (1860–1869) – *441 Bull Street, 912-232-8205.*

An antiques shop with wraparound cast-iron balcony. Noble Hardee began building this mansion in 1860, but died before its completion. After the Civil War, President Chester Arthur visited here twice and no doubt enjoyed a stroll in Monterey Square. A major scene in the movie *Something to Talk About*, with Julia Roberts, was filmed here. Alex Raskin owns the house, and his antiques shop extends to all four floors.

❿ Scudder's Range (c. 1852) – *East Gordon Street between Bull and Drayton Streets.*

An outstanding row of town houses overlooking Monterey Square. Built by brothers John and Ephraim Scudder, construction is stucco-over-Savannah-gray bricks with ornamental iron balconies. The buildings exemplify merchant town housing, characteristic of the mid-nineteenth century.

 Drive east on Gordon Street to …

Calhoun Square

Named for one of the south's great statesmen, this square was added in 1851. John Calhoun served his country as vice president, secretary of state, and secretary of war. Each year schoolchildren gather here to "dance the Maypole" in front of Massie Heritage Center, a tradition that began in the 1850s to celebrate the arrival of spring.

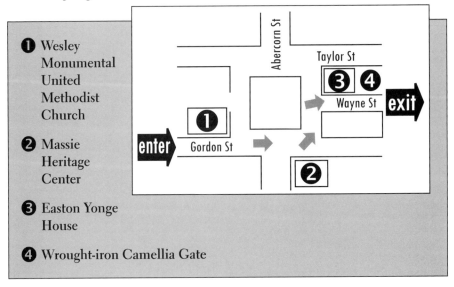

❶ Wesley Monumental United Methodist Church

❷ Massie Heritage Center

❸ Easton Yonge House

❹ Wrought-iron Camellia Gate

Points of interest:

1 **Wesley Monumental United Methodist Church** – *429 Abercorn Street, 912-232-0191.*

Brothers John and Charles Wesley were honored in the naming of this church. Begun in 1868, the church was not dedicated until 1890, because of Reconstruction money woes and a yellow fever epidemic.

2 **Massie Heritage Center (c. 1855)** – *207 East Gordon Street, 912-201-5071.*

Rosy-beige school buildings with connecting walkways, named for Peter Massie, a Scottish planter who settled in Georgia. Thanks to a bequest from Mr. Massie, plans were drawn by architect

Wesley Monumental United Methodist Church

John Norris for a school for less fortunate children. These buildings are a resource center in living history, offering exhibits of the city plan, Savannah in the Victorian era, and elements of Greek, Roman, and Gothic architecture. Recently renovated, Massie is now a hands-on learning center for Georgia history. Open daily and weekends for tours. Gift shop.

3 **Easton Yonge House** – *426 Abercorn Street.*

This doctor saved lives during the yellow fever epidemic of 1878. Dr. Easton Yonge, born in 1822, built this house in 1855. He was the son of William Philip Yonge and Ann Easton.

 Exit the square east on Wayne Street. On your left, pause at the …

4 Camellia Gate – *on Wayne Street on the side of the Easton Yonge house.*

Iron artwork is one of Savannah's distinguishing features. John Boyd Smith has adorned the Historic District with forged wrought-iron gates and ornamental ironwork. The camellia gate was commissioned in 1987 by Murray Galin in memory of his uncle Emanuel Kronstadt.

 Go two blocks east on Wayne Street to …

Whitefield Square

This square was named for the spirited English clergyman Reverend George Whitefield, who was minister to the colonists. He succeeded the Reverend John Wesley as Church of England minister to the Georgia colony. He is also remembered as the founder in 1740 of Bethesda Home for Boys, until recently, America's oldest orphanage in continuous operation. Bethesda is now a private boarding and day school for boys in grades six through twelve. The gazebo is a favorite spot for exchanging "I do's."
Frame houses with wide porches and Victorian gingerbread add romantic charm to this neighborhood.

Point of interest:

⭐ **First Congregational Church**
– *421 Habersham Street,*
912-232-0191.

This Gothic-style building replaces the original frame meeting house. The First Congregational Church is an outgrowth of the Alfred E. Beach Institute, a school where white missionary teachers taught African American children. Organized in 1869, shortly after the Civil War, the congregation acquired this property in 1878. This structure of brick covered with stucco was built in 1895. The original steeple blew off during a hurricane in 1940 and was replaced in 1992.

Gazebo in Whitefield Square
Courtesy of the artist, Pamela Lee

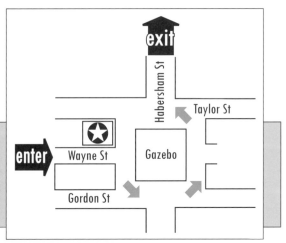

Exit north on Habersham Street, go two blocks to ...

Troup Square

Poised on six iron turtles in the center of the square is an armillary sphere, an ancient instrument for telling time. A horizontal bar, or gnomon, casts a shadow on the Roman numerals underneath, telling the hour. The sphere is decorated with the signs of the zodiac painted in gold. Laid out in 1851, this square commemorates Governor George Michael Troup, who welcomed the Marquis de Lafayette to Savannah in 1825, and later served as United States senator. Thirsty dogs, after being walked in Savannah's oppressive heat, appreciate the water fountain on the east side of the square with its two low-slung lapping bowls.

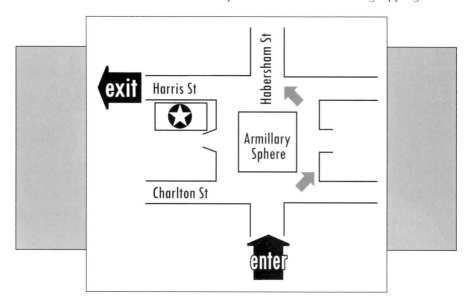

Point of interest:

⭐ **Unitarian Universalist Church** – *311 East Harris Street, 912-234-0980.*

Built as Saint Stephen's, with an African American Episcopal congregation. In 1892, in this church, Robert Bright was the first African American Episcopal priest to be ordained in America. In 1850, James Lord Pierpont (1822–1893), director of music here, composed the popular Christmas carol "Jingle Bells." Born in Boston, he longed for snow and traditional New England customs.

 Continue west on Harris Street to ...

Lafayette Square

Courtesy of the artist, Pamela Lee

Lafayette Square

The name honors the Marquis de Lafayette, aide to George Washington in the War for American Independence. The Marquis visited Savannah in 1825 and spoke to cheering crowds. Lafayette Square dates from 1837. The fountain was given by the Savannah Town Committee of the National Society of the Colonial Dames of America in the state of Georgia.

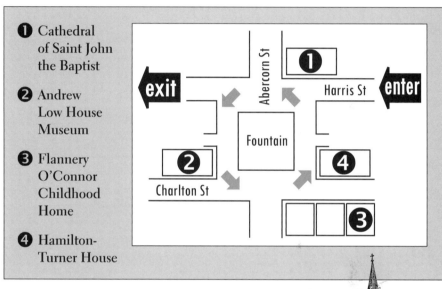

❶ Cathedral
   of Saint John
   the Baptist

❷ Andrew
   Low House
   Museum

❸ Flannery
   O'Connor
   Childhood
   Home

❹ Hamilton-
   Turner House

Points of interest:

❶ **Cathedral of Saint John the Baptist** – *222 East Harris Street,* 912-233-4709.

The oldest Roman Catholic Church in Georgia. Twin spires with chiming bells rise high above this French Gothic cathedral, the seat of the Diocese of Savannah. Dedicated in 1876, it was destroyed by fire in 1898, then rebuilt from the original plans of Francis Baldwin, architect. The interior is rich with Italian marble, Austrian stained glass, and opulent Persian rugs. The first event of Saint Patrick's Day on March 17

Cathedral of Saint John the Baptist

Courtesy of the artist, Pamela Lee

-65-

each year is Mass in the cathedral. Then the Hibernians head for Forsyth Park to march in a parade, now the largest in the United States. Visitors welcome.

❷ Andrew Low House Museum – *329 Abercorn Street, 912-233-6854.*

Georgia headquarters of the National Society of the Colonial Dames of America. Andrew Low and his wife Sarah built this house in 1848 with architect John Norris. Their plan to live here with their three children was dashed, first by the death of four-year-old Andrew, and then by the death of Sarah. Later, Andrew married Mary Stiles, who produced four daughters and a son, William Mackay Low.

William was called "Billow" by Juliette "Daisy" Gordon, whom he married in 1886. They lived here. Although the marriage was not ideal and produced no children, Daisy had daughters aplenty when she founded the Girl Scouts of the United States of America in 1912. The Andrew Low House was visited by William Makepeace Thackeray and General Robert E. Lee. Visitors welcome. Gift shop.

Andrew Low House Museum
Courtesy of the artist, Jill Howell

❸ Flannery O'Connor Childhood Home (c. 1855) – *207 East Charlton Street, 912-233-6014.*

A high-stooped house museum with lectures and readings. This three-story house was home to Edward and Regina O'Connor, whose only child, Mary Flannery, became a well-known author. She died in 1964 of lupus, which had also claimed her father in 1941. Now a house museum, readings of her works and other lectures are presented regularly. Visitors welcome. Gift shop.

❹ **Hamilton-Turner House** – *330 Abercorn Street, 912-233-1833.*

An outstanding example of Second Empire architecture with four iron balconies across the front. Commissioned by Samuel

Hamilton-Turner House
Courtesy of the artist, Jill Howell

Hamilton, this mansion was constructed by Abraham Snedeker. The exterior brick was later covered with stucco. Do admire the elaborate Victorian ornamentation, from the mansard roof on down. It is now the elegant Hamilton-Turner Inn.

 Exit the square west on Harris Street to ...

Madison Square

This square was named for the fourth president of the United States, James Madison. On the monument is Sergeant William Jasper, Revolutionary War hero, holding aloft the banner he recaptured for his company. Unveiled in 1888, it is the work of sculptor Alexander Doyle. Around the base are scenes from this gallant soldier's life. In one, he is wounded and dying, cradled in the arms of a comrade. Cannon on the south side of this square mark colonial roadways, including the old route to Darien, Georgia, mapped out in 1733 with the help of Tomochichi, the Yamacraw Indian chief, and the colonial road to Augusta. Madison Square was added in 1837.

Points of interest:

❶ **The Sorrel Weed House** – *6 West Harris Street, 912-257-2223.*

A stuccoed building with welcoming-arms staircases. Charles Blaney Cluskey, an Irish architect, designed this mansion for shipping merchant Francis Sorrel. Mr. Cluskey's love of Greek Revival design is seen in accents of Doric columns, the sweeping double entrance, and the marble floors. Later, the house was owned by the Weed family. A. J. and Kelly Cohen bought the house in 1941, and in the

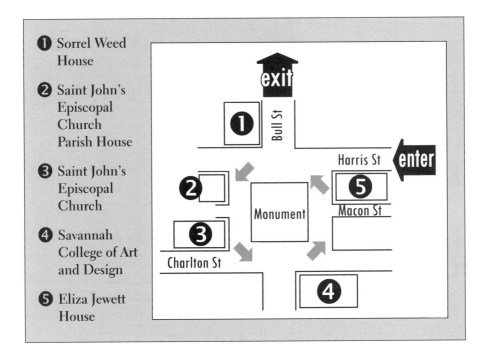

- ❶ Sorrel Weed House
- ❷ Saint John's Episcopal Church Parish House
- ❸ Saint John's Episcopal Church
- ❹ Savannah College of Art and Design
- ❺ Eliza Jewett House

rear opened The Lady Jane Shop, where they sold ladies' apparel for forty years. Open for tours.

❷ **Saint John's Episcopal Church Parish House (Green-Meldrim House Museum)** – *1 West Macon Street, 912-232-1251.*

Known as the Green-Meldrim House, it displays Medieval-style architecture with unusual oriel windows. From its crenellated parapet to the metal-studded portal, the design is Gothic and the mood medieval. The first owner was cotton merchant Charles Green. John Norris was the builder-architect. The Union General William Sherman headquartered here when Savannah surrendered toward the end of the Civil War. Serving as mayor pro tem of Savannah at the time was alderman George Washington Wylly, the great-great-grandfather of one of this book's authors. General Sherman sent this telegram to President Lincoln in December 1864:

To his Excellency.

Dear Sir, President Lincoln,

I beg to present you as a Christmas gift the city of Savannah with 150 heavy guns and plenty of ammunition and also about 25,000 bales of cotton.

—W. T. Sherman, Maj. Gen.

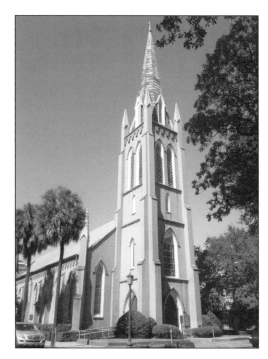

Saint John's Episcopal Church

❸ **Saint John's Episcopal Church** – *1 West Macon Street, 912-232-1251.*

A Gothic-style church with connecting garden to the parish house. Gothic in design and dating from the mid-1850s, the church was designed by Calvin Otis. Dark wood and rich colors contribute to an atmosphere of quiet beauty. The sound of St. John's carillon is a melodious gift to the neighborhood. In 1960 Macon Street between the church and parish house was closed to make room for a garden.

❹ **Savannah College of Art and Design (SCAD)** – *342 Bull Street, 912-525-5100.*

Romanesque red brick with upended cannon flanking the entrance, and originally built to be the Savannah Volunteer Guards Armory. Just south of Madison Square on Bull Street is the first building acquired by the Savannah College of Art and Design, designed in 1893 by William Gibbons Preston. Combined are red brick and molded terra-cotta. The growth of this college has brought vitality to the downtown neighborhood. ShopSCAD, at the corner, sells students' work.

❺ **Eliza Jewett House** – *326 Bull Street, 912-234-7257.*

A classic residence with a bookstore on the street level. The prosperous realtor Eliza Jewett built this house of stucco over brick. It is enhanced by the expanse of Madison Square in front and E. Shaver Bookseller below. In the 1950s the monocled character actor Charles Coburn came here often to visit his sister, Zoe.

 Exit the square north on Bull Street, cross Liberty Street to ...

Monument of General James Oglethorpe
Courtesy of the artist, Pamela Lee

Chippewa Square

The square honors the victory of American troops under General Jacob Brown in the Battle of Chippewa in the War of 1812. In the center is a bronze sculpture by Daniel Chester French of James Oglethorpe in the full dress uniform of a British general. His right hand rests on his unsheathed sword; his eyes gaze southward toward Florida, guarding Georgia from the threat of the Spaniards. Henry Bacon, who designed the base, also teamed with Daniel Chester French to create the Lincoln Memorial in Washington, D.C.

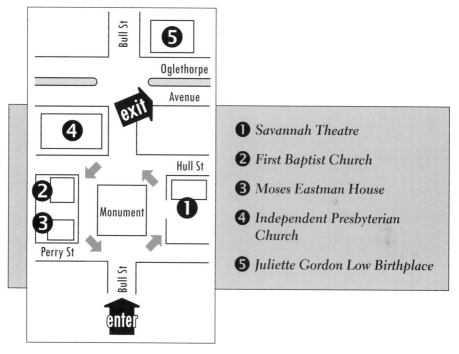

1 *Savannah Theatre*

2 *First Baptist Church*

3 *Moses Eastman House*

4 *Independent Presbyterian Church*

5 *Juliette Gordon Low Birthplace*

Points of interest:

1 Savannah Theatre – *222 Bull Street, 912-233-7764.*

Today you'll see 1950s Art Deco architecture, but the first structure on this site was a Greek Revival theater that seated a thousand spectators. It was designed in 1818 by English architect William Jay and built by Amos Scudder of New Jersey. Traveling on an oxcart loaded with his carpentry tools, Mr. Scudder took three months to get to Savannah.

This location is considered to be the oldest theater site in continuous operation in the United States. The first plays performed there, in December 1818, were the comedy *The Soldier's Daughter* and the farce *Raising the Wind.*

First Old Savannah Theatre in Greek Revival Style

Current Savannah Theatre

In 1906 the theater was almost completely destroyed by a fire "of incendiary origin." Only two exterior walls remained. Newspaper accounts of the day reported that Thomas Dixon's play *The Clansman* was scheduled to be performed and that the Ku Klux Klan may have started the fire.

Later that same year the theater was rebuilt, with some of the old walls still intact, and it survived until 1948, when it was completely destroyed by fire. The current theater reopened as a movie house in 1950, with a screening of *Mister Eighty-Eight*, starring Burt Lancaster and Dorothy McGuire. Today the Savannah Theatre offers live performances of musicals, comedy, and drama. In the lobby you'll find an interesting museum.

Over its nearly two-hundred-year history, having survived numerous fires and subsequent remodelings, the Savannah Theatre has persevered as a center for the arts and entertainment. Its stage and screen have hosted such stars as Edwin Booth, Sarah Bernhardt, Lillian Russell, Oscar Wilde, W. C. Fields, Fanny Davenport, Joseph Jefferson, James Hackett, E. H. Southern, Julie Marlowe, Otis Skinner, Henry Irving, Ellen Terry, Tyrone Power, Savannah's own Charles Coburn, and even Ty Cobb and possibly John Wilkes Booth.

❷ First Baptist Church (1833) – *223 Bull Street, 912-234-2671.*

Of Greek temple design with six massive columns built by Mathew Lufburrow, the church was based on a design by Elias Carter. This is a missionary Baptist congregation with the motto "Established in Faith; Nurtured in Hope; Continuing in Love."

A city ordinance of 1791 established a Baptist society at Houston and Duke (now Congress) Streets. The first minister, Dr. Henry Holcombe, organized this church in 1800. Under the leadership of Sylvanus Landrum, the church remained open during the Civil War.

❸ Moses Eastman House – *17 West McDonough Street.*

Tall columns accent this elegant round porch. This house was designed by architect Charles Cluskey and construction began in 1844. Moses Eastman was a watchmaker and jeweler. The building was owned by John Stoddard from 1848 to 1870.

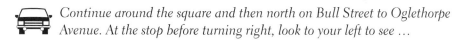 *Continue around the square and then north on Bull Street to Oglethorpe Avenue. At the stop before turning right, look to your left to see ...*

❹ Independent Presbyterian Church – *207 Bull Street, 912-236-3346.*

Note the soaring steeple with clocks on all four sides, topped by a gleaming brass weather vane. Organized in 1755, this congregation has strong Scottish ties. In 1818 architect John Greene won a design competition with his plans for this building. Its appearance is similar to St. Martin in the Fields in London. When the church burned in 1889, William Gibbons Preston directed the rebuilding.

Lowell Mason, who wrote favorite hymns such as "Nearer My God to Thee" and "Joy to the World," served as organist here in the 1820s. Reverend I. S. K. Axson was minister in 1868. His granddaughter Ellen Axson was married here to Woodrow Wilson on June 24, 1885. Folks wondered what she saw in "that unknown lawyer from Atlanta."

It was here that funeral services were held for the six Savannah soldiers who died in combat at the First Battle of Manassas.

At the beginning of the movie *Forrest Gump*, a feather floated down in front of this steeple, glided over a car fender, and landed between two dirty tennis shoes worn by actor Tom Hanks.

Independent Presbyterian Church
Courtesy of the artist, Pamela Lee

 Turn right on Oglethorpe Avenue. Look left at the four-story house on the northeast corner …

❺ Juliette Gordon Low Girl Scout National Center (Wayne-Gordon House Museum, c. 1818) – *10 East Oglethorpe Avenue,* *912-233-4501.*

Juliette Low founded the Girl Scouts of the United States in 1912. She was born here on Halloween night in 1860. This elegant town house was built for James Moore Wayne, a mayor of Savannah and Supreme Court Justice, who sold it to Juliette's grandfather William Washington Gordon in 1831. The furnishings reflect the years of Juliette's youth, including her portrait and family treasures. Visitors welcome. Gift shop.

 Continue east on Oglethorpe Avenue for two blocks; look to your right and you will see …

Colonial Park Cemetery – *Abercorn Street and Oglethorpe Avenue.*

The gates were given by the Daughters of the American Revolution. Established in 1750 for Christ Church parish, Colonial Park was enlarged in 1789 to include all denominations. Many distinguished Savannah residents are buried here, including seven hundred victims of the 1820 yellow fever epidemic.

Duels were fought here, including one between Lachlan McIntosh and Button Gwinnett, a signer of the Declaration of Independence. Mr. Gwinnett was mortally wounded. Opponents in life, they're neighbors in death in the cemetery. The cemetery was closed to burials before the Civil War; no Confederate soldiers are buried here. However, Union troops camped here during the war and

Juliette Gordon Low Birthplace

Courtesy of the artist, Pamela Lee

rearranged headstones, sometimes changing the dates in their spare time. The Trustees' Garden Club has done much to maintain the cemetery.

 On your left, across the median is …

Mary Marshall Row – 230 to 244 East Oglethorpe Avenue.

These four houses were saved from demolition in 1960. They were to be torn down for their valuable Savannah gray bricks and marble steps. The carriage houses had already been flattened when Mrs. F. Bland Tucker (Polly) sounded an alert that someone was about to wreck these houses built by Mary Marshall. The pioneer preservationists Albert Stoddard, Lee Adler, Karl Roebling, and Harry Duncan quickly bought all four, thus realizing one of the first victories for the Historic Savannah Foundation. One of the houses was later occupied by Pulitzer prize–winning poet and author Conrad Aiken and his wife, Mary, when they returned to Savannah in 1962. The house at 228 East Oglethorpe Avenue had been Conrad Aiken's childhood home.

 Continue east on Oglethorpe Avenue through two lights to Houston Street; turn right to …

Crawford Square

Here you'll find a mix of restored houses and new construction. Cisterns were built throughout the city in the 1830s and '40s. Built by Amos Scudder and Charles Cluskey, they trapped and stored rainwater for fire emergencies. This square was named for Savannahian William Harris Crawford, who ran for president of the United States in 1816. It was laid out in 1841.

Point of interest:

✪ **Cistern** – An interesting long-domed structure in a dugout area. Trapped rainwater, sometimes to a depth of nine feet, was stored here for fighting fires. Imagine the clouds of bloodthirsty mosquitoes breeding in this much stagnant water! Savannah houses were always in danger of burning, as so many were built of highly flammable heart pine.

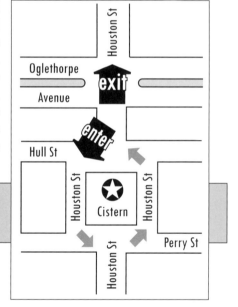

 Exit the square north on Houston Street leading to Greene Square ...

Greene Square

This square was named for General Nathanael Greene, aide to George Washington in the Revolutionary War. The general was also honored by the obelisk in Johnson Square, where he and his son are buried. In gratitude for his service, he was given Mulberry Grove Plantation, where he died at age 44 of sunstroke, leaving behind his widow, Catherine. It was there in 1793 that Eli Whitney, along with the children's tutor, Phineas Miller, invented the cotton gin, which revolutionized the cotton industry.

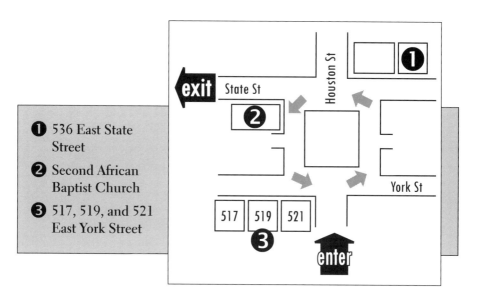

1 536 East State Street

2 Second African Baptist Church

3 517, 519, and 521 East York Street

The John Dorsett House
536 East State Street

Courtesy of the artist, Jill Howell

Points of interest:

1 536 East State Street

A teeny red frame house built for John Dorsett, 1845. It was moved here by pioneer preservationist Stella Henderson. This is the tiniest of Savannah's little crooked houses, with only 511 square feet.

2 Second African Baptist Church – *123 Houston Street, 912-233-6563.*

The first gathering of free slaves took place here in 1865. The Reverend Henry Cunningham (1759–1852), a free man of color, founded this church in 1802 and was the first pastor. The main sanctuary is on the second floor with heart-pine floors and curved pews.

❸ 517, 519, and 521 East York Street

517 East York Street – *The Clarke-Davenport House, 1799.*

This house was built by Stephen Clarke for his wife, Susannah. It is one of only a few eighteenth-century houses still standing. Susannah raised two children here after her husband's death, and her daughter Sarah married Isaiah Davenport, a master builder. In 1913, Thomas Holly, an African American realtor, owned the house as an investment.

519 East York Street

A mustard-colored house built in 1799 for Edward White from Brookline, Massachusetts. Mr. White was a major in the Revolutionary army and a member of the Society of the Cincinnati, an organization of men who fought with George Washington in the Revolution. The house was restored by preservationist Stella Henderson in 1971.

521 East York Street

A two-story brick house (1840) made of Savannah gray bricks. These coveted bricks were handmade at the Hermitage Plantation built by Henry McAlpin, c. 1825.

 Exit west on State Street to ...

Columbia Square

The fountain was given by Eudora and Wainwright Roebling in memory of her parents, Augusta and Wymberley DeRenne. It came from Wormsloe Plantation, home of Noble Jones, who sailed to America with James Oglethorpe in 1733. Columbia Square and Greene Square were added to the original town plan in 1799.

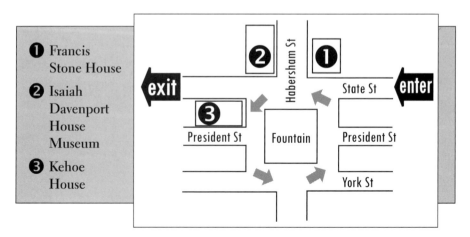

❶ Francis Stone House

❷ Isaiah Davenport House Museum

❸ Kehoe House

Points of interest:

❶ Francis Stone House (1821) – *402 East State Street.*

A high-stooped, white frame house with black trim built for city alderman Francis Stone. Mr. Stone was given five shares of Central Railroad stock in gratitude for his heroic service during the yellow fever epidemic of 1854.

❷ Isaiah Davenport House Museum – *324 East State Street, 912-236-8097.*

The first house saved by the seven ladies to whom this book is dedicated. It was the threat of its destruction in 1955 that outraged seven ladies enough to halt the wrecking ball. Thus began the Historic Savannah Foundation.

In 1818 Isaiah Davenport became an alderman and began construction of this Federal-style brick house for himself and his wife Sarah. Today it is a fine museum. The Davenport House is owned by the Historic Savannah Foundation. Visitors welcome. Gift shop.

Isaiah Davenport House Museum

❸ Kehoe House – *123 Habersham Street, 912-232-1020.*

Red brick, iron, and terra-cotta, built for William Kehoe, founder of Kehoe Iron Works; DeWitt Bruyn was the architect. Mr. Kehoe, an Irishman, had nine children.

When the eldest daughter and her five children came home to live, he often packed up rosary and newspaper and climbed to the cupola for a respite. The mood is Romantic Revival with carved-oak woodwork inside and twelve marble mantles. The stairs, sills, and columns are all made of iron.

The Kehoe House was later a funeral home, and then owned by investors, including Joe Namath of football fame. It is now the Kehoe House Inn.

Kehoe House

Courtesy of the artist, Jill Howell

 Exit the square west on State Street, and go two blocks to …

Oglethorpe Square

When first laid out, it was called Upper New Square. The Owens-Thomas House is one of the stately mansions to survive the test of time. The Moravian Marker honors the service of the Moravians, who were in Savannah from 1736 to 1740. Arriving in Savannah to unite Christians and convert non-Christians, the Moravian community was never very large and did not last long. They had hoped to assist the persecuted Lutheran refugees from Salzburg, but the Lutheran leaders in Germany sent the Salzburgers upriver to Ebenezer instead. The Moravians had hoped to convert Native Americans to Christianity. Although their mission was not successful, their work marked the beginning of the group's work in North America.

Points of interest:

❶ **Cluskey Buildings** – *127–129 Abercorn Street.*

Two brick office buildings with leafy ironwork, blue-green shutters. The Irish architect Charles Blaney Cluskey designed these buildings. Mr. Cluskey greatly influenced the Classical Revival in the South.

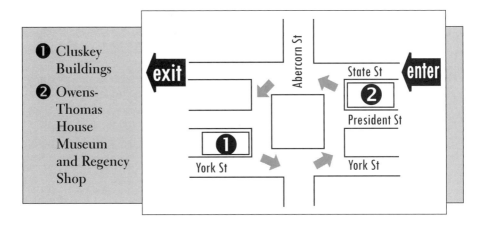

1 Cluskey
Buildings

2 Owens-
Thomas
House
Museum
and Regency
Shop

2 Owens-Thomas House – *124 Abercorn Street, 912-790-8879.*

Outstanding Regency architecture. The English architect William Jay designed and supervised construction of this building for cotton broker Richard Richardson in 1817. In 1825 the Marquis de Lafayette spoke from the side balcony to cheering Savannahians. Miss Meta Thomas, granddaughter of the previous owner, George Owens, willed the house to the Telfair Academy for a museum. Visitors welcome. Gift shop.

Owens-Thomas House
Courtesy of the artist, Jill Howell

 Exit the square west on State Street, and go two blocks to …

Wright Square

Originally this was Percival Square, in honor of the colonists' friend in Parliament, the Right Honorable John Lord Viscount Percival, Earl of Egmont, and president of the trustees of the colony.

In the southeast quadrant is a granite boulder (❹) given by the Colonial Dames to honor Chief Tomochichi, who was buried nearby in 1739. James Oglethorpe was a pallbearer at his funeral. Centering the square are the pink Georgia marble columns of the monument to William Washington Gordon, founder and president of the Central of Georgia Railroad and grandfather of Juliette Gordon Low.

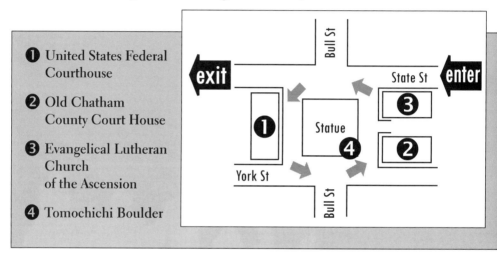

❶ United States Federal Courthouse

❷ Old Chatham County Court House

❸ Evangelical Lutheran Church of the Ascension

❹ Tomochichi Boulder

Points of interest:

❶ United States Federal Courthouse (former Post Office Building)
– 125 Bull Street.
A massive Georgia marble and granite building with an intricate frieze under the eaves. Many architectural ideas are combined here. Look up at the tower with its marble arches and intriguing details.

❷ Old Chatham County Court House (1889) *– 124 Bull Street.*
Romanesque yellow brick and terra-cotta on a granite base. The new Chatham County Courthouse is on Montgomery Street and the old Court House is now the administrative legislative center for the city of Savannah. William Gibbons Preston was the architect.

❸ Evangelical Lutheran Church of the Ascension (1879) *– 120 Bull Street.*
With soaring French Gothic spires, this church was founded by Lutherans from Salzburg, Austria. Salzburgers, led by Pastor John Martin Boltzius, gathered on Georgia's sandy soil in 1734 to organize this parish. In 1771 the Lutherans (Salzburgers) bought the site. They then bought the wooden courthouse on the south trust lot and rolled it across President Street on palmetto logs and added a steeple and a bell. They built a new Greek Revival structure here with six Doric columns in 1836. It was completed in 1844. It was used as a hospital for soldiers

during the Civil War. The present structure was begun in 1875. The Ascension window was installed in 1878.

 Continue west on State Street to …

Telfair Square

This became Telfair Square in the 1880s in honor of the Telfairs, a family of scope and vision. The original name was St. James Square, after the square in London. It is the fourth of James Oglethorpe's original four squares.

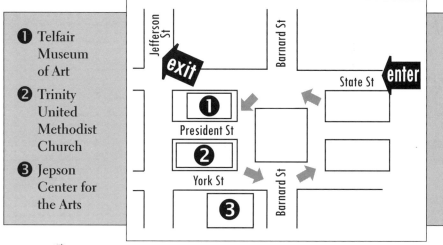

❶ Telfair Museum of Art

❷ Trinity United Methodist Church

❸ Jepson Center for the Arts

Telfair Museum of Art
Courtesy of the artist, Pamela Lee

Points of interest:

❶ **Telfair Museum of Art** – *124 Barnard Street, 912-790-8800.*

A Regency mansion designed by English architect William Jay. Governor Edward Telfair's son, Alexander, commissioned William Jay to design this house. As specified in the will of his sister, Mary, the Telfair home became the Telfair Academy of Arts and Sciences in 1886. Expansion was overseen by the architect Detlef Leinau, who preserved Mr. Jay's classical Greek design while providing space for exhibits, concerts, and lectures. Visitors welcome. Gift shop.

❷ Trinity United Methodist Church – *225 West President Street, 912-233-4766.*

Two Corinthian columns in front welcome visitors to the oldest Methodist church in Savannah. Inside is hand-hewn Georgia pine. The church is built of stucco-over-Savannah-gray bricks along the lines of Wesley Chapel in London. John Hogg was the architect. Trinity Church remained open through the Civil War, even as Union soldiers camped out in the square. After a major restoration project, the "Mother Church of Methodism" has received a preservation award from the Historic Savannah Foundation.

❸ Jepson Center for the Arts – *207 West York Street, 912-790-8800.*

This building features a soaring, sunlit atrium and offers many attractions for art lovers. This 64,000-square-foot center, designed by Moshe Safdie, was opened in 2006 as a modern expansion of the Telfair Museum of Art. It features traveling exhibits, African American art, photography, community gallery, a two-hundred-seat auditorium, a café, and more. Don't miss *Artzeum*, the "hands-on" children's gallery. Visitors welcome. Gift shop.

Continue around the square and exit west on State Street for one block, turn right onto Jefferson Street for one block, cross Broughton Street for two blocks. Turn left onto Bryan Street to …

Franklin Square

Laid out in 1790, Water Tank Square was renamed to honor Benjamin Franklin, the colonists' agent in London. Mr. Franklin sent seeds of the Chinese tallow tree to Noble Jones in Georgia, with a note saying he hoped they'd flourish. Indeed they did! Now this tree grows wild with leaves like Chinese lanterns and "popcorn" seedpods. The bronze figures on the monument, sculpted by James Mastin, honor the more than five hundred Haitians who fought with Casimir Pulaski in the Siege of Savannah in 1779.

Point of interest:

⭐ **First African Baptist Church** (1859) – 23 *Montgomery Street, 912-233-6597.*

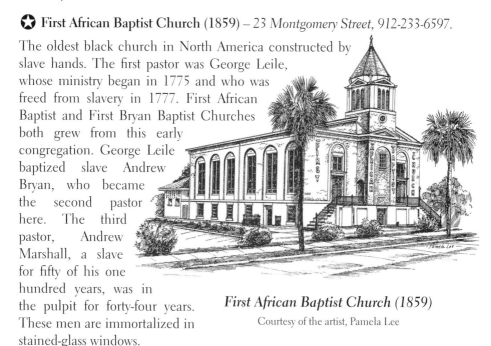

The oldest black church in North America constructed by slave hands. The first pastor was George Leile, whose ministry began in 1775 and who was freed from slavery in 1777. First African Baptist and First Bryan Baptist Churches both grew from this early congregation. George Leile baptized slave Andrew Bryan, who became the second pastor here. The third pastor, Andrew Marshall, a slave for fifty of his one hundred years, was in the pulpit for forty-four years. These men are immortalized in stained-glass windows.

First African Baptist Church (1859)

Courtesy of the artist, Pamela Lee

The remnants of slavery can be seen inside. In the floor downstairs are breathing holes used by slaves fleeing to freedom via a secret tunnel to the river. On pews

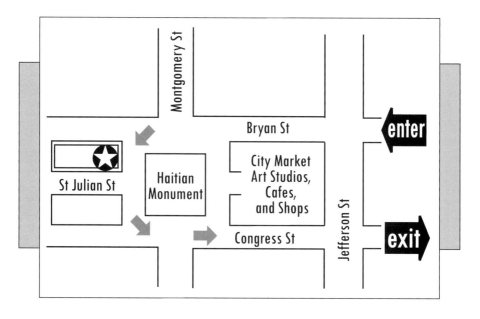

in the balcony, enslaved artisans scratched their African signatures—silent mementos of souls in chains.

 Exit the square east on Congress Street to Ellis Square. Pass by buildings that formerly served as seed and feed warehouses, and are now cafes, shops, and artists' studios ...

Ellis Square

This was one of the original four squares and the site of Savannah's colorful city market. Farmers came in mule wagons full of peaches, persimmons, watermelons, scuppernongs, butterbeans, and okra. Women carried baskets of vegetables on their heads. Fresh fish, crabs, and oysters were for sale. Sounds of bargaining and laughter and the aroma of boiling peanuts filled the air.

Over loud objections, the market was torn down in 1954 for a parking garage. It was this terrible mistake that sparked the strong preservation movement that has made our Historic District a national treasure. Today this urban plaza is a popular spot for relaxing while exploring the artists' studios in the area of the old market. A life-size bronze statue of Johnny Mercer, Savannah's famed lyricist, by local sculptor Susie Chisholm, stands at the west end. A visitor center and restrooms are located in this square.

 Continue east on Congress Street. On your left is Paula Deen's restaurant. Johnson Square is next.

Johnson Square

Johnson Square was the first square laid out by Oglethorpe in 1733, and was named for Robert Johnson, friend and helper to Oglethorpe and governor of South

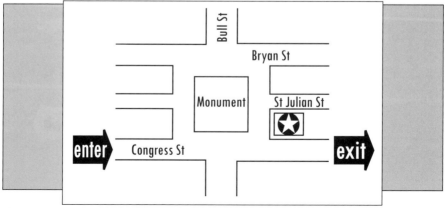

Carolina. The obelisk is a monument to General Nathanael Greene, Revolutionary War hero and chief of staff to General George Washington. The cornerstone was laid by the Marquis de Lafayette in 1825.

Point of interest:

⭐ **Christ Church Episcopal** – *18 Abercorn Street, 912-236-2500.*

The "Mother Church of Georgia" held its first service on February 12, 1733, at the colony's founding. This Greek Revival building was designed by James Hamilton Couper and completed in 1840. It is the third structure on this site chosen by Oglethorpe upon his arrival. The bell in the belfry was made by Revere and Son in 1819.

The first minister to the colonists was the Reverend Dr. Henry Herbert, chaplain on the ship *Ann*. Later came Reverend John Wesley and Reverend George Whitefield. Reverend Whitefield, with his friend James Habersham, was the founder in 1740 of the Bethesda Home for Boys, until recently America's oldest existing orphanage. John Wesley started America's first Sunday school in 1736, and his brother Charles Wesley wrote the first hymnal.

 No need to circle this square. Continue east on Congress Street for two blocks to …

Reynolds Square

Mapped out in 1734, Reynolds Square was home to the Filature, where cocoons were brought, and from them silk was woven. Hopes for a silk industry never materialized, and fire burned the Filature in 1758. The square was named for

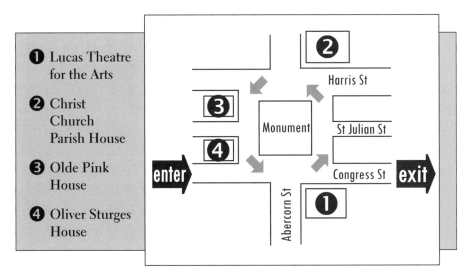

① Lucas Theatre for the Arts

② Christ Church Parish House

③ Olde Pink House

④ Oliver Sturges House

Lucas Theatre for the Arts

Courtesy of the artist, Jean Lim

John Reynolds, the first royal governor of Georgia. The statue by sculptor Marshall Daugherty is of the Reverend John Wesley and was dedicated by the Methodist Church in 1969. Mr. Wesley wears the clerical vestments of the Church of England.

Points of interest:

❶ **Lucas Theatre for the Arts** – *32 Abercorn Street. 912-525-5040.*

A 1920s movie palace restored to former glory.
Arthur Lucas built this grand movie palace, which hosted vaudeville's finest acts, as well as movies—first silent films, then "talkies." The Lucas Theatre for the Arts was formed in 1989 to undertake a magnificent restoration. Today it is owned by the Savannah College of Art and Design (SCAD), and offers live theater and films. Open for tours.

❷ **Christ Church Parish House** – *18 Abercorn Street.*

This church house features fourteen arched windows on a former cigar factory. Who knows how many stogies were rolled in this stucco-over-brick building when it housed the Cortez Cigar Company? Christ Church bought it in 1949 for offices and a Sunday school.

Through the generosity of Emmaus House, an outreach project of a number of parishes and denominations, the hungry and homeless come here for a hot breakfast during the week.

❸ Olde Pink House – *23 Abercorn Street, 912-232-4286.*

One of few buildings to survive the inferno of 1796, when over two hundred houses burned to ashes. Built for James Habersham Jr. and his wife Esther Wylly in 1771, this house brightens the neighborhood with rose-pink stucco. Toward the end of the Civil War, it was headquarters for Union General Zebulon York. Now it is a fine restaurant and tavern. Notice the Palladian window above the columned entrance. Both authors of this guidebook are related to the original owners.

❹ Oliver Sturges House – *27 Abercorn Street.*

Masterful masonry with earthquake rods and dolphin downspouts. Built for the wealthy merchant Oliver Sturges in 1813, this house stands where John Wesley's parsonage stood in 1736. Mr. Sturges met here with Captain Moses Rogers to plan the voyage in 1819 of the SS *Savannah*, the first steamship to cross the Atlantic. Now it houses the offices of a newspaper publishing corporation, Morris Multimedia.

 Continue east on Congress Street for two blocks to …

The Olde Pink House
Courtesy, Dan Kaufman/Studio Kaufman LLC

Warren Square

This square was named for General Joseph Warren, a Revolutionary War hero who died in the Battle of Bunker Hill in 1775. Warren Square and neighboring Washington Square were added in 1790.

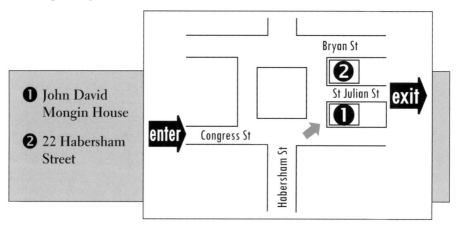

Points of interest:

❶ **John David Mongin House** – *24 Habersham Street.*

This home was a hospital when yellow fever struck in 1876. Mr. Mongin was a planter of Sea Island cotton. His father-in-law lived at Bloody Point on Daufuskie Island, near Hilton Head. The Mongins inherited the Daufuskie property but lived here on Warren Square. The house once served as the rectory for Christ Church.

❷ **22 Habersham Street.**

A frame house that escaped the terrible fire. Miraculously, this house was not consumed by the fire that gobbled up more than two hundred houses in four hours in 1796. The fire began in Mr. Gromet's bake house on Market Square (Ellis Square) and, pushed by strong winds, rolled from one rooftop to the next. Water thrown from buckets was useless.

Exit east on St. Julian Street, two blocks to Washington Square ... (notice the tabby street of oyster shells). On your right in the second block is the ...

Hampton Lillibridge House (c. 1796) – 507 East St. Julian Street.

This house features a widow's walk on the gambrel roof of a frame house. Built by New Jersey native Hampton Lillibridge, it's rumored to be haunted. Even after the bishop of Georgia performed a rite of exorcism, the ghost stories persisted.

The widow's walk, seen on many eighteenth- and early-nineteenth-century New England houses, is a platform on the roof used as a lookout for the sails of incoming ships against the horizon.

Washington Square

Added in 1790, this square was named for George Washington, the first president of the United States. There's no monument here, only benches and a sense of tranquility.

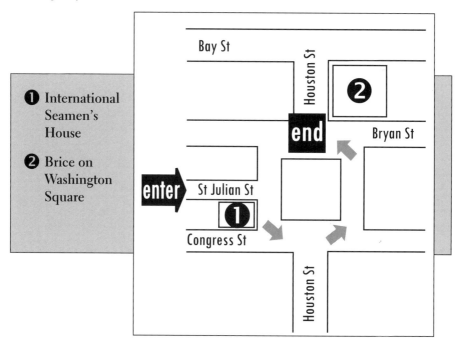

Points of interest:

❶ International Seamen's House – *25 Houston Street, 912-234-2438.*

A welcoming place for sailors. Seafaring men in Georgia's state port come here to find a warm welcome and to enjoy games, music, television, and the Holy Bible in many languages. Run by the Port Authority, the International Seamen's House offers a large dose of Savannah's famous hospitality.

❷ Brice on Washington Square – *601 East Bay Street, 912-238-1200.*

A popular place for tourists to stay. This building was once a livery stable for boarding and hiring riding horses and carriages. Later it became the Coca-Cola Bottling Plant and then the Mulberry Inn. Today it is a very nice hotel.

Georgia Historical Society
Courtesy, Herb Woo family

*For more in-depth information on any of
the buildings on this driving tour, visit the*

Georgia Historical Society
at 501 Whitaker Street
(Gaston and Whitaker Streets)
912-651-2125

*This building houses a rare collection of old manuscripts, books, maps,
architectural drawings, photos, and artifacts related to Georgia history.
www.georgiahistory.com.*

Hours: Wednesday–Friday, noon–5 p.m. and
every first and third Saturday 10:00 a.m.–5:00 p.m.

Hitting the
High Spots on Foot

*Allow about an hour and a half for this pleasant walk through twelve
of Savannah's twenty-two famous squares. For more details on the points of
interest along your walk, consult the preceding chapter, "Savannah Panorama,"
in this guidebook. Follow the easy directions and the map.*

 Begin at the north end of Bull Street at …

Johnson Square (A)

❶ This was the first square laid out by our
founder James Oglethorpe. The monument in
the center is dedicated to **General Nathanael
Greene**, General George Washington's valued
aide in the Revolutionary War.

❷ **Christ Church (Episcopal)** is the "Mother
Church of Georgia," where John Wesley started
the first Sunday school. Juliette Gordon,
founder of the Girl Scouts, married William
Low in this church. Both authors of the
Savannah Guidebook were married here.

 *Walk east on Congress Street just two
blocks to …*

General Nathanael Greene
1742-1786

Courtesy, Georgia Department
of Archives and History

SAVANNAH SQUARES

Savannah River

start

RIVER ST

BAY ST

BRYAN ST

end

Franklin Square

City Market

Ellis Square

ST JULIAN ST

CONGRESS ST

Johnson Square

A

H

Wright Square

BROUGHTON ST

JEFFERSON ST

BARNARD ST

WHITAKER ST

BULL ST

MARTIN LUTHER KING JR BLVD

PRESIDENT ST

Telfair Square

K

OGLETHORPE AVE

MONTGOMERY ST

HULL ST

McDONOUGH ST

PERRY ST

Orleans Square

J

WHITAKER ST

Chippewa Square

I

LIBERTY ST

-94-

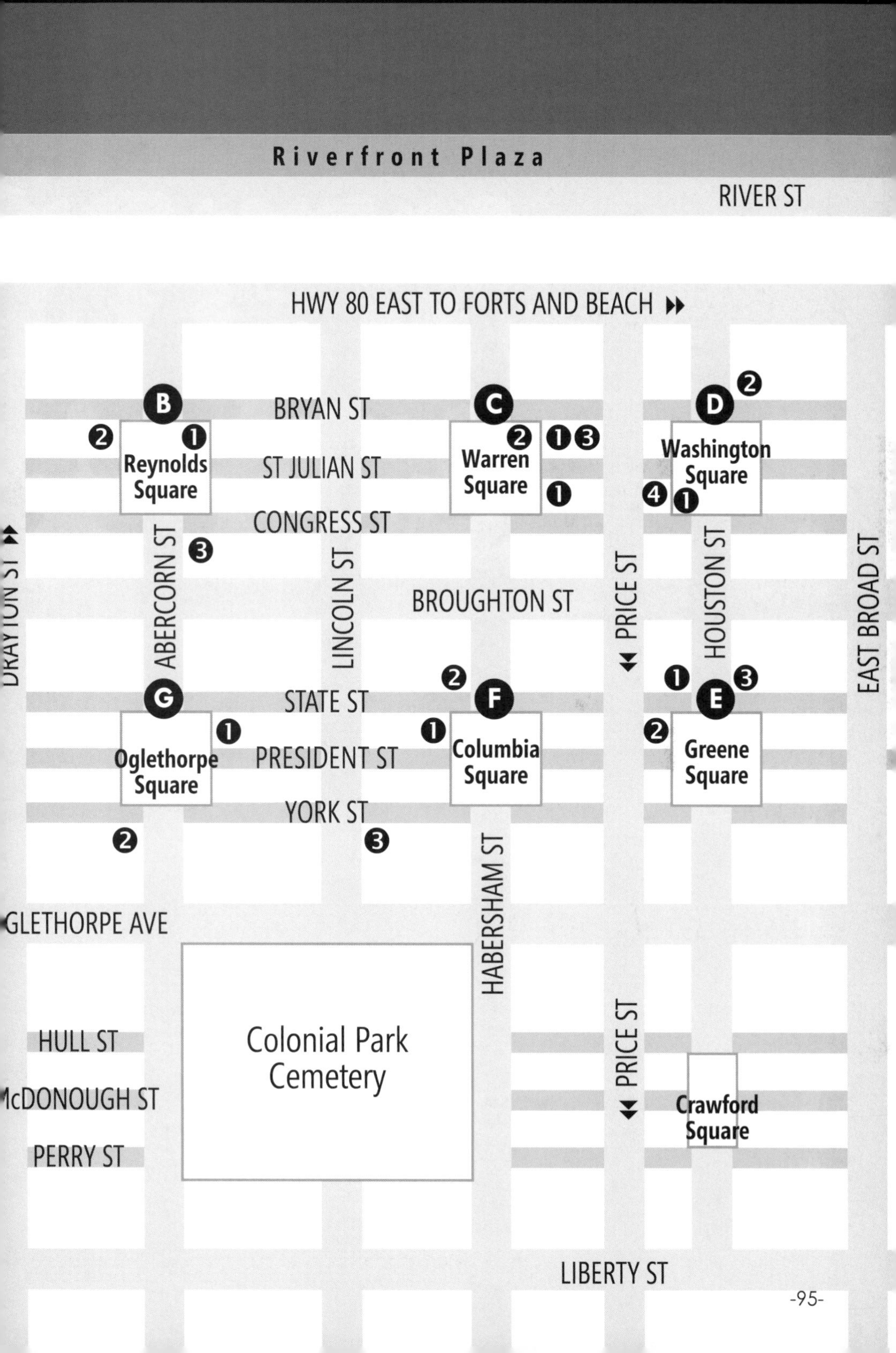

Riverfront Plaza

RIVER ST

HWY 80 EAST TO FORTS AND BEACH ▶▶

B BRYAN ST **C** **D** **2**

2 **1** ST JULIAN ST **2** **1** **3**

Reynolds Square

Warren Square

Washington Square

1

4 **1**

CONGRESS ST

3

DRAYTON ST

ABERCORN ST

LINCOLN ST

PRICE ST

HOUSTON ST

EAST BROAD ST

BROUGHTON ST

G STATE ST **2** **F** **1** **3**

1 **E**

Oglethorpe Square

1 PRESIDENT ST **1** Columbia Square

2 Greene Square

2 YORK ST **3**

GLETHORPE AVE

Colonial Park Cemetery

HABERSHAM ST

HULL ST

PRICE ST

McDONOUGH ST

Crawford Square

PERRY ST

LIBERTY ST

Reynolds Square (B)

❶ Here stands the bronze statue of **Reverend John Wesley**, who seems to be delivering a sermon. He was the third rector of Christ Church and the founder of Methodism.

❷ **The Olde Pink House** was built in 1771 by James Habersham Jr., one of three sons of James Habersham, who shipped the first cotton from Savannah to England. He lived here with his wife, Esther Wylly, and their family until his death. It is now a first-class restaurant.

The Olde Pink House
Courtesy of the artist, Jill Howell

❸ **The Lucas Theatre** is a restored 1920s movie palace. Clint Eastwood threw a party here after the filming of *Midnight in the Garden of Good and Evil.* Guests were entertained by the World Famous Crabettes, Savannah's own home-grown music group, complete with gutbucket, clarinet, keyboard, accordions, and singers.

 Continue east on Congress Street for two blocks to ...

Warren Square (C)

❶ On the east side, look for two restored eighteenth-century clapboard houses numbered 22 and 24 Habersham Street.

❷ On the north side, at 404 East Bryan Street, is an example of a house that was moved to a safe location and tastefully restored by its owners.

 Exit square on St. Julian Street and ...

❸ Notice the simple wooden house at 426 East St. Julian Street on your left. This little cottage was built in the late 1700s. **Jane DeVeaux** had a secret school in the attic for slave children before the Civil War.

Cross Price Street. On your right is …

❹ The Hampton-Lillibridge House, at 507 East St. Julian Street, reputed to be the most haunted house in the city, has a widow's walk on top of the gambrel roof.

 Just ahead is …

Washington Square (D)

❶ **The International Seamen's House**, on the west side, offers southern hospitality to visiting seamen.

❷ The Brice on Washington Square, once a livery stable and later a Coca-Cola bottling plant, became the Mulberry Inn, and is now a comfortable hotel.

 Walk two blocks south on Houston Street to …

Greene Square (E)

❶ The green double house on the right at 7 and 9 Houston Street was owned in 1810 by Betsey and Henry Cunningham, free people of color. This neighborhood is known as the Old Fort Community.

❷ The **Second African Baptist Church** is where General Sherman met with the newly freed slaves during his occupation of Savannah near the end of the Civil War. He offered each of them forty acres and a mule, although few were able to actually take advantage of that opportunity.

The John Dorsett House

Courtesy of the artist, Jill Howell

❸ The teeny-weeny red frame house at 536 East State Street was built in 1845 for John Dorsett.

 Now, walk west on State Street to …

Columbia Square (F)

❶ On the west side of the square is the **Victorian Kehoe House**, once a funeral home and today a classic inn. At one time it was partly owned by Joe Namath of football fame. This inn was built by the owner of Kehoe Iron Works for his large Irish family.

Davenport House

Courtesy of the artist, Jill Howell

❷ **Davenport House**, on the north side of the square, is an example of Federal-style architecture. It was saved from destruction by the seven women to whom this book is dedicated.

 Exit the square on York Street, stopping to admire the ...

❸ **Orange Tree Gate**, which was forged by ironsmith Ivan Bailey. Iron artwork such as this is an attractive feature of the Historic District.

 Just ahead is ...

Oglethorpe Square (G)

❶ The **Owens-Thomas House Museum** is a fine example of Regency architecture. General Lafayette spoke to cheering townspeople in 1825 from the low balcony on the south side of the house.

❷ The large beige building, now the **Urban Health Center**, was once a United States Marine Hospital.

Keep walking on York Street to …

Wright Square (H)

1 You can't miss the large granite boulder given by the Colonial Dames in honor of **Tomochichi**, the Creek Indian chief who befriended James Oglethorpe upon his landing in the New World in 1733.

2 The monument in the center honors **William Washington Gordon**, founder of the Central of Georgia Railroad and grandfather of Juliette Gordon Low, founder of the Girl Scouts.

3 The **Lutheran Church of the Ascension** was completed in 1879 and had a congregation of Salzburgers. If the front door is open, enter and sit in the sanctuary upstairs and admire the Austrian stained-glass windows.

Tomochichi Boulder

4 The 1898 **United States Post Office and Courthouse,** with its massive columns, stands on the west side. The current post office is a block behind this building.

5 The old Romanesque-style **Chatham County Court House** (1889) is now the administrative and legislative center for the county.

 Before you leave the square to walk south on Bull street, notice the plaque on York Street indicating Savannah's first burial ground. Now walk one block south on Bull Street. On your left, you'll pass a famous building. It's the …

6 **Juliette Gordon Low Girl Scout National Center** (Wayne Gordon House Museum c. 1818). This Regency mansion was built for James Moore Wayne, mayor of Savannah and Supreme Court Justice. Juliette Low's grandfather, W. W. Gordon, bought it in 1831.

After crossing Oglethorpe Avenue, look right at the …

❼ Independent Presbyterian Church with its cloud-piercing steeple, gleaming weather vane, and clocks on all four sides. Woodrow Wilson married Ellen Axson, granddaughter of the pastor, in this church. Remember the movie *Forrest Gump*? In the beginning, a feather floated down in front of this steeple and landed between two dirty tennis shoes worn by Tom Hanks.

Our next square is …

James Edward Oglethorpe Monument
Courtesy of the artist, Pamela Lee

Chippewa Square (I)

1 Eating his box of chocolates, Forrest sat on the famous Gump bench, telling his story to a little lady who listened with interest. A replica of the bench used in the filming is in the Savannah History Museum.

2 In the center is the splendid bronze monument to **James Edward Oglethorpe**, founder of the colony of Georgia. He is wearing the uniform of a British general.

3 The **Savannah Theatre** stages live productions in this art deco building on the site of the country's oldest theater (three buildings) in continuous operation.

4 The **First Baptist Church** (1833) was built in Greek temple design with six massive columns.

 Exit west on Perry Street for two blocks. You'll come to ...

Orleans Square (J)

1 The fountain in the center was given in 1989 by Savannah's German heritage organizations.

2 The **Champion-McAlpin-Harper-Fowlkes House** has two-story Corinthian columns on a masterpiece of Greek Revival architecture. The house is owned by the Georgia Chapter of the Society of the Cincinnati.

3 The **Civic Center** hosts everything from concerts to circuses. This site originally held the historic Bulloch-Habersham house, designed by William Jay. It was torn down to build the Municipal Auditorium, which was torn down for a parking lot for the Civic Center.

 Walk north on Barnard Street two blocks to ...

Telfair Square (K)

1 The modern **Jepson Center** is Savannah's new modern art museum with special hands-on displays for children.

2 **Trinity United Methodist Church** is the oldest Methodist church in Savannah.

3 The **Telfair Museum of Art** (1818) is a Regency mansion designed by William Jay. The Telfair has an exciting schedule of events, including the elegant Telfair Ball and auction in February.

Continue two more blocks on Barnard Street to …

Ellis Square (L)

Here, gone but never forgotten, was once Savannah's colorful and lively City Market building, which was torn down in 1954. Loud objections and pleas fell on deaf ears, and a homely parking garage arose in the market's footprint. For fifty years folks tolerated this eyesore. It was finally torn down to "bring back" this delightful open space, creating a square to reestablish Oglethorpe's original four.

City Market (Torn down in 1954)

*For more information about the squares,
you can purchase Michael Jordan's video*

Savannah Square by Square

A Guided Tour of the Hostess City of the South.

*This one-hour video and others about Savannah by Michael Jordan
are available at local gift shops and at www.cosmosavannah.com.*

Riverbank Ramble

A Riverfront Walking Tour

The colony of Georgia began on Savannah's riverfront in 1733. Learn the fascinating history of this port city by following a series of markers, plaques, and monuments along the river. It's an easy comfortable walk, wheelchair accessible, without the hazards presented by the cobblestones that surface River Street.

 Start your walk on River Street, 100 yards west of the Hyatt Hotel, at the replica of the ...

SS Savannah

The first steamship to cross the Atlantic Ocean left Savannah in 1819.

Steamship *Savannah*

Steamship *Savannah*

 Also notice behind the replica the marker for the ...

SS Savannah *and the* SS John Randolph

The SS *Savannah* was the first steamship to cross the Atlantic Ocean, sailing from this harbor in May 1819 and arriving at Liverpool twenty-seven days later. She was owned by the Savannah Steamship Company, of which William Scarbrough was the principal promoter. The SS *John Randolph*, America's first successful iron steamship in commerce, was launched here in 1834. Made for Gazaway B. Lamar of Savannah, she was the first of a great fleet of iron steamboats on the rivers of America.

 Look toward the Hyatt to see the marker designating the ...

Start of the Bartram Trail

One of forty-two markers telling of William Bartram's adventures exploring a trail through the South, from wrestling alligators in the St. John's River to sketching the flora and fauna he saw in the mountains of north Georgia. The marker designates the start of the Bartram Trail, the route traced by John and William Bartram from Savannah through Georgia from 1773 to 1777.

 Now look on the railing alongside the river ...

● Plaque 1 – Ships That Carried the Name *Savannah*

This plaque describes ships named *Savannah*, from the first steamship (1819) to the nuclear ship *Savannah* (1953).

● Plaque 2 – The Settlement of Savannah

Here is the story of Oglethorpe's arrival from England in 1733 with 114 settlers to establish the thirteenth colony. Those early days were harsh as the colonists struggled to survive against inclement weather, insects, and other hardships as they tried to cultivate crops while defending against the Spaniards to the south.

 Near the Hyatt you'll see ...

The World War II Memorial

This memorial is a huge globe, a tribute to "the Greatest Generation," and in particular to the veterans of Savannah and Chatham County who died for our country's freedom.

World War II Memorial

 In front of the Hyatt is ...

The Historic Spot Where Oglethorpe
and the First Settlers Landed in 1733

The circle embedded in the pavement marks the historic spot where Oglethorpe
and the settlers landed.

♥ Plaque 3 – Savannah and the Slave Trade

Here we learn about the slave trade in the early development of the colony.

 Look toward River Street, where you'll see …

The African American Monument

We remember those people who were brought from Africa in chains to work on
cotton and rice plantations.

African American Monument
Courtesy, Dan Kaufman/Studio Kaufman LLC

On River Street across from the mini-visitor center, you'll find …

Savannah Waterfront

This marker tells of the economic and historical importance of the Savannah River. The first dock for oceangoing ships and the first commercial house opened in 1744, and cotton was exported throughout the nineteenth century. The cotton warehouses are now used for offices, shops, and restaurants. In 1956 the last cotton office was closed, and River Street revitalization began in 1977.

 Continue walking along the riverbank, and observe on your right a plaque mounted on a granite block honoring the …

Jewish Settlers

The Jewish settlers arrived on the *William and Sarah* in July 1733, soon after Oglethorpe's arrival. Savannah Jews have been prominent in all aspects of the commercial, cultural, and political life of the community.

♥ Plaque 4 – Savannah during the American Revolution

Here is the story of the Siege of Savannah, this city's major battle in the American Revolution.

 You'll be walking over six plaques embedded in the pavement …

♥ They describe the importance of **Gray's Reef National Marine Sanctuary**, located fifty miles south-southeast of Savannah. This first plaque pictures all the Barrier Islands along the Georgia coast and Gray's Reef on the ocean floor just beyond.

♥ The second plaque, **Reef Natural History**, shows the different habitats on the ocean floor. Hard rock and soft sand provide attachment and security for diverse marine life.

♥ The third plaque, **Ocean Stewardship**, reminds us that seventy-five thousand gallons of fresh water flow from the Savannah River into the Atlantic every second, and any trash thrown in here will disturb the ecology of the sea turtles, dolphins, and two hundred species of fish that call the reef home.

 You'll pass a tribute to …

Mayor John Rousakis, who encouraged the restoration of the riverfront in 1977.

● The fourth plaque embedded in the pavement, **Ocean Wildlife**, tells about the loggerhead and leatherback sea turtles, as well as the bottlenose and Atlantic spotted dolphins in the Savannah River. Critically endangered right whales swim from New England to give birth in the warm waters of coastal Georgia.

● The fifth plaque, **Geologic History**, tells us that thousands of years ago Gray's Reef was dry land. Mammals such as the giant ground sloth, woolly mammoths, mastodons, and small horses grazed on the evergreen ground cover and fir forests. Corals and other marine life have now covered the remains of these prehistoric animals.

● The sixth plaque, **Savannah River Watershed**, shows how the watershed transports sediments, nutrients, and pollutants from its origin in the mountains of north Georgia to the coast and beyond. Gray's Reef offers protection to 350 invertebrate species as well as to the fish within the sanctuary.

 Keep walking east along the rail to …

● Plaque 5 – Confederate Savannah

Learn the story of Savannah during the Civil War, 1861–1865, and the struggles of the people here during that chaotic time.

 Look behind you at the …

Anchor Memorial

A tribute to all merchant seamen who have perished at sea.

Note: Located in Laurel Grove Cemetery North, several miles away, is the Sailor's Burial Ground. In this burial ground, hallowed to the "men who go down to the sea in ships and occupy their business in great waters," are interred ship captains and seamen from many lands – America, Norway, Sweden, England, Scotland, Ireland and Germany. It serves as a burial place for seafarers "who may die in this Port."

Anchor Memorial

A commemorative service for the officers and men of the merchant marine whose mortal remains lie here is held annually at this site on the Sunday nearest National Maritime Day, May 22nd, which is the anniversary of the departure of the Steamship *Savannah* from this Port on her epoch-making voyage across the Atlantic in 1819.

♥ Plaque 6 – Savannah Cobblestones

These stones served as the ballast of ships from all over the world, which is why there are so many different types. Taken from the hulls of ships to make room for exports, they were used to surface Savannah's sandy streets, as well as construct buildings and retaining walls on the bluff.

♥ Plaque 7 – Christmas in Savannah, 1864

A miserable Christmas it was for weary citizens when General Sherman and his troops marched into town and presented our beloved city to President Lincoln as a Christmas gift. Coauthor Polly Cooper's great-great-grandfather, mayor pro tem George Washington Wylly, was one of the dignitaries who handed over the key of the city to General Sherman to avoid its destruction.

♥ Plaque 8 – Savannah's Wharves

This plaque illustrates how the riverfront has changed over the past 280 years. The early settlers faced a steep bank and a fast-moving tide.

♥ Plaque 9 – Shipping in the Port of Savannah

Along this walk you have probably seen at least one huge container ship and any number of tugs coming into Savannah's port, one of the busiest on the East Coast.

 You've now run out of riverwalk. Cross River Street and walk along the tabby sidewalk past the shops. In a few minutes, the riverwalk picks up again at the ...

Lions Club Flagpole

The three flags—the Lions Club flag, the American flag, and the state flag of Georgia—begin the rest of your walk.

Look beyond the flags to see the stone with the Liberty plaque on the south side of River Street.

The Liberty

The armed schooner *Liberty*, the first American naval vessel officially commissioned in 1775, sailed from this port commanded by Oliver Bowen and Joseph Habersham. Flying the Liberty flag—a white banner with a red border—she captured the British vessel *Phillipa*, commanded by Captain Richard Maitland, off the coast of Tybee that same year.

 Walk toward the railing alongside the river ...

♥ Plaque 10 – Ironclads and Gunboats of the Savannah River Squadron

The CSS *Georgia* was called the *Ladies Gunboat* when it was commissioned in 1862, because Confederate women earned the money to build it by sewing during the war. They also contributed to the CSS *Savannah*, completed in 1863. Both gunboats were part of the Savannah River Squadron, which protected the city from a Union attack by river.

♥ Plaque 11 – Crossing the Savannah

The old Talmadge Bridge has been replaced by a spectacular bridge giving romantic ambience to the riverfront. Some have suggested a new name for the bridge, perhaps honoring Oglethorpe or Tomochichi. Linking Georgia to South Carolina, the bridge could symbolize the link between the Native Americans and the colonists, just as those two leaders enjoyed a friendship that transcended vast differences.

 Look behind you at ...

The Statue of the Waving Girl

Here you will learn the story of Florence Martus (1868–1943), who waved at every ship coming in or leaving the Savannah Harbor for forty-four years. She lived with her brother, the lighthouse keeper, on nearby Elba Island.

 *Next ...*

The Olympic Cauldron

This cauldron was sculpted by ironsmith Ivan Bailey. The flame commemorates the yachting venue of the 1996 Olympics held in Atlanta and Savannah.

 Continue on to ...

Waving Girl Statue

Olympic Cauldron

🛡 **Plaque 12 – Native Americans on the Georgia Coast**

When Oglethorpe arrived, the Native Americans had been hunting and fishing on this coastal plain for ten thousand years. They had been building canoes and hunting with spears, eating deer and alligators, as well as turtles, eels, mussels, clams, and oysters.

🛡 **Plaque 13 – Savannah's Early Economy**

The first colonists identified products that they could export to England to establish an economy. They cultivated rice, tobacco, indigo, timber, and naval stores. Later, Sea Island cotton became the major crop that shaped Georgia's economy.

🛡 **Plaque 14 – Savannah's Liberty Ships and the Atlantic Bridge**

During World War II Savannah shipbuilders constructed eighty-seven Liberty Ships. At peak production, they could build a ship in forty days. The first was the SS *James Oglethorpe*, and among the later ships was the SS *Joseph Habersham.*

Coauthor Laura Lawton's mother, Josephine Connerat, smashed a bottle of champagne on the bow of the *Joseph Habersham*, the Liberty ship named for her great-great-great-grandfather, constructed here in 1943. A video by Michael Jordan of Cosmos Mariner Productions, *Ships for Victory: Liberty Ships of the Georgia Coast*, tells the story of the Savannah shipyards that arose overnight to meet wartime needs. The video is available in local shops or at www.cosmosavannah.com.

Mrs. Spencer Connerat (coauthor Laura Lawton's mother) shown on October 12, 1943 christening the Liberty Ship S.S. Joseph Habersham, named for her great-great-great-grandfather.

🛡 Plaque 15 – King Cotton

Growing mulberry trees to produce silk was not profitable for the colonists, but cultivating cotton led to great wealth and prosperity. The invention of the cotton gin by Eli Whitney on nearby Mulberry Grove Plantation gave the industry a huge boost. At its peak in World War I, cotton production averaged 1.7 million bales per year.

Cotton Wharves

 Walk up the ramp to the Marriott Hotel to the outside veranda and admire the bronze bust of ...

Hernando DeSoto (1495–1542)

This impressive portrait bust was sculpted by Billy Nelson in 1992. It honors the Spanish age of exploration and was commissioned by the Armstrong State University Hispanic Society.

End of Walk

Sculptor Billy Nelson in 1992 with his clay model of Hernando DeSoto before the piece was cast in bronze.

Courtesy of Billy Nelson

The Upper Factors Walk Walking Trek

A View of Historic Lower Factors Walk

Another stroll steeped in history awaits you on the upper level of the bluff/Bay Street, but the pathway upward is not necessarily an easy one. If you wish to continue, stand near the Olympic Cauldron and look towards the bluff and stone wall.

Walk toward the vehicular ramp below the stone wall. The first staircase (on the right) to greet you has been condemned and closed. There is another staircase toward your left – DO NOT climb this staircase.

There is a steep staircase a short distance to your RIGHT from the condemned staircase on Lower Factors Walk in front of the Olde Harbor Inn which DOES lead to Bay Street. Or, if you wish, you may walk up the vehicular ramp straight ahead. The ramp is narrow and without a sidewalk, but leads to Bay Street and the Old Harbor Light. The Upper Factors Walk Walking Trek begins at the Old Harbor Light.

Upper Factors Walk
Walking Trek

Discover More Monuments and Markers

HERB WOO '84

Steep Stone Staircase
Courtesy, Herb Woo family

This walk begins at the east end of Emmet Park. Walk into the park from Bay Street, or begin at the east end of River Street at the East Broad Street ramp.

Old Harbor Light

Circled by ship anchors, this light was built in 1858 and stands seventy-seven feet above sea level. One of a few gas lamps still standing, it was a rear-range light to aid ships navigating around the hulls of vessels sunk by the British in 1779 to close the harbor to French ships.

Follow the red brick walk to the ...

Bust of Dr. Noble Wimberly Jones

Dr. Jones came to Georgia as a boy with his father, Noble Jones, on the ship *Ann* in 1733, and he lived at their plantation *Wormsloe* on the Isle of Hope. He was elected to the Commons House, but loyalist governor James Wright viewed him as a threat and dissolved the Assembly. He organized the Georgia Medical Society, becoming its first president.

Walk down the middle of the grassy park.

Old Harbor Light
Courtesy, Herb Woo family

Savannah Cotton Exchange
With a View of the Upper and Lower Factors Walk

Courtesy of the illustrator, Pamela Lee

Chatham Artillery Monument

This combat militia unit was formed in 1786 and served during the Civil War. It exists today as the 1st Battalion of the 118th Field Artillery Unit in the Georgia National Guard.

The recipe for Chatham Artillery punch has been treasured for generations. Guests have demonstrated wobbly gaits and mumbling speech after imbibing its mixture—gin, rum, brandy, rye whiskey, Catawba wine, Benedictine, Maraschino cherries, green tea, lemons, orange juice, and brown sugar.

 Look for a marker near Bay Street dedicated to …

Jane Cuyler (1738–1799)

Jane Cuyler came to Savannah in 1768 and hosted meetings of Savannah's Liberty Boys, among them her son, Henry. The British governor James Wright called for her arrest for supporting the revolutionaries.

 Continue on the grass to the …

Vietnam Memorial

Two flags are on one pole, with the American flag on top and a black and white flag beneath. The lower flag displays the initials MIA (missing in action) and POW (prisoner of war), to lament the loss of our troops. The helmet on top of the rifle is a poignant reminder of this war. Local citizens who contributed to the memorial are acknowledged with bricks in the pavement.

 Walk along the sidewalk to a …

Marker Honoring Savannah's Irish and Robert Emmet

Robert Emmet led an unsuccessful Irish uprising in Dublin and was executed for treason. He was a hero to Savannah's Irish community, many of whom lived in the nearby Old Fort neighborhood.

 Continue down the center to the …

Celtic Cross

This Irish limestone cross was crafted in County Roscommon, Ireland. It was placed here in 1983 to honor those of Irish descent. Every year, as part of the St. Patrick's Day festivities, people of Irish heritage march with the Savannah Pipe and Drum Corps from the Cathedral to the Celtic Cross to lay a wreath.

Celtic Cross

 Walk to see on your left a …

Marker Honoring
Prince Hall, Mason

Savannah was the birthplace of the Prince Hall Masonry in Georgia. These masons organized in Savannah in 1866. Prince Hall was an immigrant from Barbados, who became a Mason in 1776. With fourteen associates he started the African Lodge #459 and served as the Worshipful Master. After his death the name of the lodge was changed to Prince Hall Grand Lodge.

 Continue to the …

Korean War Monument

This monument honors the members of D Company, 10th Infantry Battalion, USMCR, killed in this war.

 Step around the hedge of azaleas toward the sidewalk, cross Rossiter Street, and walk twenty yards to see on your right the …

Georgia Hussars Monument

These mounted rangers, organized by James Oglethorpe, protected the colony from Spaniards and Indians. They are remembered with a marker and a cannon strapped onto a block.

 Continue down the sidewalk, cross the Lincoln Street ramp, and thirty yards on the right is the …

Salzburger Monument

A plaque on the stone monument says, "Denied religious freedom, they were forced to leave their homeland." The sculptor was Anton Thuswaldner. A marker near the monument acknowledges the thirty-seven Salzburgers who came to Georgia in 1734.

Continue on the sidewalk, cross Abercorn Street, walk one block, then cross the Abercorn Street ramp. On the right is the …

Old City Exchange Bell

The bell was cast in 1802 and hung in the bell tower of the old City Exchange building. When it was torn down for a new City Hall, the bell was moved. Later this replica steeple was built a block from the present City Hall to house the bell.

 Continue on the sidewalk and cross the unmarked street that makes a semicircle. On the right is the …

Old Savannah Cotton Exchange and the Winged Lion

This terra-cotta winged lion is a symbol of how important cotton was to the local economy. The mythological winged lion is surrounded by an iron fence with medallions of poets, presidents, and statesmen. The fountain was constructed in 1889.

 To the right of the lion is the …

Marker for the Old Savannah Cotton Exchange

Designed by William Gibbons Preston, a nationally known Boston architect, the Cotton Exchange was completed in 1887, when Savannah ranked first on the Eastern Seaboard in cotton production and second in the world.

Old Savannah Cotton Exchange

Courtesy of the artist, Jill Howell

To the right is a smaller …

Marker Honoring Eli Whitney and the Cotton Gin

Eli Whitney invented the cotton gin on nearby Mulberry

Grove plantation. He discovered that a hooked wire could pull the cotton lint through a slot in a basket, leaving the cotton seeds inside.

 Return to the sidewalk and notice another marker to the left of the lion. It's the …

Solomon's Lodge Marker with Masonic Symbol

This lodge is the oldest continuously operating English-constituted lodge in the western hemisphere. James Oglethorpe was the first Worshipful Master when it was founded in 1734. Solomon's Lodge now occupies the old terra-cotta Cotton Exchange.

 Return to the sidewalk and cross the Drayton Street ramp. On your right is the …

Marker for the Birthplace of the University of Georgia

The Georgia Legislature met in the coffeehouse across the street in 1785 to establish a public institution of learning in Georgia. The charter establishing the University of Georgia was the first issued in the United States to a state university.

 Continue to walk west on the sidewalk. On your right are the …

Washington Guns

The guns (known locally as George and Martha) were captured from the British in the Battle of Yorktown and presented to the Chatham Artillery by General George Washington in 1791. In 1861, at the beginning of the Civil War, they were buried under the armory floor, then dug up after all Federal troops had left in 1872.

 At the end of the block is a …

Marker Next to the City Hall Building

One of the Washington Guns

This marker to the right of City Hall explains that Savannah's City Hall was constructed in 1906. Its gold dome marks the center of the business district.

City Hall

Courtesy, Dan Kaufman/Studio Kaufman, LLC

 On the City Hall building are two ...

Plaques at the Entrance to City Hall

They commemorate two important ships. The *Savannah* was the first steamship to cross the Atlantic Ocean. Leaving Savannah's port in 1819, it arrived in Liverpool a month later. The *John Randolph* was the first iron vessel seen in American waters. The parts made in England were riveted together here, and the ship was launched from this port in 1834.

 Just inside the front door of City Hall is a ...

Time Capsule Chest

This copper-hammered chest, put on display in 1976, was fashioned by ironsmith Ivan Bailey. It is to be opened in 2076, and an effort will be made to the greatest extent possible to return the contents to descendants of the original owners. The key is stored at the Georgia Historical Society.

Time Capsule Chest

 Next door to City Hall is the Hyatt Regency Hotel. At the end of the little park in front of the hotel is a …

Monument to the Landing of Oglethorpe and the Colonists

The plaque on a small granite monument designates this area as Yamacraw Bluff, where the colony of Georgia was founded. The DAR (Daughters of the American Revolution) put the monument here to honor Oglethorpe, declaring this spot to be the most historic in Georgia.

 Look back toward the sidewalk for the …

Marker for the Landing of Oglethorpe and the Colonists

James Edward Oglethorpe, the founder of Georgia, landed at the foot of this bluff in 1733 with 114 colonists. The site where he pitched his tent is marked by the stone bench 100 feet west of the marker.

 In the same little park is the …

Oglethorpe Bench

It was erected in 1906 by the Georgia Society of Colonial Dames of America to honor James Edward Oglethorpe, founder of the Georgia colony. The bench is here on Yamacraw Bluff, named to honor the tribe of Indians who greeted Oglethorpe on his arrival.

 Walk a few more yards and cross the street to the …

Joel Chandler Harris Marker

Mr. Harris (1845–1908) was the author of *Uncle Remus: His Songs and His Sayings*, *Stories of Georgia*, and others. He was the associate editor of the *Savannah Morning News* and later the associate editor of the *Atlanta Constitution*. Uncle Remus stories were the basis for the well-loved film *The Song of the South*. These books are available at several local shops.

Continue walking for one block on Bay Street until reaching Jefferson Street. In the grassy area you will find the historical marker explaining the complicated Confederate withdrawal from Savannah.

Evacuation of Savannah

On December 13, 1864, General Sherman and his troops arrived at Fort McAllister after a long and destructive march through Georgia. The fort was well fortified from the east, but Sherman's approach from the west enabled the fort to be captured with only a brief battle. Lt. General W. J. Hardee, who was in charge of the Confederate troops in Savannah, ordered his troops to leave the city in hopes the city would be spared. The Confederate troops constructed a pontoon bridge across the Savannah River from the foot of West Broad Street (now Martin Luther King Jr. Blvd.) to Hutchinson Island, and another to the South Carolina shore. They escaped to South Carolina just before General Sherman's arrival.

 End of Walk. One block west (it's not a comfortable walk) on Bay Street is the historical marker for the …

John Ryan Excelsior Bottle Works

On this site in 1852 stood the Excelsior Bottle Works operated by John Ryan for the manufacture of soda water and other carbonated beverages. Ryan's soda, in colorful bottles embossed with his name and location, was known throughout Georgia. His operations expanded to Augusta, Columbus, and Atlanta. Today Ryan's bottles are prized by collectors nationwide.

John Ryan, with his contemporaries, Thomas Maher and James Ray, is commemorated for his pioneer contribution to the soda water industry in Georgia and the United States. Ryan retired from business in 1879 and passed away in Savannah on March 23, 1885.

Highly collectible, James Ray and John Ryan bottles from the 1860s

Printed on the bottles to the right:

Georgia Brewing Association, ALU, Tivola, Savannah, GA

James Ray, Lager Beer, Savannah, GA

Printed on the bottles below from Excelsior Bottle Works (left to right):

Excelsior Soda Works, Savannah, Geo

John Ryan, 1866

Excelsior, Ginger Ale

African American Journey

by Jamal Touré of Day Clean Journeys

A self-guided driving tour.
Thank you for joining us on this journey.
(Gullah = Tenk hunnah fa jine we on da jurnee!)

With this sampling of the Gullah language, we embark on our journey into the life and history of Africans in Savannah, beginning in 1733 with the new colony of Georgia. Charleston and Savannah are major centers of Gullah/Geechee culture. You'll find a sprinkling of colorful Gullah language (Gullah = *unrabble mout* or *krak en teet*) throughout the text.

Gullah/Geechee people are African Americans who live on the coastal mainland and barrier islands of southeastern North Carolina, South Carolina, Georgia, and northeastern Florida. They have spoken an African-based Creole language for centuries. The ancestors of the Gullah/Geechee people were largely from West and Central Africa, in an area ranging from Mauritania to Angola. They were sought after by Georgia and South Carolina planters because of their experience (Gullah = *speriunce*) with growing rice and other cash crops.

Africans were unofficially in the colony from its beginning. The trustees anticipated that everyone in the Georgia colony would be free and equal, and in their liberal ideals they had placed restrictions on African captivity. An act of 1735 prohibited the importation of "black Africans or Negros." However, as help came from South Carolina in the building of the new colony, Africans came also. By 1750 the colonists had persuaded the trustees in England that Africans were needed to work on southern plantations, and the 1735 law was repealed. By 1760 the population of Georgia consisted of 6,000 whites and 3,578 Africans.

This journey will take you through the era of captivity, emancipation, and beyond. You will see buildings and sites marking African struggles and achievements.

This driving adventure will bring to life the "King Cotton" era and highlight the persistence of captive Africans as they built the First African Baptist Church at night and in their free time. You'll see monuments to influential African Americans, including the church in which Martin Luther King Jr. practiced part of his "I Have a Dream" speech in 1963 and where General Sherman issued his Field Order No. 15, promising forty acres and a mule to freed Africans.

Our journey (Gullah = *jurnee*) begins in the parking lot of the Visitor Center, once the Central of Georgia Railroad depot. The buildings on the south side are passenger and freight buildings, now housing the Savannah History Museum and Visitor Center. They are built of Savannah gray bricks made by Africans on the Hermitage Plantation on the Savannah River, now part of the Georgia Ports Authority. The railroad used these buildings until 1972.

 Leaving the rear of the parking lot, turn right onto Fahm Street for one block. Take the first right onto Turner Blvd. Look left to see the …

Granite Monument

This monument honors Bishop Henry McNeal Turner, pastor of Saint Philip Monumental African Methodist Episcopal Church, which once stood behind the monument. Later the congregation moved to Park Avenue and Jefferson Street, where Saint Philip Monumental A.M.E. stands today. Bishop Turner was a chaplain in the U.S. Army during the Civil War, and also a leader at Saint James A.M.E. Church on East Broad Street. We'll drive by both churches.

Bishop Turner

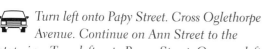 *Turn left onto Papy Street. Cross Oglethorpe Avenue. Continue on Ann Street to the stop sign. Turn left onto Bryan Street. On your left is the …*

First Bryan Baptist Church – 525 West Bryan Street, 912-232-5526.

Here is the oldest black church in continuous operation in North America. The church was originally one and the same with First African Baptist, which we'll see soon. The monument to the first pastor, Father George Lisle, is on the right side of the entrance. This building was built in 1873 under the pastoral leadership of Reverend Ulysses Houston.

Father Andrew Bryan was the second pastor, until his death in 1812. A plaque on the right honors him. Father Bryan bought the lot for the church in 1793 for 30 pounds sterling (about $150.)

 On your right is the …

Yamacraw Art Park

This park was conceived by Savannah artist Jerome Meadows. It features three life-size bronze statues of dancing children. After a national search for sculptors, Mr. Meadows was chosen. He was inspired by the dynamic duo of Andrew Bryan, church pastor, and Tomochichi, Yamacraw Native American chief.

Father Andrew Bryan

The newest addition to the park is the Georgia Historical Society's marker for John C. Fremont (1813–1890), a native Georgian who served as a general in the United States Army during the Civil War. He was known for his daring and successful expeditions on the western frontier. He was the first candidate of the antislavery Republican party for president of the United States. The house in which he was born is gone, but the marker is on the approximate site.

 Turn right onto Fahm Street and right onto busy Bay Street. Stay in the right lane. At the second traffic light turn right onto Montgomery Street. Ahead is …

Franklin Square

Named for Benjamin Franklin—printer, scientist, inventor, statesman, and Georgia's colonial agent in England—this square was also called Water Tower Square. There was once a huge tank holding the city's water supply here. We have given this square the nickname "Haitian Square."

 On the west side of the square is the …

First African Baptist Church – 23 Montgomery Street, 912-233-6597.

Our African ancestors built the church at night after their daily work was done. African women walked up from the river carrying (Gullah = *totin* or *cayum*) bricks in their aprons, and men rolled heavy wheelbarrows (Gullah = *weelbarruh*) full of bricks up the steep ramps.

Father George Leile (spelled *Lisle* at First Bryan Church) was the first pastor here. First African Baptist and First Bryan Baptist are the oldest continuous black congregations in North America, dating back to 1773. First African Baptist is the oldest standing brick church in Georgia.

Stained Glass of Reverend George Leile in First African Baptist Church

To Gullah/Geechee and African people a door painted red means that we own the property free and clear, with no mortgage. At Geechee Kunda, the Gullah Geechee Museum and Cultural Center, in Riceboro, Georgia, the doors are painted red.

A court ruling determined that Africans could worship between dawn (Gullah = *day clean*) and dusk (Gullah = *daaky* or *sun fall down*). Father Andrew Bryan was the second pastor of this congregation. He was allowed by his owner, Jonathan Bryan, to preach at Brampton Plantation. He became an ordained minister in 1788. Father Andrew Marshall was the third pastor.

Inside, the balcony pews are marked with signs harkening back to the Arabic script of our West African ancestors.

Diamond patterns of holes in the floor allowed runaway captives to hide under the floor while planning the next leg of their escape. March Haynes, a deacon and river pilot, operated a "maritime underground railroad" assisting Africans to escape to Fort Pulaski and on to Hilton Head during the Civil War (Gullah = *Big Shoot*).

 In the center of the square you'll find the ...

Andrew Marshall

Haitian Monument

In 1779 more than five hundred free blacks from Haiti fought with the colonists in an effort to win freedom from England during the Revolutionary War.

Three of the bronze Haitian soldiers have rifles pointing ahead. The model for the soldier with his rifle raised is Jamal Touré (the author of this journey.) The drummer is young Henri Christophe, who later became King Henri I of Haiti. This is the work of sculptor James Mastin from Miami.

 Continue around the square. Pause at the City Market courtyard, the site of the …

Haitian Monument
Courtesy, Dan Kaufman/Studio Kaufman LLC

City Market

Here was once a thriving market in an open brick building. Farmers came in mule wagons full of peaches, persimmons, figs, scuppernongs, sweet potatoes (Gullah = *yalluh yam*), and fresh vegetables (Gullah = *vegitubble*) like okra, black-eyed peas, boiled peanuts (Gullah = *byal gubas*), and collards. Women carried baskets of vegetables on their heads. Hucksters sold fresh shrimp, crabs, oysters, and fish.

Hucksters like Shorty George had their own singsong calls: "Crab sweet, crab sweet! Hilton Head crab meat. Pope, Baygall, dey have a Fishhaul. Crab sweet, Crab sweet! Daufuskie crab meat! Ayy swimp! Crab oyster buy … yuh! Lanna Jurnul Paypuh!"

In 1954 the market was torn down—a horrendous mistake. But out of this loss came Savannah's nationally recognized preservation movement. Today, folks can visit artists' studios and cafes and take horse-drawn carriage rides. Ellis Square, where the market building stood, has been "brought back" to rejoin James Oglethorpe's original squares.

 Exit the square on Bryan Street (on the right side of the church) for one block. Turn right onto Martin Luther King, Jr. Blvd. Cross busy Bay Street and continue down to the Savannah River. Before turning right at river, look to your left, toward …

The Eugene Talmadge Bridge
(new Savannah River Bridge)

One of the engineers was the Haitian American Lionel Bellevue, who was also the structural engineer for the Haitian monument in Franklin Square. Some want to change the name to the Tomochichi Bridge, after the Native American chief who befriended the colonists who landed on his Yamacraw Bluff.

The Savannah-Ogeechee Canal begins its journey from the Savannah River to connect to the Ogeechee River sixteen miles to the west. Built in 1830 by captive Africans predominantly, as well as Irish laborers, the canal was an efficient way to move cotton, rice, and bricks to be shipped to other ports. There's not much to see at this end, but the far end has a visitor center and a nature trail (Savannah Ogeechee Canal, 681 Fort Argyle Road, Route 204, 912-748-8068).

 Follow the train track along River Street. Across the river is …

Hutchinson Island

Captive Africans transported to Savannah were often held on Hutchinson Island before being brought to the city to be auctioned. During the Civil War, many Confederates escaped out of the city in rowboats (Gullah = *bateau*) ahead of the arrival of General Sherman and his Union forces. The Confederates built a pontoon bridge at the foot of Martin Luther King Jr. Blvd. so that soldiers could cross the river (Gullah = *deloe*) before General Sherman's arrival. They destroyed it as the last man leaped onto South Carolina soil.

 On your right are …

Cotton Warehouses

These tall buildings are now nightclubs, shops, and restaurants. The old part of River Street is surfaced with cobblestones (Gullah = *cobblerocks*). These are ballast stones that provided stability in the hulls of sailing ships arriving into port. They were left behind to make room for the eight-hundred-pound cotton bales exported overseas.

 Look up the sides of buildings at the …

Small Balconies

Factors (cotton merchants, investors, or middlemen) watched cotton being loaded into waiting ships. Our African ancestors were brought here for their knowledge of growing cotton, rice, and indigo. Many African longshoremen and longshorewomen worked on the waterfront in the 1700s and 1800s during the time of captivity.

WEIGHING COTTON.

BALES OF COTTON READY FOR SHIPMENT.

Just before the Hyatt, look left to see the …

Large Spherical Monument

This twenty-foot-tall split globe, erected in 2011, honors the five hundred men and women of all races and religions from Chatham County who died in World War II. It reminds us of the sacrifices made by past generations.

 Just past the Hyatt, look up the street to the right to see …

City Hall

The dome of City Hall, once copper, was gold-leafed in 1987. The gold deposit causing the first gold rush in the United States was in North Georgia. According to the history told today in Dahlonega, gold was discovered by an African, who was forced to give it to his owner.

Many Africans helped build the City Hall in 1907. In 2012 Edna Jackson became Savannah's first female black mayor; she was the third black mayor, following Floyd Adams Jr. and Otis Johnson.

Not visible from here, and beyond City Hall across Bay Street behind the Custom House, is the area of Bay Lane. Here is where the business of selling captive Africans, which sustained the city's economy, took place.

 Wait! Don't drive off yet. Look left at the …

Monument to African Americans

Erected in 2002, this monument shows a family (Gullah = *famlee*) looking downriver toward Africa and embracing after emancipation. Dr. Abigail Jordan and the Consortium of Doctors were the driving force behind this powerful piece of art. It is an important monument, giving credit to the contributions by African Americans. The model for the father on the monument is Jamal Touré (author of this journey.)

Designed by SCAD professor Dorothy Spradley and her student Dan Koster, the monument was cast in bronze from their clay model. Poet Maya Angelou's words on the monument read in part:

> *We were stolen, sold and brought together from the African continent. We got on the slave ships together. … Today, we are standing up together with faith and even some joy.*

Continue along River Street for half a block. On your right is a building with green columns built over a street …

Cotton Exchange *(back side)*

Relying heavily on captive labor, cotton became the main export crop until the Civil War. World prices for cotton, lumber, and turpentine were set here. The street beneath the Cotton Exchange building was kept open so that mule wagons could haul heavy bales of cotton and raw materials to the waiting ships for export.

 On the river you'll see a …

Ferry Boat

One of the dot Savannah Belle ferries taking folks across the river to the Trade Center is named for Susie King Taylor. Born on Saint Catherines Island in 1848 and raised in Savannah by her grandmother, she was taught in one of the six black schools in the underground school network. Later she became a nurse in the United States Colored Troops. She and Clara Barton, founder of the Red Cross, served the wounded in the Union Army. In her school on Saint Simons Island she taught forty freed African American children, as well as adults eager for an education (Gullah = *edjacashun*).

Susie King Taylor

She met a black noncommissioned officer, Edward King. They married and traveled with the 33rd United States Colored Troops for three years. After he died, she returned to Savannah to start another school for freed black children. Before her death in 1912, she wrote her *Reminiscences*, published privately in 1902. *Reminiscences* is the only book written by an African woman describing her experiences during the Civil War.

For years, riverboats left from River Street for Daufuskie Island and Hilton Head. The original riverboat company was owned by Captain Sam Stevens. The youngest of twenty children (Gullah = *churn*), he was a member of the United States Army Corps of Engineers survey team and helped lay out the channels in the Savannah River. The credit union for First African Baptist Church is named after him.

Near the end of River Street, you'll pass the Waving Girl statue and the Olympic Torch on your left. Take the right fork up the hill to Bay Street. Across Bay Street is the Brice Hotel. Turn here (by the sign) onto Houston Street. Ahead is ...

Washington Square

This square was once known as Firehouse Square. A fire station stood on the south side and was demolished in the mid-1870s. Free and captive Africans fought Savannah's dangerous fires (Gullah = *diffy*) in 1796 and in 1820. Houses were built of heart pine, and hundreds were gobbled up in flames in these infernos.

 Enter the square. Look for ...

21 Houston Street

This gray house was owned by the Mirault family, free people of color from Haiti. This family formed the core of black families who were part of the first Catholic congregation in the city. Every free person of color was required to have a white guardian, someone of their choosing. Although free, they could not vote, hold political office, or own property.

Aspasia Mirault defied an 1842 law forbidding black ownership of land. She had a secret agreement with George Cally, a white man (Gullah = *buckra*) who was a carpenter (Gullah = *bitonnayl*) from up north, and she built a house. Mr. Cally was the ostensible owner. She operated an ice cream parlor at the corner of Bull and Broughton Streets for years. Generations of Miraults lived in the house.

 After passing the Mirault house, turn right onto an oyster-shell road ...

Saint Julian Street

You are driving on a tabby street made of oyster shells, sand, limestone, ash, and water. Many Africans knew how to mix this concoction, and often their cabins were built with tabby. The art of making tabby was brought from Africa.

 At the intersection, prepare to turn left. Look across Price Street at the corner house, 426 East Saint Julian Street ...

A white cottage with two dormer windows and a brick chimney

Jane Deveaux, a free woman of color, operated an underground school in the attic. It was against the law for African children to learn to read and write. This made her more determined.

At least six other schools were being run in Savannah at the same time. Jane's mother, Catherine, from Antigua, operated one. Jane's school ran for thirty years, until emancipation opened the doors for black students after the Civil War. She is buried in Laurel Grove South Cemetery.

 Turn left onto Price Street to the light. Turn left onto Broughton Street. Go one block. Turn right onto Houston Street, where you'll see a …

Two-story green house on your right – 7 and 9 Houston Street.

This was owned by Betsey Cunningham, a free woman of color. She and her husband, Reverend Henry Cunningham, owned at least ten properties (Gullah = *proputty*) in the city in the early 1800s. This neighborhood is known as the Old Fort Community.

Jane Deveaux House

 Continue around the square to the …

Second African Baptist Church – 123 Houston Street, 912-233-6163.

Reverend Cunningham was the first pastor here. After General Sherman's arrival in Savannah, he met with the African leaders at the Green-Meldrim House and discussed their needs as recently freed men. The result of this meeting was Special Field Order No. 15, which offered each man forty acres and a mule. Sherman made the announcement here to a huge crowd that overflowed the church. The order was later rescinded before many people could take advantage of it.

Dr. Martin Luther King Jr. delivered part of his "I Have a Dream" speech here in 1963 and later during the famous March on Washington.

 Just past the church, look ahead at the building made of Savannah gray bricks.

These bricks were made by Africans on the Hermitage Plantation. Pause and read the sign on the building.

 Continue south on Houston Street, cross Oglethorpe Avenue to …

Crawford Square

During segregation, this was the only square in which black children were allowed to play. Notice the underground cistern at the south end of the square for collecting rainwater for fighting fires. In 1821 seventy-five free blacks formed the Franklin Fire Engine and Hose Co. and the Union Axe and Fire Co. The city required all free blacks, ages sixteen to sixty, to enroll in fire companies. Each wore a cap with the initials F.C. (free colored) while on duty.

 Exit the square on Perry Street for one block. Turn right onto East Broad Street. Cross Liberty Street. Go one block. Turn right onto Harris Street. On your right is a …

Vacant Lot

In 1874 Benedictine monks from France arrived to tend to the spiritual (Gullah = *soul cleansin*) needs of the freed Africans during Reconstruction. A small frame church was built here at the corner of East Broad and Harris Streets, where the vacant lot is now. In 1889 a new St. Benedict's Catholic Church was built four blocks south, at East Broad and Gordon Streets, where it stands today.

In Europe, Savannahian Fredericka Law received the habit of the Missionary Franciscan Sisters of the Immaculate Conception at the Shrine of Portiuncula in Assisi, Italy, in 1882. She took the name Sister Benedict of the Angels.

 Drive on to the end of this block. On your right is the …

Beach Institute African American Cultural Center – 502 East Harris Street, 912-234-8000.

After the Civil War ended in 1865, this building was erected for the education of black children. It was built in 1867 by the Freedmen's Bureau (Gullah = *Freedmun Bruro*), the American Missionary Association, and the black Savannah Educational Alliance, which operated two black schools prior to the establishment of the Beach Institute.

Alfred E. Beach, editor of *Scientific American*, donated funds to buy the land. Black and white teachers taught the six hundred black pupils. Tuition was one dollar per month. Today it is a cultural center.

Beach Institute

Robert Sengstacke Abbott was a pupil here in 1880. He was the founder of the *Chicago Defender* newspaper (Gullah = *noozpapuh*) in 1905, which helped prompt the Black Exodus, or Great Northern Migration, of 1915–1919. He fought to abolish the Jim Crow laws and establish a nondiscriminatory society. Descendants of these black leaders spurred by his newspaper helped start the political rise of President Barack Obama and other Democratic party leaders.

 Turn left onto Price Street for two short blocks. Turn left onto Charlton Street. On your left is …

The Frank Callen Boys and Girls' Club – 510 East Charlton Street, 912-233-2939.

Frank Callen, a member of the First Congregational Church and local probation officer, formed a club for boys in 1917. Girls were allowed to join in the mid-1950s. This club continues to exert a positive influence in the lives of young people today.

 Continue to East Broad Street and turn right. Go four blocks, passing Jones, Taylor, and Gordon Streets. Turn right at Gaston Street. On your right is …

St. Benedict the Moor Catholic Church – 441 East Broad Street, 912-232-7147.

In 1874 Benedictine monks established this church, Georgia's oldest Catholic Church for freed Africans. Carrying on the mission of the Benedictine monks, the parish grew to include a convent and grammar school.

The Franciscan Sisters of the Immaculate Conception staffed the school from 1907 until it closed in 1969. In 1955 seven-year-old Clarence Thomas attended classes here. He lived with his grandfather, Myers Anderson, in downtown Savannah (Gullah = *Sabanna*). Here he learned principles of faith, justice, and equality. He transferred to Saint Pius X High School and then to a white Catholic boarding school, Saint John Vianney Minor Seminary at Isle of Hope. He later succeeded Thurgood Marshall as the second African American to serve on the United States Supreme Court.

Young Clarence Thomas

Inside is the Clarence Thomas Center for Historic Preservation, part of the Savannah College of Art and Design. The Center houses a laboratory for the study of artifacts, as well as exhibition space and lecture hall.

 Continue on Gaston Street to Price Street. Turn left and go one block. Turn left on Hartridge Street. On your left is …

St. John Baptist Church – 522 Hartridge Street, 912-232-8507.

Reverend William Gray, a member of the historic First Bryan Baptist Church, obtained permission to build a church on the east side of town. In 1885 he established St. John Baptist Church, and the building, erected by the congregation of African Americans, was completed in 1891. In 1993 a devastating fire scorched (Gullah = *scawch*) the building to ashes. Soon a new building, called "The Mighty Fortress," arose from the rubble.

 Continue on Hartridge Street to East Broad Street. Look across East Broad at the large green field and pavilion.

Mother Mathilda (Matilda) Beasley Park

Mother Beasley was the first black nun in Georgia. Born Mathilda Taylor in 1834, she established an orphanage in 1886, later called Saint Francis' Home. She founded the first group of black nuns in Georgia and together (Gullah = *tugedda*) they ran the orphanage. She gave the money she earned sewing to poor black families.

Mathilda (Matilda) Beasley, 1834-1903
First Black Nun in Georgia
Courtesy, Georgia Historical Society

In 1903 she died and was buried in Laurel Grove South Cemetery, which we'll visit soon. She had been kneeling in the chapel of her cottage next to her burial clothes, funeral wishes, and her will, when she was found. Her house has been moved to the park as an interpretive center to commemorate her life and work.

 Turn right onto East Broad for one block. Turn right onto Huntingdon Street. On your right toward the end of the block is the …

King-Tisdell Cottage – 514 East Huntingdon Street, 912-234-8000.

This is an 1896 Victorian cottage featuring a gingerbread design on its exterior. Preservationist, historian, and civil rights leader W.W. Law worked to save the cottage and move it here. Today it's a house museum and contains exhibits on African American history and culture in Savannah from the 1900s to the 1950s. Two exhibits highlight the legacies of W.W. Law and the Gullah/Geechee people.

W. W. Law

King-Tisdell Cottage

Courtesy of the artist, Dr. Preston Russell

Turn left onto Price Street for one block. Go left onto Nicoll Street to East Broad Street. Look across East Broad to your left at …

Prince Hall Masonic Lodge – 602 East Broad Street, 912-236-6030.

Prince Hall from Barbados and fourteen associates became Masons in 1776 and started the African Lodge #459. He was named Worshipful Master. After he died, the name of the lodge was changed to Prince Hall Grand Lodge. The Reverend James Merilus Simms is the father of Prince Hall Masons and Eastern Stars in the State of Georgia, establishing a chapter in February 1866. A historic marker on Bay Street in Emmet Park tells the history.

 The church ahead and to your right is …

Saint James A.M.E. Church – 612 East Broad Street, 912-236-2051.

Founded in 1865, here is another church started by Bishop Henry McNeal Turner. A remarkable piece of history hangs in the top of (Gullah = *puntopob*) the tower—a bell given to the bishop by Queen Victoria in the late nineteenth century for his work establishing churches in America and the British colonies.

 Turn right onto East Broad Street to the light. Go right onto Gwinnett Street. Go four blocks (past Kroger) to Abercorn Street. Turn left for three blocks. Turn right (by the bus stop bench) onto Park Avenue. Go one block. Cross Drayton Street. On your right is …

Forsyth Park

African American militias once marched in this park. These militias were formed in major cities during Reconstruction. They performed on ceremonial occasions. In the 1880s Savannah had one state-supported and seven unofficial black militia units. Savannah had the only African American artillery company in the United States.

Lieutenant Colonel John Deveaux of the Georgia State Troops commanded all of the African American companies in Georgia. Major Richard R. Wright, the first president of Savannah State University, was appointed the state of Georgia's historian for African American soldiers.

 Continue on Park Avenue. Cross Whitaker Street. Go two blocks. On your left is …

Saint Philip Monumental A.M.E. Church – 1112 Jefferson Street, 912-233-8547.

This church, established in 1865, is the Mother Church of African Methodism in Georgia. In the parking lot is a monument crowned with a black iron anvil made in Sweden. The anvil is the symbol of the African Methodist Episcopal (A.M.E.) Church. It represents the blacksmith shop where African Methodism was conceived by the grace of God (Gullah = *grayse ob Gawd*) in 1787.

Bishop Henry McNeal Turner was pastor (Gullah = *Table Tappa*) here. Reverend Frederick Douglas Jaudon, the "Walking Preacher," galvanized black ministers in Savannah to join (Gullah = *jine*) the growing civil rights movement in the 1960s.

 Follow Park Avenue one block to Montgomery Street. Turn left to the light at Henry Street. Turn right to the end. Go left on Martin Luther King Jr. Blvd. At the next light, turn right onto Anderson Street. On your left is …

St. Matthew's Episcopal Church (side view) – 1401 Martin Luther King Jr. Blvd., 912-233-5965.

Here is the first African American Episcopal Church parish in Georgia. In 1855 it was called St. Stephens. St. Augustine Episcopal, near Yamacraw, merged with this congregation in 1943 to become St. Matthew's. For twenty-one years Reverend Charles Hoskins from Trinidad served as pastor of this church.

 Continue on Anderson Street. On your right is …

Cuyler Junior High School (now the Economic Opportunity Authority) – 618 West Anderson Street, 912-238-2965.

Built by the Board of Education for African American children in 1914, this was the first time public funds were used to build a school for black children, and their first opportunity to get an education beyond the sixth grade. John Hubert from the Springfield community was principal for twenty-five years.

Fannie Pettie Watts was an alumna of Cuyler and a founder of Zeta Phi Beta Sorority. Today this sorority, with goals of sisterly love, scholarship, and finer womanhood, has eight hundred chapters in the United States, Africa, Europe, Asia, and the Caribbean.

Continue past the playground and turn right onto May Street. You will see on the right …

Bethlehem Baptist Church – 1008 May Street, 912-233-9040.

Here is the last of the five black congregations established in the slavery era. The others we have seen are First Bryan Baptist, First African Baptist, Second African Baptist, and St. Matthew's Episcopal.

Turn around on May Street, go back the way you came. Go left on Anderson Street. Take an immediate right onto Ogeechee Road. On the right, we pass the ...

Sweet Daddy Grace

Church of the United House of Prayer –
1805 Ogeechee Road, 912-236-8877.

Bishop Charles Grace, "Sweet Daddy Grace" (1884–1960), founded the United House of Prayer. He was born in Cape Verde, an island country off the coast of western Africa, and came to Savannah in 1926. He was a flamboyant evangelist, preaching revivals in the Pentecostal tradition, including brass "shout bands," speaking in tongues, and baptizing crowds in the waterways and later with fire hoses, spraying hundreds of people dressed in white. He held lively services here. There are House of Prayer places of worship in twenty-six states, with headquarters in Washington, D.C.

Continue on Ogeechee Road and cross the 37th Street Connector. Look for the small sign for Laurel Grove Cemetery on your right. End your journey here, and drive around this historic burial ground at your leisure.

Laurel Grove South – 2101 Kollock Street, 912-651-6772.

This (Gullah = *disyuh*) acreage was designated as a burial ground for "free persons of color and slaves" in 1853. The land was once part of Springfield Plantation, owned by the Stiles family. Many graves were moved here in 1857 from the old African Burial Ground, which lay south of Troup and Lafayette Squares, as well as in areas around Whitefield and Calhoun Squares. These original burial grounds had been used for more than a century.

The graves of Baptist ministers Reverend Andrew Bryan (1716–1812), Reverend Henry Cunningham (1759–1842) and his wife, Betsey,

Sign to graves of Baptist ministers in Laurel Grove South

and Reverend Andrew Cox Marshall (1755–1856) are here. Many other prominent black citizens are interred in this hallowed ground. Time and weather are taking a toll on headstones, ironwork, and bricks.

Sign to graves of slaves in Laurel Grove South

Plot in Laurel Grove South for black families

Road through Laurel Grove South

Westley Wallace Law (1923–2002) was a local preservationist, historian, and civil rights leader. In the 1970s he led an effort to preserve the cemetery and identify historically significant markers. He is buried beside his mother, Geneva Wallace Law.

Take care. Have strength.

Come here another time to Savannah, friend.

(Gullah = Tek' cyare. Hab skrength. Com yuh annuda tyme tu Sabanna, Padi.) Jurnee obuh!

Places to Visit Later

❧ **Beach Institute – 502 East Harris Street, 31401, 912-234-8000.**

Built in 1867 by the Freedmen's Bureau, this was a school for newly freed slaves. It is now an African American cultural center. Visit the Ulysses Davis collection of folk art—238 wood carvings whittled between giving haircuts in his barber shop. Other artists are featured periodically. In 1990 Ulysses Davis and Haywood Nichols had an exhibition of their carvings in City Market, called "Different Roots, Common Fruits."

❧ **Bynes-Royall Funeral Home – 204 West Hall Street, 31401, 912-233-2175.**

Here is the oldest black business in Georgia. Started in the 1870s by Major William Royall, a member of First Bryan Baptist Church. Bynes-Royall is the third-oldest African American–owned funeral home in the United States.

❧ **Carnegie Library – 537 East Henry Street, 31401, 912-231-9921.**

Opened in 1914 to serve the black community, this library was a gift from Andrew Carnegie. As a child, Supreme Court Justice Clarence Thomas did his homework here. He spoke in 2004 at the reopening ceremony after the library's remodeling. Open Monday–Thursday, 10–6; Friday, 2–6; Saturday, 10–6; closed Sunday.

❧ **Day Clean Journeys – 912-220-5966. www.daycleansoul.com.**

Here you'll find tours for everyone: the I Love Savannah History Tour (general history); the African American History and Gullah Geechee Tours (tours that share the history of African people here and beyond); and the Drums 'n Spirits Tour (an evening folklore journey.) We offer specialized tours in Savannah and the lowcountry of Georgia and South Carolina. Come join us! (Gullah = *Wa jine we*.) Family, go back into your past and reclaim that which has been misplaced. (Gullah = *Fanmi se woa were fina sankofa ayinke*.)

❧ **First African Baptist Church – 23 Montgomery Street on Franklin Square, 31401, 912-233-6597. www.firstafricanbc.com.**

This congregation evolved from the oldest Negro congregation in the United States, as did First Bryan Baptist Church. The building dates back to 1859, and is said to be the first brick building in Georgia built and owned by African Americans. Images of the early pastors are depicted in the stained-glass windows, which date from 1885. The original lectern and pews are still in use. Some of the pews in the balcony are marked with African writing on the ends.

The church's history dates back to 1774, when George Leile, a Virginia-born African, came to spread the Gospel along the Georgia coast.

❧ Geechee Kunda Cultural and Interpretive Center – 622 Ways Temple Road, Riceboro, Ga., 31323 (45 minutes south of Savannah), 912-884-4440. jim@bacote.com.

Geechee Kunda is the interpretive center and museum for Gullah/Geechee and African culture in the United States, the Americas, and Africa. It was started by Jim and Pat Bacote. Day Clean Journeys is the tour component of Geechee Kunda.

Annual festivals include The Gathering, a homecoming for you (Gullah = *fa hunnah*), the third Saturday in April, and Sugarcane Harvest and Crafts Expo, the Saturday after Thanksgiving.

❧ King-Tisdell Cottage – 514 East Huntingdon Street, 31401, 912-234-8000.

This classic Victorian cottage was saved from demolition by civil rights leader and preservationist W. W. Law, among others. It features furnishings of a typical family in the early twentieth century. Open Tuesday–Saturday, noon–5:00 p.m.

❧ Massie Heritage Interpretation Center – 207 East Gordon Street on Calhoun Square, 31401, 912-201-5070. www.massieschool.com.

Savannah's first public school opened here in 1856. Forty students paid a small tuition, and the rest attended free, thanks to a $5,000 bequest from Scotsman Peter Massie. Only white students living east of Whitaker Street were allowed to attend.

When Sherman's troops occupied Savannah during the Civil War, many families fled the city, and Massie was used as a hospital for wounded soldiers. For a time in 1865, it was designated a school for black children by the Federal Army authorities in control of the city. Open Monday–Saturday, 10-4; Sunday, noon–4:00 p.m. Admission fee.

❧ Owens-Thomas House, with the Old Stables and Urban Quarters – 124 Abercorn Street, 912-790-8889.

Designed by William Jay and built in 1819 for cotton merchant and banker Richard Richardson, this mansion retains the original carriage house, stables, and intact slave quarters. This house museum offers daily tours.

❧ Penn Center National Historic Landmark, P.O. Box 126, Saint Helena, S.C. 29920, 843-838-2432. www.penncenter.com.

Penn Center is the site of one of the first schools for freed Africans and is considered a significant African American historical and cultural institution. The center is on fifty acres in the heart of the South Carolina Sea Islands. Buildings are nestled under the silvery moss-draped limbs of giant live oaks beside the salt marsh of Capers Creek.

❧ Pin Point Oyster Factory Heritage Museum – 9924 Pin Point Avenue, 31406, 912-667-9176. www.pinpointheritagemuseum.com.

For many years the residents of Pin Point, descendants of slave families from Ossabaw Island, made their living harvesting oysters along the banks of the Skidaway River. Their culture has been preserved in a museum eight miles south of Savannah's Historic District. It was here at Pin Point that Supreme Court Justice Clarence Thomas was born. Admission fee. Open Thursday, Friday and Saturday.

❧ Ralph Mark Gilbert Civil Rights Museum – 460 Martin Luther King Jr. Blvd., 31401, 912-231-8900.

The museum is named for Ralph Mark Gilbert, a civil rights leader who, for sixteen years, was pastor of First African Baptist Church on Franklin Square. He was also president of the NAACP Savannah chapter from 1942 to 1950. The museum chronicles the civil rights struggle of Georgia's African American community from their beginnings to the present.

❧ Savannah State University – 3219 College Street, 31404, 912-358-4778.

Founded in 1890, it is the oldest public black college in Georgia. Originally Georgia State Industrial College for Colored Youth, it functioned in Athens, Georgia, for a few months before moving to Savannah with eight students and five faculty members. Reverends James M. Simms and E. K. Love were instrumental in the institution's being located in Savannah and Thunderbolt. During the 1960s many civil rights activities took place here, and many of the NAACP members were educated here.

❧ Ships of the Sea Museum – 41 Martin Luther King Jr. Blvd., 31401, 912-232-1511.

The building was designed by William Jay and built in 1819 for William Scarbrough, who invested heavily in the SS *Savannah*, the first steamship to cross the Atlantic Ocean. Mr. G. W. J. DeRenne bought the house in 1878 and gave it to the Savannah Board of Public Education to be used as a school for black children. It became the second school for black children in the city. Today it is a museum filled with ship models. Stroll through the largest formal garden in the city.

❧ Walter O. Evans Center for African American Studies – 601 Turner Blvd., 31401, 912-525-7204.

The center is inside the SCAD Museum of Art. It houses important works of art by renowned African American artists.

Historic Churches

Savannah is known for its historic and architecturally significant churches. The impressive Gothic architecture of the Cathedral of St. John the Baptist, the Independent Presbyterian Church with its Corinthian-style columns and cloud-piercing steeple, the First African Baptist Church, the oldest standing brick church in Georgia, and many others add to the rich religious tapestry found in the Historic District.

Beth Eden Baptist Church – *302 East Gordon Street, 31401, 912-233-9115.* N32° 04. 212′ W081° 05. 490′. Sunday services at 11:00 a.m.

This fine example of neo-Gothic architecture was designed for an African American congregation by Berlin-born architect Henry Urban in 1893. An associate of Boston architect William Preston, Mr. Urban rebuilt the interior of Christ Church after the fire of 1897 and supervised the intricate brick detailing of the Foley House Inn.

 &

Cathedral of St. John the Baptist – *222 East Harris Street, 31401, 912-233-4709. www.savannahcathedral.org.* N32° 04. 394′ W081° 05. 490′.

Roman Catholic Mass on Saturday at 5:30 p.m. On Sunday at 8:00 a.m., 10:00 a.m., and 11:30 a.m.

Destroyed by fire in 1898, this cathedral was rebuilt using the original plans of architect Francis Baldwin. Open daily.

Christ Church Episcopal

Christ Church Episcopal – *28 Bull Street, 31401,* 912-236-2500. *www.ccesavannah.org.* N32° 04. 774′ W081° 05. 465′. Sunday services at 8:00 a.m. and 10:30 a.m.

The "Mother Church of Georgia" held its first service on February 12, 1733.

Evangelical Lutheran Church of the Ascension – *120 Bull Street, 31401,* 912-232-4151. *www.elcota.org.* N32° 04. 671′ W081° 05. 508′. Sunday services at 8:30 a.m. and 11:00 a.m.

Salzburgers, led by Pastor John Boltzius, organized this parish in 1734. Construction of the present structure was begun in 1875.

ᚨ

First African Baptist Church – *23 Montgomery Street, 31401,* 912-233-6597. *www.firstafricanbc.com.* N32° 04. 883′ W081° 05. 759′. Empowerment hour, Sunday at 8:30 a.m. Worship service at 10:00 a.m.

This church was built by slaves at night after their daily duties were done.

ᚨ

First Baptist Church – *223 Bull Street, 31401,* 912-234-2671. *www.fbc-sav.org.* N32° 04. 560′ W081° 05. 617′. Sunday service at 11:00 a.m.

Completed in 1833, this structure is Savannah's oldest standing house of worship.

First Bryan Baptist Church
Courtesy of the painter, Augusta Oelschig

First Bryan Baptist Church – *575 West Bryan Street, 31401, 912-232-5526. www.fbbcsav.org.* N32° 04. 959´ W081° 06. 035´. Sunday service at 11:00 a.m.

The oldest continuous black congregation in North America.

ငh

First Congregational Church (*United Church of Christ*) – *421 Habersham Street, 31401, 912-236-6521. www.ucc.org.* N32° 04. 235´ W081° 05. 436´. Call for times of services.

Organized in 1869, the church has occupied this property since 1878. The original steeple blew off in the hurricane of 1940 and was replaced in 1992.

ငh

Independent Presbyterian Church – *207 Bull Street, 31401, 912-236-3346. www.ipcsav.org.* N32° 04. 607´ W081° 05. 565´. Sunday service at 11:00 a.m.

Woodrow Wilson was married here to Ellen Axson, granddaughter of the minister, in 1885.

ငh

St. Benedict the Moor Catholic Church – *441 East Broad Street, 31401, 912-232-7147. www.stbenedictthemoor. com.* N32° 04. 121´ W081° 05. 271´. Mass on Sunday at 9:00 a.m. and 11:30 a.m.

This is the oldest African American Catholic church in Georgia. The church opened the first Catholic school for blacks in Savannah in 1875.

Independent Presbyterian Church

ငh

St. James A.M.E. Church – *632 East Broad Street, 31401, 912-236-2051. www.stjamesame.com.* N32° 03. 975´ W081° 05. 326´. Sunday services at 7:30 a.m. and 11:00 a.m.

The bell in the tower was a gift to Bishop Henry McNeal Turner from Queen Victoria.

St. John Baptist Church – *522–528 Hartridge Street, 31401, 912-232-8507. www.stjohnthemightyfortress.org.* N32° 04. 092´ W081° 05. 365´. Sunday services at 8:00 a.m. and 11:45 a.m.

In 1993 the building burned to ashes. Soon "The Mighty Fortress" arose from the rubble.

૮ઽ

St. John's Episcopal Church – *1 West Macon Street, 31401, 912-232-1251. www.stjohnssav.org.* N32° 04. 420´ W081° 05. 658´. Sunday services at 8:00 a.m., 10:30 a.m., and noon.

The parish house (Green-Meldrim House) is one of the finest examples of Gothic Revival architecture in the south. General Sherman headquartered here during the occupation of the city during the Civil War.

૮ઽ

St. Matthew's Episcopal Church – *1401 Martin Luther King Jr. Blvd., 31401, 912-233-5965. www.stmatthewssav.georgiaepiscopal.org.* N32° 03. 817´ W081° 06. 216´. Sunday services at 8:00 a.m. and 10:00 a.m.

This church has celebrated over 150 years of worship in the Diocese of Georgia.

૮ઽ

St. Philip A.M.E. Church – *613 Martin Luther King Jr. Blvd., 31401, 912-233-2083. www.stphilipame.org.* N32° 04. 215´ W081° 06. 064´. Traditional worship, Sunday at 8:00 a.m. Contemporary worship at 11:00 a.m.

Through video ministries this church reaches fifty thousand people weekly.

૮ઽ

St. Philip Monumental AME Church – *1112 Jefferson Street, 31401, 912-233-8547.* N32° 03. 939´ W081° 06. 037´. Sunday service at 10:00 a.m.

Established in 1865, this is the mother church of African American Methodism in the state of Georgia. Bishop Henry McNeal Turner was a pastor here. A historical marker is dedicated to him on the site.

૮ઽ

Second African Baptist Church – *123 Houston Street, 31401, 912-233-6163. www.secondafrican.org.* N32° 04. 594´ W081° 05. 174´. Sunday service at 11:00 a.m.

Dr. Martin Luther King Jr. gave part of his "I Have a Dream" speech here and later in Washington, D.C., during the March on Washington.

Temple Mickve Israel – *20 East Gordon Street, 31401, 912-233-1547. www.mickveisrael.org.* N32° 04. 257´ W081° 05. 668´. Services Friday at 6:00 p.m., Saturday at 11:00 a.m.

In the museum is a rare fifteenth-century Torah brought to this country by early settlers. Gift shop.

ત

Trinity United Methodist Church – *225 West President Street, 31401,* 912-233-4766. *www.trinity1848.org.* N32° 04. 718´ W081° 05. 696´. Service Sunday at 11:00 a.m.

The Mother Church of Methodism moved back in after the devastating fire of 1991.

Unitarian Universalist Church
Courtesy of the artist, Pamela Lee

Unitarian Universalist Church – *311 East Harris Street, 31401, 912-234-0980. www.uusavannah.org.* N32° 04. 364′ W081° 05. 385′. Sunday service at 11:00 a.m.

In 1850, James Lord Pierpont, director of music, composed the song "Jingle Bells" here.

 &

United House of Prayer For All People – *1805 Ogeechee Road, 31415, 912-236-8877. www.tuhopfap.org.* N32° 03. 724′ W081° 06. 546′. Call for times of services.

Bishop Charles Grace (Sweet Daddy Grace, 1884–1960) was the church's founder.

&

Wesley Monumental United Methodist Church – *429 Abercorn Street, 31401, 912-232-0191. www.wesleymonumental.org.* N32° 04. 234′ W081° 05. 586′. Sunday services at 8:45 a.m. and 11:00 a.m.

A magnificent Noack organ was dedicated in 1985. With its Gothic-style organ case, it is compatible with the architectural style of the building.

Museums, Historic Sites, Monuments, Memorials & Places of Interest

ℰ𝒜ℬ

African American Monument – At Rousakis Plaza behind City Hall on River Street is a monument honoring African American contributions to the Savannah community. N32° 04. 905′ W081° 05. 455′

Anchor Monument to Chatham County Seamen – On River Street at Abercorn Street.

This monument is a tribute to American merchant seamen who died at sea. N32° 04. 871′ W081° 05. 321′

Andrew Low House – *329 Abercorn Street, 31401, 912-233-6854. www.nscda.org.*

Built in 1848 for cotton merchant Andrew Low, this house was designed by John Norris, who designed many other Savannah historic houses. It is now headquarters for the

Andrew Low House

National Society of the Colonial Dames of America in the state of Georgia. Visitors welcome. Gift shop.

A video by Michael Jordan of Cosmos Mariner Productions, *Savannah's Historic Homes,* offers an inside look at more than a dozen of Savannah's historic mansions. The video is available at local shops or at *www.cosmosavannah.com.* N32° 04. 379′ W081° 05. 526′

Aquarium, UGA Marine Extension Service – 30 Ocean Science Circle, 31411, 912-598-2496. *www.marex.uga.edu.*

Watch live fish, turtles, and invertebrates in saltwater tanks. The aquarium and nature trails are handicapped accessible. Cases display fossils of sharks, giant armadillos, whales, mastodons, and woolly mammoths. There is a "Touch Tank" with sea snails, turtles, and hermit crabs. Gift shop. N31° 59. 271′ W081° 01. 430′

Armillary Sphere – In Troup Square, at Habersham and Charlton Streets, is a giant sundial featuring signs of the zodiac painted in gold. The square is named for George Michael Troup, who served as governor of Georgia from 1823 to 1827. N32° 04. 346′ W081° 05. 376′

℘ *B* ℂ

Bamboo Farm – *See* **Coastal Georgia Botanical Gardens**.

Bartow, General Francis – In the center of Forsyth Park is a bust of General Bartow, the first Savannahian killed in the Civil War in the Battle of Manassas in 1861. N32° 04. 023′ W081° 05. 782′

Battlefield Memorial Park – This park is across the street from the Visitor Center at the southwest corner of Louisville Road and Martin Luther King Jr. Blvd., 31401, 912-651-6840. *www.chsgeorgia.org.*

On October 9, 1779, one of the significant battles of the American Revolution, the Siege of Savannah, was fought here. Americans aided by French troops tried unsuccessfully to take control from the British soldiers occupying the city. Over eight hundred soldiers were killed on this hallowed ground in less than one hour. N32° 04. 559′ W081° 06. 025′

Beach Institute – 502 East Harris Street, 31401, 912-234-8000.

Here you'll find the offices of the King-Tisdell Cottage Foundation and artwork by Ulysses Davis. The museum is an African American cultural center and offers a full schedule of programs and exhibits. N32° 04. 347′ W081° 05. 302′

Beacon Range Light – In Emmet Park on East Bay Street, this beacon was erected in 1858 to guide ships passing over the hulls of ships scuttled years earlier. The navigational hazards consisted of ships deliberately sunk by the British in 1779 to block the harbor while they occupied the city. N32° 04. 758´ W081° 05. 058´

Bethesda Academy – 9520 Ferguson Avenue, 31406, 912-351-2040. *www.bethesdaacademy.org.*

A private boarding and day school for boys in grades six through twelve. Bethesda was formerly an orphanage founded in 1740 by evangelist George Whitefield, and was later known as the Bethesda Home for Boys. N31° 57. 588´ W081° 05. 753´

Bethesda Museum – *See* **William H. Ford Sr. Museum and Visitor Center**.

Big Duke Fire Alarm Bell and Monument – On the East Oglethorpe Avenue median at Abercorn Street is a bell named for alderman Marmaduke Hamilton, chairman of the City Council Fire Committee, 1871–1873. N32° 04. 591´ W081° 05. 465´

Beacon Range Light

Bishop Henry McNeal Turner Monument – At the northeast junction of Fahm and Turner Streets, this monument honors Bishop Turner (1834–1915), the first southern bishop of the African Methodist Episcopal Church. N32° 04. 692´ W081° 06. 058´

Bonaventure Cemetery – 330 Bonaventure Road, 31404, 912-651-6843. *www.bonaventurehistorical.org.*

Featuring mature trees, flowering azaleas, and graceful marble sculptures, this historic cemetery encompasses one hundred acres alongside the Wilmington River. Many famous people have been laid to rest here, including Conrad Aiken, Johnny Mercer, Noble Jones, "Little Gracie" Watson, and Confederate soldiers and generals. Open daily 8:00 a.m.–5:00 p.m. N32° 02. 707´ W081° 03. 039´

Botanical Garden of Tiles – *See* **Children's Botanical Garden of Tiles**.

Botanical Gardens – *See* **Savannah Area Council of Garden Clubs Botanical Gardens**.

Botanical Gardens at the Historic Bamboo Farm – *See* **Coastal Georgia Botanical Gardens**.

Candler Oak

Button Gwinnett Monument–In Colonial Park Cemetery is a monument to Button Gwinnett, one of three signers from Georgia of the Declaration of Independence. N32° 04. 533′ W081° 05. 392′

ജ *C* ൜

Candler Oak – On the southeast corner of Gaston and Drayton Streets is a mossy giant oak tree shading the parking lot of the Savannah School of Law. It was a seedling at the time of the founding of the colony in 1733. The Savannah Tree Foundation oversees the care of the tree. A premier tree of Savannah's Forest City, it is approximately 270 years old with a spread of crown of 107′, circumference of 16′ and height of 50′. N32° 04. 154′ W081° 05. 668′

Cathedral of St. John the Baptist – 222 East Harris Street, 31401, 912-233-4709. *www.savannahcathedral.org*. Founded in the late 1700s by the first French colonists, this cathedral is the seat of the Diocese of Savannah. Destroyed by fire in 1898, then rebuilt, it is open to visitors. N32° 04. 394′ W081° 05. 490′

Catholic Cemetery – 1720 Wheaton Street, 31404, 912-201-4100.

Many priests and bishops are buried here, in addition to veterans of the Civil War, the Spanish-American War, the two World Wars, and the Korean and Vietnam conflicts. The cemetery gates honor the Rizza family. N32° 03. 663′ W081° 04. 222′

Celtic Cross – *See* **Irish Monument**.

Champion-McAlpin-Fowlkes House – *See* **Harper-Fowlkes House**.

Charles H. Morris Center at Trustees' Garden – 912-443-3253.
www.trusteesgarden.com.

The Charles H. Morris Center at Trustees' Garden is a versatile and flexible facility that can be used for business meetings, trade shows, art fairs, church and school gatherings, and visual and performing arts. It is located at 10 East Broad Street behind the Pirates' House.

The Trustees' Garden was set aside in 1733 as an experimental farm where peaches, rice, cotton, grapes, and mulberry trees essential to the silk culture were grown. The high bluff on the northeastern corner was used as a fortification and named Fort Wayne in 1812. In 1830 an iron foundry, later known as the Kehoe Iron Works, opened on the Broughton Street side of the garden, and in 1945 the Savannah Gas Company acquired the property.

In 1945 Mary Hillyer, wife of gas company president Hansell Hillyer, began a restoration of the old houses in the Trustees' Garden. The area's newly restored houses and apartments were an inspiration for the preservation movement in Savannah.

In 2004 Charles Morris bought 6.3 acres of the original garden and restored the Charles H. Morris Center, the former Hillyer Building. He has plans to restore other buildings at the site. N32° 04. 718′ W081° 05. 003′

Chatham Artillery Monument

Chatham Artillery Monument – This monument in Emmet Park on East Bay Street at Drayton Street honors this standing militia formed in 1785.
N32° 04. 787′ W081° 05. 147′

Chatham County Court House (the old one) – 124 Bull Street, 31401.

This Romanesque yellow brick and terra-cotta building sits on a granite base. The new courthouse is on Montgomery Street. This building is now the administrative and legislative center for the county. William Gibbons Preston designed the building. N32° 04. 656´ W081° 05. 527´

Children's Botanical Garden of Tiles – 650 West Jones Street, 31401 (next to the Garrison School of the Visual and Performing Arts), 912-395-5975.

Gates are open 8:00 a.m. to 5:00 p.m. during school days. This 30-by-90-foot walled garden was designed by sculptor Haywood Nichols, who created the bronze *Lamb and Lion under the Tree of Knowledge* at the entrance. Georgia red clay tiles lining the walls were made by children in 1996 as a tribute to the Olympic sailing events held in Savannah. The tile workshop was conducted by Polly Cooper and Sandy Thompson. Emmeline Cooper kept records of donations, and Helen Downing and Zelda Tennenbaum were the prime fundraisers. According to Jim Heater, there are plans to build an auditorium using the garden as the entrance. N32° 04. 471´ W081° 06. 193´

Features from the Children's Botanical Garden

Children's Museum – *See* **Savannah Children's Museum**.

Christ Church Episcopal – 28 Bull Street, 31401, 912-236-2500. *www.christchurchsavannah.org.*

This was the third building built on the site chosen by James Oglethorpe in 1733. It is the "Mother Church of Georgia." N32° 04. 774´ W081° 05. 465´

City Exchange Bell – The "bell-founding" took place in 1802. It hung in the tower of the Old Exchange building, which was demolished in 1900 and replaced by the City Hall building. Today it hangs in a replica of the tower on East Bay Street at Drayton Street. N32° 04. 841´ W081° 05. 075´

City Hall Rotunda Fountain – At Bay and Bull Streets, an ornamental fountain was installed in 1904–1906 in the new City Hall, representing prosperity in the city. N32° 04. 864´ W081° 05. 452´

Civic Center – 301 West Oglethorpe Avenue, 31401, 912-651-6550. *www.savannahga.gov.*

This venue hosts trade shows, concerts, ballet performances, and theater, as well as circuses and more. The Johnny Mercer Theater is located here. N32° 04. 610´ W081° 05. 849´

Coastal Georgia Botanical Gardens at the Historic Bamboo Farm – 2 Canebrake Road, 31419, 912-921-5460. *www.coastalgeorgiabg.com.*

Fifty-one acres of historic plants, ornamental gardens, lakes, farm buildings, and pick-your-own-berry fields. N31° 59. 768´ W081° 16. 076´

Coastal Heritage Society at Tricentennial Park – 303 Martin Luther King Jr. Blvd., 31401, 912-651-6840. *www.chsgeorgia.org.*

The Coastal Heritage Society is a nonprofit organization dedicated to preserving the history and culture of coastal Georgia. CHS is located at the Savannah Visitor Center and manages the Savannah History Museum and Battlefield Memorial Park, the Georgia State Railroad Museum, the Savannah Children's Museum, Pin Point Heritage Museum, Old Fort Jackson, and the Whistlestop Café.

The Savannah History Museum contains interesting historical artifacts from the industrial, military, and fashion life of early Savannah. Musical, cultural, and artistic contributions are highlighted. The shops of the Georgia State Railroad Museum are considered to be the oldest and most complete antebellum railroad repair and manufacturing facility in the United States.

The recently opened Savannah Children's Museum is a creative and interactive environment, encouraging learning through play. The Pin Point Heritage Museum, recently opened in an old oyster and crab factory, celebrates the life, work, and culture of a Gullah Geechee community settled by one hundred freed slaves and their families.

Old Fort Jackson is a beautifully preserved fort along the Savannah River, and is Georgia's oldest standing brick fortification. The site existed as an earthen fort during the Revolutionary War. Built of brick in 1808, the fort was strengthened between 1845 and 1860. It served as headquarters for the Confederate river defenses during the Civil War. N32° 04. 578´ W081° 05. 960´

Cockspur Island Lighthouse – Off the eastern edge of Fort Pulaski, Tybee Island, 31328.

During the Civil War, this little beacon suffered only minor damage. After the Civil War, it was relit and operated until 1909. It was transferred from the United States Coast Guard to the National Park Service in 1949. Access to the lighthouse is limited by the tides and the terrain of the island. An overlook trail is available to visitors from Fort Pulaski. Ask for the trail guide booklet. In recent years concerned citizens like Harvey Ferrelle, John Wylly, and others have helped raise funds to preserve this crucial remnant of history. N32° 01. 349´ W080° 52. 962´

Cockspur Island Lighthouse
Courtesy of the artist, Pamela Lee

Lachlan McIntosh, 1727-1806
Courtesy, Library of Congress

Button Gwinnett, 1735-1777
Courtesy, Library of Congress
Ole Erekson, Engraver

Colonel William Bull Sundial – In Johnson Square, the sundial honors Colonel Bull of South Carolina, who helped choose the site for the new city of Savannah and helped James Oglethorpe survey and lay it out.
N32° 04. 786′ W081° 05. 488′

Colonial Park Cemetery – Abercorn Street and Oglethorpe Avenue, 31401.

The gates were donated by the Daughters of the American Revolution. This burial ground was used for a hundred years beginning in 1750. In 1777 a duel was fought between Lachlan McIntosh and Declaration of Independence signer Button Gwinnett, who died a few days later. Opponents above ground in life, they're neighbors below ground in death. Union soldiers camped here during the Civil War and during idle moments amused themselves by changing the names and dates on some of the headstones. The Trustees Garden Club greatly improved the grounds. N32° 04. 570′ W081° 05. 420′

Confederate Monument – Located in Forsyth Park, this monument was completed in 1879. It honors all the Confederate soldiers who lost their lives during the Civil War. N32° 04. 037′ W081° 05. 770′

Cotton Exchange Fountain – At Bay and Drayton Streets, this terra-cotta winged lion (1889) in front of the Cotton Exchange building symbolizes the prosperous era of "King Cotton." N32° 04. 852′ W081° 05. 394′

Count d'Estaing/Benjamin Lincoln Memorial – A concrete monument in Madison Square commemorates the Siege of Savannah on October 9, 1779, when

**Winged Protector of
the Cotton Exchange**

Courtesy of the photographer, Robb Helfrick

the British holding the city were assaulted by French and American troops. Thirty-five hundred French troops under Count Charles d'Estaing and fifteen hundred Continental troops under Benjamin Lincoln failed to take back the city. The southern line of the British defenses ran right through where Madison Square stands today. N32° 04. 423 W081° 05. 642′

ஐ *D* ௧

Daffin Park – 1500 East Victory Drive, 31404.

This eighty-acre park was opened in 1907 and named for Philip Daffin, who served as chairman of the Park and Tree Commission. Come play tennis, baseball, football, and basketball, or swim, jog, and fish. Rotarian and generous public citizen Herb Traub made possible the restoration of the fountain and also the weather vane by John Boyd Smith on the gazebo in the lake. In the northwest corner of the park is a granite monument (N32° 02. 865′ W081° 05. 075′) honoring those killed in battle during World War I. It explains that Victory Drive's palm trees were planted in their honor. N32° 02. 821′ W81° 05. 017′

Davenport House – 324 East State Street, 31401, 912-236-8097. *www.davenporthousemuseum.org.*

This historic house museum was built in 1820 by Isaiah Davenport. Its rescue from destruction marked the beginning of Savannah's preservation movement. Tour the house, or attend one of the special programs. Gift shop. N32° 04. 636′ W081° 05. 268′

DeSoto, Hernando (c. 1496–1542) – Located on the river side of the Marriott Hotel, this bronze portrait bust by local sculptor Billy Nelson was commissioned by the Spanish Club at Armstrong State University. N32° 04. 748′ W081° 04. 890′

Dog Parks

Herty Pines Dog Park – 2961 Bee Road, 31404.

Two shaded acres with pines allow plenty of romping room. The park has picnic tables and is open daily from 8:00 a.m. to 9:00 p.m. N32° 02. 618′ W081° 04. 665′

Beasley Dog Park – 523 East Broad Street, 31401.

In this park, dogs may run off-leash on dirt and grass in a fenced-in area. N32° 04. 154′ W081° 05. 240′

Savannah Dog Park – 11 East 41st Street, 31401.

The park hosts several dog events each year. It offers shade and chairs, as well as running water. Members only. N32° 03. 207′ W081° 06. 046′

ℰ

Early Roads to Augusta and Darien – In Madison Square at Bull and Charlton Streets are two cannon, marking the origin of these early Georgia roads. N32° 04. 408′ W081° 05. 616′

ℱ

First African Baptist Church – 23 Montgomery Street, 31401, 912-233-6597. *www.firstafricanbc.com.*
Empowerment hour, Sunday at 8:30 a.m. Worship service at 10:00 a.m. This church was built by slaves at night after their daily duties were done. N32° 04. 883′ W081° 05. 759′

First Bryan Baptist Church – 575 West Bryan Street, 31401, 912-232-5526. *www.fbbcsav.org.*
Sunday service at 11 a.m. The oldest continuous black congregation in North America. N32° 04. 959′ W081° 06. 035′

First Burial Ground – 5 West York Street, 31401.

The two lots on which this building stands were a burial ground in 1733. William Cox, a surgeon who arrived on the *Ann* with the first settlers, is buried here. It was used until 1750, when Colonial Park Cemetery was established. N32° 04. 664′ W081° 05. 566′

First African Baptist Church
Courtesy, Dan Kaufman/Studio Kaufman LLC

Flannery O'Connor Childhood Home – 207 East Charlton Street, 31401, 912-233-6014. *www.flanneryoconnorhome.org.*
Visit the house dedicated to this novelist and short story writer, one of the most important writers of the twentieth century. Flannery O'Connor lived here from her birth in 1925 until 1938. Check the schedule for lectures and readings. Gift shop. N32° 04. 353′ W081° 05. 482′

Fowlkes-McAlpin Champion House – *See* **Harper-Fowlkes House**.

Forsyth Park – Located at Bull Street between Gaston Street and Park Avenue. 912-651-6610. *www.savannahga.gov.*
These acres are for walking, jogging, tennis, frisbee, soccer, football, and pigeon feeding. A vision conceived by William Brown Hodgson, the park dates from 1851. The name honors John Forsyth, American statesman and governor of Georgia in 1828.

It was designed by Frederick Law Olmsted, who also designed Central Park in New York City. In the center of the promenade is the monument to Confederate Dead in the Civil War. The gift of G. W. J. DeRenne, this monument by British sculptor David Richards was installed in 1879. It bears these poignant words:

Come from the four winds, O Breath, and breathe
upon these slain that they may live.

There is a mini-visitor center in the nearby restaurant, the Fort Café, that offers restrooms and lunch with indoor or outdoor seating. N32° 04. 150´ W081° 05. 738´

Forsyth Park Arboretum – Located in the north section of the park, at the south end of Bull Street and Gaston Street at Forsyth Park, 912-651-6610. *www.savannahga.gov.*

Stroll through twelve acres of trees, including fifty species of native and adaptive exotic species identified on a map in the park. You can print a brochure from a link on the website. N32° 04. 108´ W081° 05. 756´

Forsyth Park Braille Garden – Southwest of the fountain in Forsyth Park is a lovely and often fragrant garden. With support from the Junior League of Savannah and the Trustees Garden Club, the garden is well maintained. Plant names are in English and in Braille. N32° 04. 108´ W081° 05. 756´

Forsyth Park Fountain – In the center of Forsyth Park, this "playing" fountain is reminiscent of urban renewal of Paris in the 1800s, when broad boulevards and parks were created in major cities. The fountain is similar to the one at the Place de la Concorde in Paris. N32° 04. 150´ W081° 05. 738´

Fort Jackson – *See* **Old Fort Jackson**.

Fort Pulaski National Monument – U.S. Highway 80 East, 31410, 912-786-5787. *www.nps.gov/fopu.*

Construction of this masterpiece of masonry on Cockspur Island was begun in 1829 and completed in 1847. It bears the name of Count Casimir Pulaski, the gallant Polish cavalry officer who died in the Siege of Savannah. This was the first post for young Robert E. Lee after he completed his studies at the U.S. Military Academy at West Point. N32° 01. 131´ W80° 53. 984´

Fragrant Garden for the Blind – *See* **Forsyth Park Braille Garden**.

෨ G ෬

Georgia Historical Society – 501 Whitaker Street, 31401, 912-651-2125. *www.georgiahistory.com.*

Within these walls is one of the oldest collections of manuscripts, books, maps, architectural drawings, photographs, and artifacts relating to Georgia history. N32° 04. 235´ W081° 05. 793´

Georgia State Railroad Museum (Roundhouse Museum) – 655 Louisville Road, 31401, 912-651-6840. *www.chsgeorgia.org.*

This museum is located in the old Central of Georgia Railway Savannah Shops and Terminal Facilities. The Central, chartered in 1833, was one of the oldest railroads in America. The museum is one of the most complete operational historic railroad sites in the world. Gift shop. N32° 04. 535´ W081° 06. 035´

German Memorial Fountain – Located in Orleans Square on Barnard and McDonough Streets, this fountain was given in 1989 by Savannah's German heritage organizations to honor their ancestors. N32° 04. 583´ W081° 05. 724´

Girl Scout First Headquarters – 330 Drayton Street, 31401 (behind the Andrew Low house), 912-232-8200 or 888-223-3883. *www.gshg.org.*

This building housed the family horses and carriages for driving around town. When Juliette Low died in 1927, it was willed to the local Girl Scouts as a museum, program center, and gift shop. Archives are kept here documenting the history of the Girl Scouts from 1912 to the present. Gift shop. N32° 04. 381´ W081° 05. 562´

First Girl Scout Headquarters

Gordon, William Washington – The monument in Wright Square at Bull and President Streets honors William Washington Gordon, founder of the Central of Georgia Railroad and grandfather of Juliette Gordon Low.
N32° 04. 685´ W081° 05. 540´

Grayson Stadium – 1401 East Victory Drive, 31404, 912-351-9150.

Originally built as the Municipal Stadium in 1926, it supported the Savannah Indians baseball team for many years. Hank Aaron, Babe Ruth, Mickey Mantle, and Jackie Robinson have slugged balls halfway to Tybee from here. Today the stadium is the oldest working minor league ballpark in America. N32° 02. 735′ W081° 04. 731′

Great Savannah Races Museum – 411 Abercorn Street, 31401, 912-398-4785. *www.greatsavannahraces.com.*

Savannah is the original venue of the American Grand Prix, and a hundred years ago it was the hub of automobile racing. See memorabilia from racing days. Gift shop. N32° 04. 287′ W081° 05. 539′

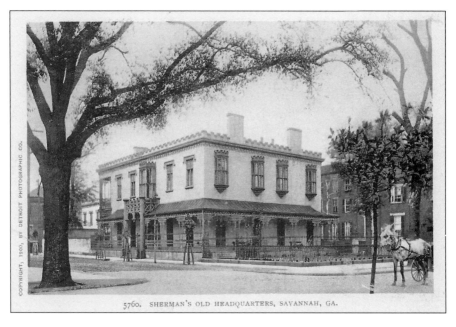

5760. SHERMAN'S OLD HEADQUARTERS, SAVANNAH, GA.

The Green-Meldrim House served as Sherman's Headquarters

Green-Meldrim House Museum – 14 West Macon Street, 31401, 912-233-3845 or 912-232-1251. *www.stjohnssav.org.*

Designed and built by architect John Norris between 1853 and 1861, this house is one of the best examples of Gothic Revival style. It served as the headquarters for General Sherman when he occupied Savannah toward the end of the Civil War. It is now the parish house of St. John's Episcopal Church. N32° 04. 408′ W081° 05. 616′

Greene, Nathanael – A monument in Johnson Square at Bull and Congress Streets honors Brigadier General Nathanael Greene, George Washington's second-in-command in the Revolutionary War. In gratitude for his service in the war, the state of Georgia gave him Mulberry Grove Plantation.
N32° 04. 802´ W081° 05. 500´

Herb House

❧ *H* ❧

Haitian Monument – Located in Franklin Square, this monument by James Mastin honors the five hundred Haitians, the Chasseurs de Saint-Domingue, who fought bravely with the American and French forces against the British in the Siege of Savannah. N32° 04. 866′ W081° 05. 755′

Harbor Light – *See* **Beacon Range Light**.

Harper-Fowlkes House – 230 Barnard Street, 31401, 912-234-2180. *www.harperfowlkeshouse.com.*

This mansion on Orleans Square was designed by Irish architect Charles Cluskey and constructed of scored stucco over Savannah gray bricks with two-story Corinthian-style columns. It is owned by the Society of the Cincinnati, and it may be the inspiration for the house featured in *The Damned Don't Cry*, by Harry Hervey. Visitors welcome. N32° 04. 568′ W081° 05. 704′

Herb House – 20 East Broad Street, 31401.

This small house on East Broad Street is part of the Pirates' House restaurant. Erected in 1734, it is said to be the oldest house in Georgia. The building originally housed the gardener of Trustees' Garden. His office and tool room were in the front section; his stable occupied the back room, and a hayloft was upstairs. The bricks used in the construction of the Herb House were manufactured only a short block away under the bluff by the Savannah River, where brick making began as early as 1733.

Historic Railroad Shops – *See* **Georgia State Railroad Museum**.

Hussars' Memorial Monument – In Emmet Park at the east end of Bay Street is an artifact from the Siege of Savannah—a British six-pounder case-iron cannon strapped to a concrete block. N32° 04. 808′ W081° 05. 256′

❧ *I* ❧

Independent Presbyterian Church – 207 Bull Street, 31401, 912-236-3346. *www.ipcsav.org.*

The first Presbyterian Church in Georgia was founded in 1755 on land deeded by King George II. The current one is modeled after St. Martin's in the Field in London. N32° 04. 607′ W081° 05. 565′

Irish Monument – Located in Emmet Park on East Bay Street at Habersham Street, this Celtic cross was placed here in 1983 to commemorate Georgians of Irish ancestry. N32° 04. 800´ W081° 05. 200´

ℰᴑ𝑱ᴄᴕ

James Johnston plaque – You'll find this plaque on the side of the building next door to (just west of) the Marshall House Hotel at 123 East Broughton Street, 31401. The plaque is located at the site of the printing office of James Johnston, the official printer in colonial times and founder of Georgia's first newspaper, the *Georgia Gazette*. The first issue was printed on April 7, 1763. The *Georgia Gazette* was revived 215 years later by Albert and Marjorie Scardino, who published an urban weekly newspaper with the same name from 1978 to 1985. They won a Pulitzer Prize for editorial writing. The plaque was placed here by the Georgia Society of the Colonial Dames of America in 1931. N32° 04. 709´ W081° 05. 441´

Jasper Monument – In Madison Square at Bull and Charlton Streets, this monument was erected in 1888 in memory of Sergeant William Jasper of the 2nd South Carolina Regiment, who was killed in the Siege of Savannah in 1779. N32° 04. 408´ W081° 05. 616´

Jasper Springs Marker – This marker is located on Augusta Avenue at the junction with I-516. Here is where Sergeant William Jasper and Sergeant Newton rescued two American prisoners and killed two British soldiers, capturing eight more while making the rescue. N32° 05. 378´ W081° 07. 684´

Jepson Center for the Arts – 207 West York Street, 31401, 912-790-8800.

Facing Telfair Square, this building was designed by architect Moshe Safdie and completed in 2006. The building provides 7,500 square feet of exhibit space for contemporary art and exhibits from the permanent collection. Visit the fascinating hands-on museum for children. Attractive gift shop and café. N32° 04. 703´ W081° 05. 707´

Jewish Cemetery Marker – In the median of Oglethorpe Avenue at Bull Street is a marker on the original 1733 burial plot allotted by James Oglethorpe to the Jewish community. N32° 04. 618´ W081° 05. 568´

The Old Jewish Burial Ground, known as de Lyon–de la Motta Cemetery – Cohen Street and Spruce Street behind Savannah Station, 31401.

Here is the burial ground of the Levi Sheftall family. Dedicated in 1773, it was used for eighty years. Stand with this cemetery on your left, and to the right you'll

**de Lyon–de la Motta Cemetery,
Burial Ground of the Levi Sheftall Family**

Courtesy of the photographer, Jill Howell

see an older, larger walled cemetery endowed by Mordecai Sheftall as a public Jewish burial ground in 1746. N32° 04. 343´ W081° 06. 212´

Jewish Section of Bonaventure Cemetery –
Bonaventure Road, 31404, 912-651-6843.

Enter the main gate and go to the right to the Jewish section, established in 1907 by the congregation of Temple Mickve Israel. The ashes of victims of the World War II Holocaust are interred next to the burial chapel. Pebbles placed on headstones show that family and friends have visited. Open daily 8:00 a.m.–5:00 p.m.
N32° 02. 508´ W081° 02. 792´

Walled Jewish Burial Ground

Johnny Mercer Bench – On the east side of Johnson Square at Bull and Congress Streets is a bench given by the Johnny Mercer Foundation. It is crescent-shaped and includes a silhouette profile done by Johnny himself, who wrote over fifteen hundred songs. A duplicate bench is located at his gravesite in Bonaventure Cemetery. N32° 04. 786′ W081° 05. 476′

Johnny Mercer Statue – In Ellis Square at Barnard and Saint Julian Streets, this bronze sculpture pays tribute to Savannah's own Johnny Mercer, who wrote "Moon River," "The Days of Wine and Roses," and many other songs. The sculptor was Savannah native Susie Chisholm. N32° 04. 848′ W081° 05. 647′

Johnny Mercer Statue

Sculpture by Susie Chisholm, NSS

Johnny Mercer Statue

Courtesy of the photographer, Daniel L. Grantham, Jr.
Sculpture by Susie Chisholm, NSS

John Wesley Bronze Statue – In Reynolds Square at Abercorn and Congress Streets, this sculpture pays tribute to Reverend John Wesley, who came from England to minister to the colonists. He was the third rector of Christ Church and later founded Methodism.
N32° 04. 762′ W081° 05. 363′

Jones, Noble Wimberly – This bust by Kevin Conlon in Emmet Park at East Bay and Houston Streets was erected in 2004, at the bicentennial celebration of the founding of the Georgia Medical Society by Dr. Jones.
N32° 04. 762´ W081° 05. 071´

Juliette Gordon Low Birthplace – 10 East Oglethorpe Avenue, 31401, 912-233-4501.

Also known as the James Moore Wayne House, this home was designated as Savannah's first National Historic Landmark in 1965. William Washington Gordon, founder of the Central of Georgia Railway, bought it in 1831. His granddaughter, Juliette Gordon Low, founder of the Girl Scouts, was born here on Halloween night in 1860. The site is visited by Girl Scouts from around the world. Gift shop. N32° 04. 612´ W081° 05. 533´

ଓ *K* ଔ

"King" Oliver marker – This marker can be found on the side of the restaurant at 514 Martin Luther King Jr. Blvd., 31401.

King Oliver (1885–1938) was one of the great early New Orleans trumpet players. He was a friend and mentor to jazz great Louis Armstrong, and he spent his last years living in a rooming house a few blocks from where this tribute stands.

King-Tisdell Cottage – 514 East Huntingdon Street, 31401, 912-234-8000.

This African American heritage museum is named for its early owners, Eugene and Sarah King, and Sarah and Robert Tisdell. Inside are furnishings typical of a nineteenth-century home. N32° 04. 048´ W081° 05. 368´

Korean War Monument – Emmet Park on East Bay Street at Abercorn Street.

Here you'll find the list of members of D Company, 10th Infantry Battalion, killed in Korea. N32° 04. 812´ W081° 05. 245´

ଓ *L* ଔ

Laurel Grove Cemetery, North – 802 Anderson Street, 31415, 912-651-6772. *www.savannahga.gov.*

All lots were sold during the Victorian era, resulting in a concentration of Victorian-period cemetery architecture. Juliette Low is interred here, along with mayors, judges, generals, and many famous citizens. Open daily 8:00 a.m.–5:00 p.m. N32° 03. 884´ W081° 06. 419´

Plot in the Laurel Grove Cemetery, North

Laurel Grove Cemetery, South – 2101 Kollock Street, 31415, 912-651-6772. *www.savannahga.gov.*

In 1852 land was set aside for the burial of slaves and free people of color. At rest here are ministers, civil rights leaders, and other well-known people. Open daily 8:00 a.m.–5:00 p.m. N32° 03. 679´ W081° 06. 773´

Lucas Theatre For the Arts – 32 Abercorn Street, 31401, 912-525-5040 or 912-231-9998. *www.lucastheatre.com.*

This 1920s movie palace has been restored to its former glory. Built by Arthur Lucas, it has hosted vaudeville acts and movies, first silent films, then talkies. Today it is owned by the Savannah College of Art and Design. Open for tours. Live theater and films. N32° 04. 742´ W081° 05. 364´

ಬ M ೞ

Marine Monument – On Bull Street at the north end of Forsyth Park is a monument honoring the twenty-four U.S. Marines from Chatham County killed in World War II. N32° 04. 207´ W081° 05. 711´

Massie Heritage Center – 207 East Gordon Street, 31401, 912-201-5070. *www.massieschool.com.*

Designed by architect John Norris, Massie is on the National Register of Historic Buildings. After serving as a school for over one hundred years, it is now an interactive museum for local history and architecture. Gift shop. N32° 04. 224´ W081° 05. 543´

McAlpin-Champion-Fowlkes House – *See* **Harper-Fowlkes House**.

McIntosh House (1770) – 110 East Oglethorpe Avenue, 31401.

This was the home of General Lachlan McIntosh, Revolutionary War hero. The first constitutional session of the Georgia Legislature was held here in 1782, after the British had left the city. George Washington visited his friend here in 1791. N32° 04. 602´ W081° 05. 473´

McLaws, General Lafayette – This bust in the center of Forsyth Park honors General McLaws, president of the Confederate Veterans' Association in Georgia. N32° 04. 045´ W081° 05. 773´

McQueen Trail – Highway 80, past the Bull River Bridge, 31410.

Enjoy six miles of nature along what was once the route for the Central of Georgia Railroad from Savannah to Tybee. It is now known as *Rails to Trails* and is popular with walkers and cyclists. N32° 02. 393´ W080° 56. 694´

Mercer-Williams House – 429 Bull Street, 31401, 912-238-0208. *www.mercerhouse.com.*

This Italianate mansion was designed by John Norris for General Hugh Mercer prior to the Civil War. The story of antique dealer Jim Williams, who restored the house, is told in John Berendt's book *Midnight in the Garden of Good and Evil.* Open for tours. Gift shop. N32°04. 282´ W081° 05. 709´

Mickve Israel Synagogue – *See* **Temple Mickve Israel Synagogue and Museum**.

Moravian Marker – Installed in 1933 in Oglethorpe Square at Abercorn and State Streets, this marker honors the Moravian colonists in Savannah who maintained a mission to the Indians from 1733 to 1740. N32° 04. 656´ W081° 05. 388´

Mother Mathilda (Matilda) Beasley Park – 407 East Broad Street, 31401.

The park that extends for many blocks along East Broad Street has been transformed from a dingy junkyard into a grassy athletic field for football or baseball practice. Named for Georgia's first black nun, Mother Mathilda Beasley, the park includes a playground, a dog park, and a pavilion for community activities. The former home of Mother Mathilda Beasley on Price Street has been moved to the park to be restored and used as an interpretive site. N32° 04. 282′ W081° 05. 709′

ಹೊ N ಛ

National Museum of the Mighty Eighth Air Force – 175 Bourne Avenue, Pooler, 31322, 912-748-8888. *www.mightyeighth.org.*

Here you'll find exhibits dedicated to the story of the Eighth Air Force of the U.S. Army Air Corps serving in the European Theater during World War II. Gift shop. N32° 06. 919′ W081° 14. 149′

Noble Hardee House – 441 Bull Street, 31401.

General Noble Hardee died before completion of his house in 1869. President Chester Arthur visited here twice. It is an antiques shop today. The house has fifteen fireplaces and was designated "exceptional" by the Historic Savannah Foundation. N32 °04. 270′ W081° 05. 697′

ಹೊ O ಛ

Oatland Island Wildlife Center – 711 Sandtown Road, 31410, 912-395-1212. *www.oatlandisland.org.*

Observe animals in their natural habitats. See alligators, bison, white-tailed deer, owls, red foxes, goats, and more. Bring a picnic, and you may need bug spray. Gift shop. N32° 03. 139′ W081° 00. 845′

Ogeechee Canal (at the west end of River Street) – This is one end of the Savannah Ogeechee Canal. The other end is located on Highway 204 near I-95. (*See* **Savannah Ogeechee Canal.**) In the early 1800s, slaves and Irish laborers dug the sixteen-mile canal to link the Savannah and Ogeechee Rivers so that cotton and rice could be transported. N32° 05. 188′ W081° 06. 046′

Ogeechee Canal and Nature Center – *See* **Savannah Ogeechee Canal and Nature Center.**

Oglethorpe Bench – A bench on Yamacraw Bluff near the Hyatt Hotel on West Bay Street marks the spot where James Oglethorpe pitched his tent upon his arrival in 1733. It was a gift from the Colonial Dames in 1906.
N32° 04. 896′ W081° 05. 521′

Oglethorpe Monument – In Chippewa Square is the sculpture of James Oglethorpe by Daniel Chester French unveiled in 1910. He is in the full dress of a British military general. N32° 04. 543′ W081° 05. 592′

Old Fort Jackson – 1 Fort Jackson Road, 31404, 912-232-3945. *www.chsgeorgia.org.*

Named for James Jackson (1757–1805), the fort dates to 1808. It stands along the Savannah River and is Georgia's oldest brick fort. Born in England, twenty-five-year-old James Jackson fought for the patriots in the American Revolution. Jackson accepted the surrender of the British in Savannah at the close of the war. He later became governor of Georgia. The fort is open to visitors, who can see Civil War and other military exhibits. Cannon firings are held daily at the fort year-round, and daily interactive programs are held March through October. Gift shop.
N32° 04. 087′ W081° 03. 002′

Olde Pink House – 23 Abercorn Street, 31401, 912-232-4286.

The Pink House is so named for the pink stucco that covers its old brick. This Georgian mansion on Reynolds Square was built in 1789 for James Habersham Jr., one of Savannah's early cotton brokers, and his wife, Esther Wylly. It is now a first-class restaurant. N32° 04. 785′ W081° 05. 375′

Olde Pink House
Courtesy, Dan Kaufman/Studio Kaufman LLC

Olympic Torch – On the east end of River Street is the Olympic Torch. In 1996 Atlanta hosted the Olympic Games, and the sailing events took place in waters around Savannah. On the first day of these events, the torch was lit with the original flame from Olympia, Greece. N32° 04. 799′ W081° 05. 020′

Owens-Thomas House – 124 Abercorn Street, 31401, 912-790-8889. *www.telfair.org/owens-thomas.*

Here is one of the finest examples of Regency architecture in America. It was designed by William Jay for cotton merchant/banker Richard Richardson and his wife Francis Bolton. In 1825 the Marquis de Lafayette spoke from this side balcony to cheering Savannahians. The house is open to the public as a house museum, and the carriage house contains the original historic slave quarters. Gift shop. N32° 04. 629′ W081° 05. 352′

Owens-Thomas House, side balcony

ℰ *P* ℭ

Pei Ling Chen Gallery and Garden for the Arts – 322 and 324 Martin Luther King Jr. Blvd., 31401, 912-525-5000. *www.SCAD. edu.*

This is one of the Savannah College of Art and Design's many galleries. The others are in Atlanta, France, and Hong Kong as well as Savannah.
N32° 04. 489′ W081° 05. 961′

Peter Tondee's Tavern plaque – *See* Tondee's Tavern plaque.

Pink House – *See* **Olde Pink House**.

Pin Point Heritage Museum – 9924 Pin Point Avenue, 31406, 912-667-9176. *www.pinpointheritagemuseum.org.*

In 1890 one hundred freed slaves and their families came from Ossabaw Island to the mainland, settling in Pin Point to fish, crab, shrimp, and harvest oysters in the creeks and sounds. In 1926 A. S. Varn & Son Oyster Factory was opened at Pin Point and became the main source of work and income for the community. The museum offers exhibits on oyster harvesting and includes interactive oral histories as told by local residents. The museum is open to the public on Thursday, Friday and Saturday and during the week for scheduled groups. Gift shop. N31° 57. 236′ W081° 05. 426′

Police Officers' Monument – In the median of East Oglethorpe Avenue at Habersham Street is a bronze statue in memory of police officers from Savannah and Chatham County who have died in the line of duty.
N31° 04. 550′ W081° 05. 321′

Pulaski Monument – In Monterey Square at Bull and Gordon Streets stands the monument to Count Casimir Pulaski, who is remembered for his loyalty to the cause of liberty during the American Revolutionary War.
N32° 04. 277′ W081° 05. 678′

℘ R ℘

Ralph Mark Gilbert Civil Rights Museum – 460 Martin Luther King Jr. Blvd., 31401, 912-231-8900.

Named for the civil rights leader and NAACP president, the museum honors the man who was the pastor of the historic First African Baptist Church for sixteen years. Built in 1914, the building was home to one of the largest black-owned banks in Georgia. The museum houses the history of Savannah's civil rights movement. Gift shop. N32° 04. 329′ W081° 06. 021′

Rotary Centennial Clock – Located in City Market, the clock was dedicated in 2005 to honor the one hundredth anniversary of the founding of Rotary International. N32° 04. 840′ W081° 05. 678′

Rotary Club Marker – In the median at Bull and Liberty Streets is a monument in the shape of a gear or wheel, placed by the Rotary Club of Savannah in 1925. The spokes indicate the Rotary four-way test related to truth, fairness, goodwill, and helpfulness. N32° 04. 480′ W081° 05. 610′

Roundhouse Museum – *See* **Georgia State Railroad Museum**.

℘ S ℘

SS *Savannah* replica – The model of the SS *Savannah* is located on River Street at the foot of the Barnard Street ramp. The ship stands in the center of the

Maritime Fountain donated by the Propeller Club. The SS *Savannah* was the first steamship to cross the Atlantic Ocean, leaving Savannah on May 22, 1819, and reaching Liverpool, England, twenty-seven days later.
N32° 04. 944′ W081° 05. 584′

Saint Andrews Monument – A small monument in the median of Oglethorpe Avenue at Bull Street honors Scottish forebears of members of the Saint Andrews Society in Savannah. N32° 04. 616′ W081° 05. 556′

Salzburger Monument – Between the Lincoln Street and Abercorn Street ramps on Bay Street is a stone monument given by the city of Salzburg, Austria, in 1994 to honor Salzburgers who landed on Georgia's sandy soil in 1734.
N32° 04. 823′ W081° 05. 305′

Savannah Area Council of Garden Clubs Botanical Gardens – 1388 Eisenhower Drive, 31406, 912-355-3883. *www.savannahbotanical.org.*

Located next door to Hospice House, the Botanical Garden includes camellias, ferns, and native plants, as well as the Ann Douglas White Memorial Rose Garden. The garden is open every day, and the walkways are wheelchair accessible. The garden is maintained by volunteers from fifteen of the city's garden clubs, along with the Coastal Master Gardener Association and the Savannah Rose Society. There is no admission charge, but donations are always appreciated. Dogs are allowed, as long as they are on a leash and well behaved.
N32° 00. 273′ W081° 05. 486′

Savannah Children's Museum—Exploration Station – 655 Louisville Road, 31401, 912-651-4292. *www.savannahchildrensmuseum.org.*

Located in Tricentennial Park, Savannah Children's Musuem is the perfect place for families to explore and play! The museum is entirely outdoors and located adjacent to the Georgia State Railroad Musuem. This great learning museum features exhibits designed to expand the imaginations of children, including an exploration maze, reading nook and sensory garden. Ideal for ages 2-10.
N32° 04. 535′ W081° 06. 180′

Savannah College of Art and Design (SCAD) – 342 Bull Street, 31401, 912-525-5100. *www.scad.edu.*

The Volunteer Guards Armory, designed in 1893 by William Gibbons Preston, was the first building acquired by SCAD. The growth of this college has brought vitality to downtown neighborhoods. Countless buildings throughout the Historic District are owned by the college and used for dorms and classrooms.
N32° 04. 380′ W081° 05. 650′

Savannah College of Art and Design Museum of Art – 601 Turner Street, 31401, 912-525-5000. *www.scadmoa.org.*

Founded in 2002 as part of SCAD, the museum includes drawings, paintings, sculpture, photography, prints, and the Walter O. Evans Center for African American Studies. Gift shop. N32° 04. 674´ W081° 05. 989´

Savannah History Museum – 303 Martin Luther King Jr. Blvd. 31401, 912-238-1779. *www.chsgeorgia.org.*

Inside the old 1860 Central of Georgia Railway train shed are Revolutionary War exhibits, one of Johnny Mercer's Academy Awards, and a replica of the bench used in filming *Forrest Gump*. Here are thousands of interesting historical artifacts from the industrial, military and fashion life of early Savannah. Almost 300 years of history. Savannah's musical, cultural and artistic contributions are highlighted. Impressive steam locomotive. Eighteen-minute film on Savannah history. Gift shop. N32° 04. 578´ W081° 05. 960´

Savannah Mural – The Augusta Oelschig Mural, 45 feet long by 6 feet tall, is on permanent display at the Savannah Area Chamber of Commerce, 101 East Bay Street, 31401, 912-644-6400. *www.savannahchamber.com.*

The mural depicts Savannah scenes ranging from Bethesda and Wormsloe to Savannah churches, the old City Exchange, and the Central of Georgia Railway Station. Some are three-dimensional, and many of the images depict places long since torn down. The mural is a gift from Mary R. and Howard J. Morrison Jr., who rescued it from a bank on Telfair Square that was being renovated and could no longer use it. Augusta Oelschig lived and painted in Savannah until her death in 2000. N32° 04. 820´ W081° 05. 394´

Savannah National Wildlife Refuge – 694 Beech Hill Lane, Hardeeville, South Carolina, 29927, 843-784-2468. *www.fws.gov/savannah.*

Established in 1927, the refuge encompasses 29,000 acres of freshwater marshes, tidal rivers, creeks, and bottomland hardwoods. It's ideal for looking for coastal birds and other wildlife at various times of the year. Along the four-mile Laurel Hill Wildlife Drive, you can listen to an audio tour of the refuge on your car radio by turning to 1600 on the AM dial. While observing alligators on the canal banks and bald eagles flying overhead, you can hear several three-minute talks on the refuge, its habitats, and its history. The introductory stop starts the tour at the entrance off of S.C. 170. Other stops powered with solar energy are the history stop, including Gullah music, a wildlife talk, and a description of habitats at the refuge. The last stop encourages visitors to stop at the visitor center. The Savannah Wildlife Visitor Center is in Jasper County, South Carolina, on U.S. 17, six miles north of downtown Savannah. Gator Hole Gift Shop.
N32° 10. 390´ W081° 04. 570´

Savannah Ogeechee Canal and Nature Center – 681 Fort Argyle Road, 31419, 912-748-8068. *www.savannahogeecheecanalsociety.org.*

Completed in 1830, the canal was built to connect the Savannah and Ogeechee Rivers. Cotton, rice, bricks, and peaches were transported to the coast for export to other countries. This end of the canal has a half-mile walk along the tow path to the river and a nature museum. There are four additional miles of trails through the river, swamp, pine forest, and sand hill environments. Gift shop.
N32° 01. 375′ W081° 18. 997′

Savannah Theatre – 222 Bull Street, 31401, 912-233-7764. *www.savannahtheatre.com.*

Today you'll find 1950s architecture on this site, but the first structure built here was a theater designed in 1818 by William Jay. Other buildings designed by William Jay include the Telfair Museum of Art and the Owens-Thomas House, so you can imagine the beautiful Regency building that originally stood on this site. Today the theater is used for musicals, comedy, and drama.
N32° 04. 557′ W081° 05. 547′

Semiquincentenary Fountain – In Lafayette Square at Abercorn and Charlton Streets is a fountain given in 1982 by the National Society of Colonial Dames of America in celebration of the 250th anniversary of the colony.
N32° 04. 389′ W081° 05. 503′

Ships of the Sea Maritime Museum – 41 Martin Luther King Jr. Blvd., 31401, 912-232-1511. *www.shipsofthesea.org.*

The museum is located in the Scarbrough House, designed by William Jay in 1818. The mansion was built for William Scarbrough, president of the Savannah Steamship Company, builder of the SS *Savannah*, the first steamship to cross the Atlantic Ocean. The building became a school for black children in 1878. In 1997 the building was restored as a museum with a collection of ship models, paintings, and maritime antiques, as well as an extensive garden. The north garden is open daily with free wifi. Gift shop. N32° 04. 868′ W081° 05. 820′

Sorrel Weed House – 6 West Harris Street, 31491, 912-236-8888.
www.sorrelweedhouse.com.

Charles Cluskey from Ireland designed this mansion for shipping merchant Francis Sorrel. You'll see a bold Greek Revival design, featuring Doric columns, a sweeping double entrance, and marble floors. Later it was owned by the Weed family. Open for tours. N32° 04. 437′ W081° 05. 630′

Spanish American War Monument – At the south end of Forsyth Park at Park Avenue is a memorial erected in 1931 to honor Georgia veterans of the Spanish American War. N32° 03. 899′ W081° 05. 837′

Ships of the Sea Maritime Museum in the Scarbrough House
Courtesy, Herb Woo Family

ℬ*T*ℭ

Telfair Museum of Art – 124 Barnard Street, 31401, 912-790-8800. *www.telfair.org.*

Facing Telfair Square is the South's first public art museum. It was designed by British architect William Jay for Alexander Telfair in 1818. In 1875 Alexander's sister Mary left the house to the Georgia Historical Society so that it could serve as a museum. Gift shop. N32° 04. 733´ W081° 05. 692´

Temple Mickve Israel Synagogue and Museum – 20 East Gordon Street, 31401, 912-233-1547. *www.mickveisrael.org.*

This temple is the third-oldest synagogue in America. Within its Gothic-style architecture it houses a fifteenth-century Torah brought to Georgia by early settlers. Gift shop. Prints and note cards of Dan Kaufman sold here.
N32° 04. 733´ W081° 05. 692´

Mary Telfair, 1789-1875
Courtesy, Georgia Historical Society

Tomochichi – In Wright Square is a granite boulder from Stone Mountain, Georgia, to honor this chief (mico) of the Yamacraw Indians and true friend to James Oglethorpe and the colonists. N32° 04. 667′ W081° 05. 537′

Tondee's Tavern plaque – On a building on the corner of Broughton and Whitaker Streets is a bronze plaque marking the spot where Tondee's Tavern stood in Colonial times. It was here that the Liberty Boys planned the overthrow of British rule and the formation of a new government. The plaque was given by the Georgia Society of the Colonial Dames of America in 1899. The eponymously named restaurant is recommended for its food and spirits and can be found at 7 East Bay Street. N32° 04. 757′ W081° 05. 586′

Tricentennial Park – Home to Savannah History Museum, Battlefield Memorial Park, Georgia State Railroad Museum and Savannah Children's Museum – located in downtown Savannah. Don't forget to stop by the WhistleStop Café for a delicious lunch! *Savannah History Museum* is located within the historic Central of Georgia Railway passenger station and offers a glimpse into Savannah's unique past. *Battlefield Memorial Park*, just across from the History Museum, is the site of the Revolutionary War Battle of Savannah. *Georgia Railroad Museum*, believed to be the oldest and most complete railroad complex of its kind in the world offers daily interpretive tours as well as site tours by rail. *Savannah Children's Museum* is a unique outdoor learning space and is the perfect place for families to explore and play. An exploration maze, reading nook and sensory garden are among a dozen exhibits there.

Truman Trail – The Truman Linear Park Trail is under construction to extend from Daffin Park to Lake Mayer. The eight-foot-wide trail will be a handicapped-accessible trail for bikers, runners, and walkers. It will extend for almost five miles through residential neighborhoods and connect to the track around Lake Mayer.

Tybee Island Marine Science Museum – 1509 Strand Street (near the pavilion), 31328, 912-786-5917 or 866-557-9172. *www.tybeemarinescience.org.*

Group programs for beach and marsh walks. Exhibits of turtles, whalebones, fish, gators, and invertebrates. Live animals in a "touch tank." Girl Scouts can earn official badges. N31° 59. 547´ W080° 50. 809´

Tybee Lighthouse – 30 Meddin Drive, Tybee Island, 31328, 912-786-5801. *www.tybeelighthouse.org.*

The first Tybee lighthouse was ordered by James Oglethorpe and constructed in 1733. Over the years the structure was rebuilt several times, resulting in the present structure, one of the most beautifully renovated light stations on the east coast. The museum is located on Battery Garland, built in 1898, displaying artifacts and exhibits of rich island history. The lighthouse is one of seven surviving colonial era towers. Climb the 178 steps for a panoramic view. Gift shop. N32° 01. 357´ W080° 50. 715´

ഇ**V**ങ

Vietnam Veterans Memorial – In Emmet Park on East Bay Street, this memorial pays tribute to local men and women who served in the Vietnam War. N32° 04. 798´ W081 °05. 171´

ഇ**W**ങ

Washington Guns – On Bay Street just east of City Hall, these guns were captured from the British at the Battle of Yorktown. They were presented by President George Washington to the Chatham Artillery in 1791. N32° 04. 858´ W081° 05. 423´

Tybee Lighthouse

Waving Girl – At the east end of River Street is the statue of Florence Martus (1868-1943), who waved at every ship arriving or departing from the port for forty-four years. She lived with her brother, a lighthouse keeper, on nearby Elba Island. N32° 04. 798′ W081° 05. 408′

Wetland Mitigation Station (Chatham County Wetland Preserve) – 912-652-7800.

This 494-acre park is located on the Ogeechee River off U.S. Highway 17 on Chief of Love Road. This preserve has a lake, trails, algae-covered water around cypress trees, gravel roads, picnic tables, and kayak access. Open 8:00 a.m.– 8:00 p.m. No attendant. N31° 59. 225′ W081° 17. 206′

William H. Ford Sr. Museum and Visitor Center – 9250 Ferguson Avenue, 31406, 912-401-0663. *www.bethesdaacademy.org.*

The museum at Bethesda chronicles the history of Bethesda since its founding in 1733 up to the present. The museum honors the museum's former director William H. Ford Sr. and also tells the story of Barney Diamond, one of Bethesda's most distinguished alumni. N31° 57. 588′ W081° 05. 753′

World War I Memorial – At the northwest corner of Daffin Park, where Waters Avenue meets Victory Drive, this granite monument honors the brave soldiers who died in the Great War. The palm trees along Victory Drive and the Tybee Road have been planted in memory of those sailors, soldiers, marines, and men and women of the Coast Guard who lost their lives between 1914 and 1918. N32° 02. 865′ W081° 05. 075′

World War II Memorial – On River Street, just west of the Hyatt Hotel. This twelve-ton globe represents the two theaters of the war (Europe and the Pacific) and honors Americans who served in the armed forces. N32° 04. 929′ W081° 05. 529′

Wormsloe Historic Site – 7601 Skidaway Road, 31406, 912-353-3023. *www.gastateparks.org/wormsloe.*

This was the plantation of Noble Jones, who arrived in the New World in 1733 with James Oglethorpe on the ship *Ann*. Drive up the spectacular one-and-a-half-mile-long, oak-lined driveway to the museum and walk to the ruins of Noble Jones's fortified home. Gift shop. N31° 58. 830′ W081° 04. 135′

Wormsloe Fountain – In Columbia Square, at Habersham and York Streets, is a fountain from Wormsloe Plantation, the ancestral home of the Jones and DeRenne families. It honors Augusta and Wymberley DeRenne, descendants of the Jones family. N31° 04.608′ W081° 05. 284′

ஐ Y ෆ

Yamacraw Art Park – 536 West Bryan Street, 31401. The park is located on Yamacraw Bluff, where Oglethorpe founded the Georgia colony in 1733 and befriended the Yamacraw Indians. The Reverend Andrew Bryan, a freed slave, preached here in 1788 to one of the oldest black congregations.
N32° 04. 947′ W081° 05. 931′

Yamacraw Bluff Marker – On West Bay Street near Bull Street is a marker on the site where James Oglethorpe landed and declared the location to be an ideal place to establish a new town. N32° 04. 879′ W081° 05. 486′

Tybee

A Funky Island with Personality

Tybee is Savannah's sandy Riviera in the sun. Located fifteen miles from the city, and offering white beaches, dunes, and inviting surf, it became popular after the Civil War. People were eager for relaxation and diversion after the stress and hardships of the war.

Lavish hotels and pavilions accommodated folks arriving by steamboat, then trains, to this sandy spit of land. They came here to cure asthma, hay fever, and arthritis by swimming in the salty Atlantic Ocean. They came for fun, frolic, and to get married, with toes wiggling in the white sand.

In the 1920s, bandleaders like Tommy and Jimmy Dorsey and Guy Lombardo brought their big bands to the pavilions. Later, crowds were enthralled with Cab Calloway, Bob Crosby, and Ella Fitzgerald. The Big Apple and the Susie-Q, the Lambeth Walk, the rumba, and the conga were trendy dances.

The old Tybrisa Pavilion, with its skating rink, dance floor, and bowling alley, burned and fell into the ocean in 1967. Another pavilion now stands in its place.

Due to rapid growth, the flavor of this little island has changed. Remembering the good old days, seniors get ruffled by so many condos and parking meters. However, the spirit of the island still prevails. So, kick off your flip-flops and sprint to the beach for a healthy dose of Tybee fun.

Train to Tybee, the "Marsh Hen," ended its run in 1933

Directions to Tybee ...

From Savannah, take U.S. 80 East for 15 miles. Nearing the Lazaretto Bridge, the last bridge onto the island, you'll see the entrance to Fort Pulaski on your left. ...

Fort Pulaski National Monument and Museum – U.S. 80 at Cockspur Island Road, 31328, 912-786-5787. *www.nps.gov/fopu.*

Near the mouth of the Savannah River, this Confederate fort was captured in 1862 by Union forces. Confederate soldiers believed the fort to be safe, but the new rifled guns fired from Tybee by Union soldiers were too powerful. The fort surrendered after just thirty hours. Take time to visit this historic site. Open daily 9:00 a.m.–5:00 p.m. Gift shop, with books for sale. N32° 01.132′ W080° 53. 976′

Leaving Fort Pulaski …

 Return to U.S. 80. Turn left. On your left is the …

Cockspur Island Lighthouse

Off the eastern edge of Fort Pulaski. During the Civil War, this little beacon suffered only minor damage. After the Civil War, it was relit and operated until 1909. It was transferred from the United States Coast Guard to the National Park Service in 1949. Access to the lighthouse is limited by the tides and the terrain of the island. An overlook trail is available to visitors from Fort Pulaski. Ask for the trail guide booklet. In recent years concerned citizens like Harvey Ferrelle, John Wylly, and others have helped raise funds to preserve this crucial remnant of history. N 32° 01. 349′ W 080° 52. 962′.

 Continue on U.S. 80. Drive over the Lazaretto Bridge onto Tybee Island.

Stop at the highly visible pink **Visitor Center** at the first traffic light (Campbell Avenue) for information, annual events, and maps. 802 First Street, 912-786-5444 or 877-470-1864. *www.visittybee.com.* N 32° 00. 967′ W 081° 50. 932′.

Leaving the visitor center, turn left at the traffic light at Campbell Avenue, left on Solomon Avenue, then take the first right onto Meddin Drive. Stay on Meddin. You're in the …

Fort Screven Historic District

In 1855 Fort Screven was built for seacoast defense. Six concrete gun batteries, a minefield, and military buildings were constructed. From 1897 to 1947, the fort was a critical part of America's coastal defense. Troops stood guard here throughout the Spanish American War of 1898, World War I, and World War II. In 1947 the fort closed and was sold to the town of Tybee. By the 1950s many buildings had been converted to private residences. In 1961 Battery Garland became the Tybee Museum.

Tybee Island Light Station and Museum – 30 Meddin Drive, 31328, 912-786-5801. *www.tybeelighthouse.org.*

Open daily 9:00 a.m.–5:30 p.m. except on Tuesdays. No tickets sold after 4:30 p.m. Gift shop. On Tuesdays there are private tours for tour companies starting at 9:00 a.m. The light station has been guiding mariners safely into the Savannah River for 270 years. It stands on five acres, and is considered one of North America's most accurately renovated light stations with all support buildings intact. N32° 01. 357′ W080° 50. 715′

Tybee Island Light Station and Museum
Courtesy of the Artist, Pamela Lee

Leaving Fort Screven …

Go back to U.S. 80. Turn left. At the ocean go right on Butler Avenue, past City Hall, to the south end of the island. Go left on Tybrisa Street (Sixteenth Street) to the roundabout. Park here, then enjoy the shops and the beach.

Recreation and Leisure

Alligators Galore Kayaking and Nature Tours – 912-695-2305. *www.alligatorsgalore.com.*

Alligators Galore provides kayak rentals and guided tours that depart from Alley 3 on Tybee's Back River.

Brown's Reel 'em N Deep Sea Fishing – Old U.S. 80, Walsh's dock, 31328, 912-897-4990. *www.reelemn.com.*

Offering boats rigged for fishing and comfort.

Burke's Beach Rentals – 912-547-8145, 912-667-8382. *www.rentafloat.com.*

Specializing in beach rental recreational equipment: umbrellas, chairs, and lounges.

Captain Derek's Dolphin Adventure – Walsh's dock on Old U.S. 80, 31328, 912-897-4990. *www.reelemn.com.*

Watch playful dolphins and listen to a narration about the area. All ages. Captain Derek also has a tour leaving from downtown Savannah (see Dolphin Magic Tours).

Capt'n Mike's Dolphin Tours – 1 U.S. 80, 31328, 912-786-5848 or 800-242-0166. *www.tybeedolphins.com.*

See bottle-nosed dolphins, hammocks, beaches, lighthouses, sea turtles, and wading birds. Offering sunset cruises, Girl Scout tours, and offshore/inshore fishing.

Capt'n Stan's Marshland Inshore Fishing Adventures – 40 Estill Hammock Road, 31328, 912-786-5943. *www.marshlandadventures.com.*

Light tackle. U.S. Coast Guard–licensed captain. Leaves from Chimney Creek at the Crab Shack. Twenty-three-foot bay boat. Catch shark, flounder, trout, and bass.

Chimney Creek Marina – 40 Estill Hammock Road (next to the Crab Shack), 31328. Catch crabs off the dock. Boat hoist. Open daily 8:00 a.m.–5:00 p.m.

Crabbing (Do it yourself) – Crabbing is best done at low tide from a boat or a dock, around jetties and in creeks. Tybee Island Bait and Tackle, 912-786-7472, rents boats and crabbing needs.

Crab Creek Charters – 41 Estill Hammock Road, 31328, 912-658-5158. *www.crabcreekcharters.com.*

Tour inlets, creeks, and Little Tybee with Captain Solomon. See blue heron, white egrets, ospreys, pelicans, bald eagles, and dolphins.

DO IT YOURSELF CRABBING

Materials needed:
- bucket,
- chicken necks,
- scoop net,
- sticks six inches long cut from old broom handle,
- a ball of twine, and
- a few nuts or bolts as weights (sinkers).

Cut the twine long enough to reach the creek bottom. Tie one neck to each line with a weight. Tie the other end to your sticks. Drop the weighted and baited end into the water.

PATIENCE!! PATIENCE!!

(Sip s-l-o-w-l-y a large Gatorade. Crabs get feisty if rushed!) Okay, now ...

Pull the line up, inch by inch. You'll feel a slight tug when the crab is eating the bait. Lift slowly, and don't lift the crab and bait out of the water. He'll skedaddle!

Scoop up your supper. Invert the scoop net so that the crab falls into bucket. Males have blue claws. Females have red on the tips of their claws. Throw back the females and the small ones.

Dolphin Magic Tours – 312 East River Street, 31401, 912-658-2322. *www.dolphin-magic.com.*

Watch playful dolphins and listen to a narration on this tour that runs between Savannah and Tybee.

Fishing on the Pier Oceanside or Back River – Get a license online at *www.georgiawildlife.com/node/654* or at Chu's Convenience Mart, 725 First Street, 31328, 912-786-5904.

Jaycee Park – Campbell Road on Van Horne. This park offers picnic tables, a playground, a lighted soccer/softball field, a playground, restrooms, tennis courts, beach volleyball courts, basketball, a pavilion with roof, and a small cemetery.

Lazaretto Creek Marina – 1 U.S. 80, 31328, 912-786-5848. *www.tybeedolphins.com/fishing.*

Capt'n Mike's dolphin tours leave from here. Take a deep-sea fishing adventure on a cabin cruiser. Rent jet skis and kayaks.

Memorial Park – Behind City Hall on Butler Avenue, 912-472-5045. Outdoor cooking, lighted tennis/basketball/volleyball courts, jogging track, restrooms.

Miss Judy Fishing Charters – 124 Palmetto Drive, Savannah, 31410, 912-897-4921 or 912-897-2478. *www.missjudycharters.com.*

Inshore, offshore, or out to the Gulf Stream.

North Beach Birding Trail – Walk west from the lighthouse on North Beach into this bird sanctuary. Access the beach through the parking area behind Fort Screven on Meddin Drive.

Channel bass caught at Tybee

North Island Surf and Kayak – 912-786-4000. *www.northislandkayak.com.*

Kayaking eco-tours, Stand-Up Paddle Boarding (SUP) and surfboard rentals, lessons, summer camps, beach and SUP yoga, retail store.

Sally Pearce Nature Trail – On the south side of U.S. 80 at Fifth Avenue. A short trail with two footbridges. This area is a habitat for painted buntings, woodpeckers, cardinals, and brown thrashers.

Sea Kayak Georgia – 1102 U.S. 80, 31328, 912-786-8732 or 888-KAYAKGA. *www.seakayakgeorgia.com.*

Guides describe the Georgia coast, offering saltwater paddle tours daily. Kayak camp for all ages. Training, fun, games. Stand-up paddle tours. Open 10:00 a.m.– 6:00 p.m.

Sundial Fishing and Nature Tours – P.O. Box 537, 31328, 912-786-9470. *www.sundialcharters.com.*

Salt marsh ecology, shelling, birding, fishing, fossil hunting, and dolphin watching.

Sweet Lowland Tours – 1315 Chatham Avenue (at AJ's Dockside Marina), 31328, 912-786-0215. *www.sweetlowlandtybeetours.com.*

Personalized tours to Little Tybee Island, Wassaw Island, Lazaretto Creek, Fort Pulaski, Cockspur Lighthouse, Thunderbolt, Daufuskie Island, and other locations.

Tybee Beach Ecology Trips – P.O. Box 30923, Savannah, GA, 31410, 912-596-5362. *www.ceasurf.com/pages.*

Comb the beach with marine scientist Dr. Joe. Learn about animals and the ecology of the Georgia coast. Find fossils, shells, and sharks' teeth. Pull a seine net.

Tybee Island Bait and Tackle – 4 Old U.S. 80, 31328, 912-786-7472. *www.tybeeislandbaitandtackle.com.*

Live/frozen bait, boat and rod and reel rentals, crabbing needs.

Tybee Island Charters – P.O. Box 1762, 31328, 912-786-4801. *www.tybeeislandcharters.com.*

Deep-sea fishing, inshore fishing, and dolphin tours aboard the 49-foot Isabella.

Tybee Island Marine Science Museum – 1509 Strand Street (near the pavilion), 31328, 912-786-5917 or 866-557-9172. *www.tybeemarinescience.org.*

Open daily 10:00 a.m.–5:00 p.m. Gift shop. Group programs for beach and marsh walks. Exhibits of turtles, whalebones, fish, gators, and invertebrates. Live animals in a "touch tank." Girl Scouts can earn official badges.
N31° 59. 547′ W080° 50. 809′

Tybee Jet Ski and Water Sports – 180 Old U.S. 80 at Lazaretto Creek Marina. 31328. 877-9JETSKI, or 912-786-8062. *www.tybeejetski.com.*

Jump waves on Wave Runners, rent kayaks, or take a jet ski tour.

Tybee Island Library – 405 Butler Avenue, 31328, 912-786-7733.

Open Monday, Friday, and Saturday: 2:00 p.m.–6:00 p.m. Tuesday: 10:00 a.m.–8:00 p.m. Wednesday: 10:00 a.m.–6:00 p.m. Thursday and Sunday closed. Tree Tots story time Tuesdays at 11:00 a.m. Songs, stories, and finger-play for babies up to five years. A handsome chandelier by ironsmith Ivan Bailey hangs in the foyer.

POST THEATRE, FORT SCREVEN, SAVANNAH BEACH, GA.

Tybee Post Theater

Tybee Post Theater – 10 Van Horne Street, 31328, 912-663-1099. *www.tybeeposttheater.org.*

This theater was built 1930 and sat unused for years. Currently under restoration. Will reopen for live entertainment, movies, art exhibits.

Walter Parker Pier and Pavilion – At the end of Tybrisa Street, 912-652-6780.

Picnic tables, concessions, and restrooms. Bring fishing rods and bug spray. Can be rented for events.

Tybee Island Wedding Chapel – 1114 U.S. Highway 80, 31328. 800-786-5889. *www.tybeeweddingchapel.com.*

Reminiscent of a 1908 seaside chapel, featuring a large sanctuary and veranda, landscaped grounds, and a baby grand piano.

YMCA – 204 Fifth Street, 31328, 912-786-9622. *www.ymcaofcoastalga.org.*

❧ Monday–Thursday: 5:30 a.m.–9:00 p.m. ❧ Friday: 5:30 a.m.–8:30 p.m. ❧ Saturday: 8:00 a.m.–6:00 p.m. ❧ Sunday: 1:00 p.m.–5:00 p.m. Children's programs, fitness classes, gymnasium.

Parking

Meters – $1.50 per hour. **Pay stations** – A quarter for 10 minutes.

There are coin machines in the parking lots on Fourteenth Street and on the Strand, as well as along Tybrisa Street and at North Beach lot. Display receipt on dashboard. Accepts debit/credit cards. Day passes can be purchased at Pay/Display machines. $2.00 per hour on beachfront.

Decal parking – May be purchased from City Hall, 403 Butler Avenue. $100 a year. Display on driver's side windshield.

Where to Park

❧ South Beach Parking Lots at beachfront lots between Fourteenth and Eighteenth Streets.

❧ North Beach Parking at beachfront lot in Fort Screven across from the lighthouse.

❧ Van Horne and Fort Streets near dog parks and River's End Campground. A short walk to the beaches or to the lighthouse.

❧ Dune crossovers – Most streets adjacent to beach access have parking available.

Getting Around the Island

Crab Cab – 1601 Chatham Avenue, 31328, 912-786-2722. *www.tybeecrabcabs.com.* Seven-passenger minivans, private tours, bar rolls. Prompt service.

Fat Tire Bikes and Scooters – 1403 Butler Avenue, 31328, 912-786-4013; and 406 First Street, 31328, 912-786-9572. *www.fattirebikestybee.com.*

Island Hoppers – 1601 Inlet Avenue, 31328, 912-786-0805, or 912-656-0805. Electric car, scooter, and bike rentals. Offers shuttles, taxis, and tours. Service to the beach, bars, and anywhere on the island.

Tim's Beach Gear – 1101 East U.S. 80, 31328, 912-786-8467. *www.timsbeachgear.com.* Rent beach cruiser bikes, tandems, trailer bikes, pull-behinds, and beach gear.

Tybee Cruisers – 1601 Inlet Avenue, 31328, 912-786-0531 or 866-512-0531. *www.tybeecruisers.com.* Four- to six-seat environmentally friendly open bubble cars.

Lodging

Atlantis Inn – 20 Silver Avenue, 31328, 912-786-8558. *www.atlantisinn.com.*

A 1950s renovated beach-style inn. This one's a peach! Rooms with imaginative themes.

Beach House at the Dunes – 404-A Butler Avenue, 31328. 866-539-0036. *www.abetterstay.com.*

Three pools, restaurant, children's activity area. Smoke-free.

Beachside Colony – 404 Butler Avenue, 31328, 912-786-4535 or 800-786-0770. *www.beachsidecolony.com.*

Right on the ocean, with two pools and a play area. One-, two-, and three-bedroom condos.

Beachview Bed and Breakfast – 1701 Butler Avenue, 31328, 912-786-5500. *www.beachviewbbtybee.com.*

On the southern tip of the island. Once a boarding house, now an upscale inn with spacious porch, built in 1895. You may rent the facility for special events.

Carbo House – 11 Tybrisa Street, 31328, 912-786-4905.

Built in 1932, this is a sixteen-room historic boarding house. Ten of the rooms still have the original beadboard on floors and ceilings, 30 feet from the beach. Microwaves, refrigerators, and bathrooms with showers. Wraparound porch. Rent for two weeks minimum.

DeSoto Beach Hotel – 212 Butler Avenue, 31328, 912-786-4542 or 877-786-4542. *www.desotobeachhotel.com.*

Red tile roof, porthole windows, plush vegetation. Ocean views. Next door is the DeSoto Bed and Breakfast, with four rooms. Evening wine and cheese. Hot breakfast.

Dunes Inn and Suites – 1409 Butler Avenue, 31328, 912-786-4591. *www.dunesinn.com.*

100 yards from the beach. Near restaurants, shops, and night spots. Pets welcome.

Georgianne Inn – 1312 Butler Avenue, 31328, 912-786-8710, 800-596-5301. *www.georgianneinn.com.*

A preserved Tybee raised cottage. Refrigerator, microwave, cable/satellite TV.

Howard Johnson Admiral's Inn – 1501 Butler Avenue, 31328, 912-786-0700, 800-793-7716. *www.hojo.com/tybeeisland.*

Near deep-sea fishing, windsurfing, sailing, and biking. Facilities suitable for conventions or weddings. Large meeting rooms.

Lighthouse Inn Bed and Breakfast – 16 Meddin Drive, 31328, 912-786-0901 or 866-786-0901. *www.tybeebb.com.*

Preserved three-bedroom beach cottage, c. 1910, a honeymoon or hideaway haven. Locally owned. Private baths, wifi, cable TV, foodie's kitchen.

Ocean Plaza Beach Resort – 1401 Strand, 31328, 912-786-7777. *www.oceanplaza.com.*

Short walk to pavilion. Six miles to Fort Screven. Two outdoor pools, balconies, ocean or pool views. Cable TV, restaurant, and late-night bar. Near the Breakfast Club and Science Center.

Oceanfront Cottage Rentals – 717 First Street, 31328. 800-786-5889, 912-786-0054. *www.oceanfrontcottage.com.*

One to seven bedrooms, pet-friendly, pools, elevator.

Ocean Song – 404 Butler Avenue, 31328, 866-599-6674. *www.oceansongonetime.com.*

Pool and children's pool, family-friendly. One mile from the Science Center. Five miles from Fort Pulaski. On the Atlantic Ocean.

River's End Campground and RV Park – 5 Fort Avenue, 31328, 912-786-5518 or 800-786-1016. *www.riversendcampground.com.*

One hundred campsites, tent sites, and cabins, plus pool and laundry.

Blue Crab

Royal Palm Motel – 909 Butler Avenue, 31328, 912-786-5518. *www.royalpalmtybee.com.*

A budget, family motel 500 feet from the beach, near restaurants/shopping. Pool, no pets.

Sandcastle Inn – 1402 Butler Avenue, 31328, 912-786-4575. *www.sandcastle-inn.com.*

Saltwater pool, short walk to the beach, microwave, refrigerator, coffee maker, and continental breakfast. Twelve miles to golfing.

Sandy's by the Shore – 1601 Inlet Avenue, 31328, 912-786-0531 or 866-512-0531. *www.sandysbytheshore.com.*

Offers a variety of options to match the size and tastes of your family or group. Facilities for two or twenty.

Sea and Breeze Hotel and Condos – 16 Strand (Sixteenth Street), 31328, 912-786-8806. *www.tybeeseaandbreezehotel.com.*

Near the pavilion. Outdoor pool, bar, in-room wifi. Small refrigerators, cable TV, concierge, valet.

Sunrise Motel – 905 Butler Avenue, 31328, 912-786-4470.

Across from beach, outdoor pool, wifi, twenty minutes from Savannah's Historic District. Rooms have cable TV, small sitting areas. Pets okay.

Summer Winds – 404c Butler Avenue, 31328, 800-786-0770.

Cable TV, washers/dryers, children's activity area, no pets. One mile from the pier.

Tybee Beach Resort Club – 404e Butler Avenue, 31328. 888-253-1628.

Outdoor pool, children's play area and pool, restaurant, beachfront site. Pets okay.

Tybee Beach Vacation Rentals – 912-786-0100 or 800- 970-7788. *www.renttybee.com.*

Oceanfront condos, beach cottages, or island homes.

Tybee Island Inn – 24 Van Horn Street, 31328, 912-786-9255. *www.tybeeislandinn.com.*

A four-minute walk to the beach. Seven guest rooms. North end of the island.

Tybee Island Rentals – 204 First Street, P.O. Box 627, 31328, 912-786-4034 or 800-476-0807. *www.tybeeislandrentals.com.*

Variety of vacation homes. Rent weekly or daily.

Tybee Time Vacation Rental – 106 Sea Lane, 31328, 877-823-6441. *www.tybeetimevacationrentals.com.*

Accommodations range from one to six bedrooms. Nonsmoking. No pets.

Tybee Vacation Rentals – 1010 U.S. 80 East, 31328, 855- 642-4082. *www.tybeevacationrentals.com.*

One- to six-bedroom beachfront condos, sleeping up to eighteen.

Restaurants

Call for hours and up-to-date information. Restaurants change their hours, days, and prices, depending on the season.

A-J's Dockside – 1315 Chatham Avenue, 31328, 912-786-9533. Kick back with a drink, and admire the glow of sunset over the Back River. Drink specials. Happy hour daily 6:00 p.m.–7:00 p.m.

Bernie's Oyster House – 13 Sixteenth Street, 31328, 912-786-5100. *www.berniesoysterhouse.com.*

Chowders, seafood, and sandwiches. Full bar, outdoor patio. Live music. Open year-round.

Benny's Tavern – 1517 Butler Avenue, 31328, 912-786-0121. Cold beer, pool tables. Come party with Tybee characters. Karaoke.

Breakfast Club – Fifteenth Street and Butler Avenue, 31328, 912-786-5984. *www.thebreakfastclub.com.*

"Hit the spot" breakfasts. Mingle with local characters and movie stars. Free wifi. Open year-round, except major holidays.

Coco's Sunset Grille – 1 Old U.S. 80 at Lazaretto Creek Marina next to Capt'n Mike's Dolphin Adventures, 31328, 912-786-7810. *www.cocossunsetgrille.com.*

Open daily year-round. Rooftop dining. Soothing sunsets.

Crab Shack – 40 Estill Hammock Road, 31328, 912-786-9857. *www.thecrabshack.com.*

Where the elite eat in their bare feet. Gator lagoon, parrots. Outdoor dining on decks. Indoors in buggy or bad weather. Fun for children. Open daily year-round, but closed for Thanksgiving and Christmas. Gift shop.

Doc's Bar – 10 Tybrisa Street, 31328, 912-786-5506. *www.docsbartybee.com.*

The oldest bar on the island. Shag contests. Beach, boogie, blues, Buffett music. A Tybee tradition. Open year-round, noon until "yawn!"

Dolphin Reef Oceanfront Restaurant – Fifteenth Street and the ocean, 31328, 912-786-8400. *www.dolphinreef.com.*

In the Ocean Plaza Beach Resort. The only thing better than their food is the amazing view.

Fannie's On The Beach – Strand near Seventeenth Street, 31328, 912-786-6109. *www.fanniesonthebeach.com.*

Two open-air decks with broad ocean views. Lunch and supper daily. Open year-round.

Gerald's Pig and Shrimp – 1115 East U.S. 80. 31328, 912-786-4227. *www.tybeebbq.com.*

Catering, barbecue, seafood. Children welcome.

Huc-A-Poo's – Off U.S. 80 in shops at Tybee Oaks, 31328, 912-786-5900. Daily lunch, supper. Full bar, pizza. Open year-round.

Lighthouse Pizza – 15 Tybrisa Street, 31328, 912-786-9874. *www.lighthousepizza.net.*

Ribs, calzones, salads, desserts, beer, wine.

Macelwee's Seafood – 101 Lovell Avenue, 31328, 912-786-8888. *www.macelweesontybee.com.*

Beer-battered shrimp, buckets of oysters, rib-eyes. Children welcome. Enjoy watching ships from the porch.

Marlin Monroe's Surfside – At Beachside Colony at 404 Butler Avenue, 31328, 912-786-4745. *www.marlinmonroessurfsidegrille.com.*

Steaks, seafood, burgers, and salads. Ocean views.

North Beach Grill – 33 Meddin Drive, 31328, 912-786-4442. *www.northbeachbarandgrill.net.*

Eclectic fusion with Caribbean flair. Open daily year-round. Entertainment Friday and Saturday. Catering available. Kid-friendly.

Quarter Sports Bar & Grill – 601 First Street, 31328, 912-786-8966.

Sports, food, fun, "Licka drinks." Burgers, snow crab legs, seafood.

Rock House Bar and Grill – 1518 Butler Avenue, 31328, 912-786-7176. Serves and delivers food until 4:00 a.m. Extensive menu.

Spanky's Beachside – 1605 Strand, 31328, 912-786-5520. *www.spankysbeachside.com.*

Shrimp, grouper, scallops, mahi, steaks, and burgers. Open year-round. You can rent the upper deck for parties.

Sting Ray's Seafood – 1403 Butler Avenue, 31328, 912-786-0209. *www.stingraysontybee.com.*

Outdoor deck, blue crabs, beach music, full bar. Live music. Open daily.

Sundae's Cafe – 304 First Street, 31328, 912-786-7694. *www.sundaescafe.com.*

Family-owned. Lunch and supper. A favorite of locals. Open year-round.

Sugar Shack – 301 First Street, 31328, 912-786-4482. *www.tybeesugarshack.com.*

Open year-round. Breakfast, lunch, supper. Cones, shakes, sundaes, banana splits.

Tybee Island Social Club – 1311 Butler Avenue, 31328, 912- 472-4044. *www.tybeeislandsocialclub.com.*

Weekday lunch specials. Sunday club brunch with Bloody Marys and champagne cocktails. Closed Mondays. Children welcome.

Tybee Time – 1603 Strand, 31328, 912-786-7150. Frozen cocktails. Thirteen TVs. Headquarters for sporting events. Open daily year-round.

Vicki's On Tybee – 1105 U.S. Highway 80 East, 31328, 912-786-9869. *www.vickisontybee.com.*

Seafood, steaks, spirits.

Wet Willie's Bar and Restaurant -16 Tybrisa Street, 31328, 912-786-5611. *www.wetwillie.com.*

Try a cooling frozen daiquiri or two with meals.

Wind Rose Cafe – 19 Tybrisa Street, 31328, 912-786-6593.

Hearty lunches. Shepherd's pie, turkey, dressing, fried chicken, livers, gizzards, ham, and seafood. Open year-round.

Shopping

From the Lazaretto Bridge, there is a dazzling gaggle of eccentric shops on both sides of U.S. 80. Buy hats, pottery with crabs and turtles, local art, cotton outfits, sandals, shell jewelry, and painted driftwood. Park and plunder.

Caldwell's Cottage Monogramming and Gifts – 1213 U.S. 80, 31328, 912-657-5236. Offers gifts for all occasions, and will monogram anything.

Fish Art owner, Ralph Douglas Jones

Fish Art – 1207 U.S. 80, 31328, 912-472-4194.

Guitar fish, watering-can fish, clapboard fish. Fish made from surfboards, pots and pans. Antiques and 100 percent junk. Custom water fountains, metal turtles. Delightfully eccentric owner.

Gallery by the Sea – 1016 U.S. 80, 31328, 912-786-7979. *www.gallerybysea.com.*

Too much to list. Beach décor, local art, unique and upscale gifts.

Hall of Frames and Debbie Brady Robinson Signature Gallery – 1207 U.S. 80, 31328, 912-786-8944. *www.atlanticbeacongallery.com.*

Award-winning artist Debbie Brady Robinson's paintings of Tybee and other coastal islands draw the viewer into private scenes that seem like a bit of paradise. Her husband, Mark Robinson, is a custom picture framer who showcases her work and offers fine art giclee printing services and more.

High Tide Surf Shop – 406 U.S. 80, 31328, 912-786-6556. *www.hightidesurfshop.com.* A true surf shop. Paddleboards and surfing gear. Beautiful sweaters and beachwear.

Latitude 32 – 1213 U.S. 80, 31328, 912-786-9334. *www.latitude32.us* Apparel and accessories to ease you into a relaxed Tybee mood.

Lighthouse Gift Shop – 30 Meddin Drive, 31328, 912-786-5877. *www.tybeelighthouse.org.* Tybee lighthouse souvenirs, books, postcards, nautical ornaments, T-shirts, and jewelry.

Seaside Sisters – 1207 U.S. 80, 31328, 912-786-9216. *www.seasidesisterstybee.com.*
Original art, furniture. Giggle, blush, and laugh at hilarious whatnots. Sassy, brassy, and always classy. Too much to list.

Waves Beachwear Surf and Gifts – 705 U.S. 80, 31328, 912-786-0084.
Sportswear, swimwear, and accessories.

 For further adventures in shopping, continue on U.S. 80. Turn right at the ocean onto Butler Avenue, where you'll find …

The Funky Fish – 211 Butler Avenue, 31328, 912-786-4704. Surfboards, all your bait and tackle needs.

Tybee Market -1111 Butler Avenue, 31328, 912-786-4601. *www.tybeemarketiga.com.*
Full grocery store. Groceries and flowers can be delivered. Open daily.

Good Vibrations – 1514 Butler Avenue, 31328, 912-786-5103.
www.goodvibrationshealthandmore.com.
Vitamins, herbs, aroma therapy, full-spectrum lighting, crystals, detoxes, and supplements.

Atlantic Beacon Gallery – 1604 Butler Avenue, 31328, 912-786-9386.
www.atlanticbeacongallery.com.
Daily 10:00 a.m.–6:00 p.m. Closed Tuesdays. Local art, from over one hundred local and regional artists. Also pottery, stained glass, photography, sculpture, fine crafts, and collectibles.

 And don't miss Tybrisa Street (Sixteenth Street) on the south end of the island …

Many shops line this short strip, offering shells, jewelry, hats, beach chairs, live hermit crabs, beer, sno-cones, burgers, bathing suits, postcards, tattoos, souvenirs, and suntan lotion. Park and walk.

Aloha Gifts – 26 Tybrisa Street (Sixteenth Street), 31328, 912-786-0130.
Gifts, beachwear, flip-flops and sunglasses.

Salt – 24 Tybrisa Street, 31328, 912-786-8833. *www.saltartisan.com.*
Massage oils, mineral makeup, candles, hair care, baby products.

Seaside Sweets – 18B Tybrisa (Sixteenth Street), 31328, 912-786-9861.
www.seasidesisterstybee.com/seaside-sweets.
Life's sweet on Tybee. Gelato, smoothies, yogurt, and coffee, plus old-fashioned candy, pralines, and chocolates.

American Beachwear – 17 Tybrisa Street, 31328, 912-786-9954.
Sportswear, swimwear, and accessories.

Beach Bums Boutique – 7 Tybrisa Street, 31328, 912-659-0226.
U.S. items, fair trade jewelry, hats, fedoras, crabs made in Haiti, Byrd's cookies.

T. S. Chu's Department Store – 6 Tybrisa Street, 31328, 912-786-4561.
"If it's something you use, you'll find it at Chu's." This establishment is a Tybee icon reminiscent of the 1950s, with a huge variety of shells, books, beach stuff, half-rubber balls, and Tybee books.

Christy's Department Store – 1–3 Tybrisa Street, 31328, 912-786-4204.
Open year-round. Flip-flops, yo-yos, sunglasses, souvenirs, cold drinks, and sunscreen.

Medical Facilities—Pets and People

Tybee has no hospitals. In Savannah are ...

Candler Hospital – 5353 Reynolds Street, 31405, 912-819-6000.

Memorial Health Center – 4700 Waters Avenue, 31404, 912-350-8000.

St. Joseph's Hospital – 11705 Mercy Blvd., 31419, 912-819-4100.

On the island ...

Island Pharmacy – 303 First Street, 31328, 912-786-7878.
Monday, Tuesday, Thursday, and Friday: 10:00 a.m.–5:30 p.m. Wednesday: 10:00 a.m.–2:00 p.m. In the summer, open Saturdays: 10:00 a.m.–2:00 p.m.

Tybee Urgent Care 24/7 – 602 First Street, 31328, 912-786-8389. *www.urgentcare247.com.*
No appointment needed. No insurance plans. Cash and credit cards. Open daily 9:00 a.m.–5:00 p.m. On call daily, 24 hours.

Tybee Animal Care – 602 First Street, 31328, 912-786-4006. *www.tybeeanimalcare.com.*
Monday–Friday: 8:00 a.m.–6:00 p.m. Appointments at other times upon request.

Tybee Teeth Family Dentistry – 601 First Street, 31328, 912-786-9433. *www.tybeeteeth.com.*
Monday, Tuesday, Thursday, Friday: 8:00 a.m.–5:00 p.m.

Off the island …

Southern Urgent Care – 4717 U.S. 80 East, 31410, 912-898-2227.

Monday–Friday: 8:00 a.m.–8:00 p.m. Saturday–Sunday: 9:00 a.m.–5:00 p.m. Credit cards and most insurance plans. No Medicaid. Walk-ins okay. Nine miles from Tybee.

Locksmiths Serving Tybee

Islands Locksmith – 912-897-1991

Pop-a-Lock – 912-234-0810

Precision Entry – 912-412-8904

24-Hour Locksmith Tybee Island – 888-243-1970

Books about Tybee

Bitsy and the Mystery at Tybee Island, by Vonda Skinner Skelton. She writes for preteens about a tomboy who searches for hidden treasure, discovers a skeleton, and faces a kidnapper.

Hiding Places: A Memoir from the Pirate Princess of Tybee Island, by Deborah Elizabeth Merriman. This pirate princess builds forts in the dunes and spies on passersby as they stroll the shores.

A History of Tybee Island, Georgia, and a Sketch of the Savannah and Tybee Railroad, by Richardson Beale. This pamphlet published in 1886 may be found online or in the library archives. It begins with John Wesley's prayer as he set foot on Tybee's sand after fifty-seven days at sea in 1735 and ends with the completion of the railroad in 1886.

Hotel Tybee, by Harry Spirides. This is an Arcadia book with many pictures of the grand old belle, which was once touted as the finest resort between Atlantic City and Miami on the Atlantic coast. The first Hotel Tybee burned and was rebuilt twenty years later in 1909, in Spanish Revival style.

Incident at Tybee Island, by Rowan Wolfe. The author has crafted fact into fiction about the bomb dropped in 1958 off the coast of Georgia. Fast-paced and well-written.

The Mystery of Goat Island, by Polly Wylly Cooper. This is a gripping little book for ages 8–14 to read while lying in the sand dunes. It is a story about an island near

Tybee, once inhabited by goats and an old hermit. You can buy it at T. S. Chu's Department Store or Lighthouse Gift Shop.

Running with the Dolphins and Other Tybee Tales, by Micheal Elliott. This collection of short stories captures the natural beauty of the island.

A *Walk on the Beach: A True Love Story from Tybee Island*, by Buddy McCoy. Share the intimacy, humor, and trials of a true love story.

Sand Between Our Toes, by Ellen Lyle Taber and Polly Wylly Cooper. The authors recreate stories of life on Tybee. Hundreds of photographs remind folks that time may change the world, but the magic of Tybee remains the same.

Tybee Days, by Ellen Lyle Taber and Polly Wylly Cooper. In 1872, before Tybee became popular, a resort on Beach Hammock was the project of Thomas Arkwright. Steamboats took day-trippers to the hammock to dance on the pavilion, and to wade and gather shells before nature's forces destroyed Arkwright's dream. Read about the Tybee train, rum runners, T. S. Chu, half rubber, hurricanes, and lifeguards in this factual and humorous social account of the area.

Tybee Island: The Long Branch of the South, by Robert Ciucevich. This book tells the story of the island from the days of the Guale Indians and Spanish explorers to Tybee's glory days of big bands on the pavilion. An Arcadia book, it is well researched.

Tybee Island, by James Mack Adams. Covering two hundred years of history, this is another Arcadia book worth reading.

Tybee Island Terror Plot, by Glenn Smith. In this work of fiction, an Air Force bomber and fighter collide over Savannah. The bomber drops its atomic bomb into waters near Tybee. Al-Qaeda finds the bomb and blackmails the United States.

Tybee Island: The Hidden Treasure, by Dr. Gustave Kreh. An elegant coffee-table book and a photographic tribute to the island.

Wassaw Sound, by Dr. William Harris. Lose yourself in this gripping book, which centers on the Tybee bomb. It offers mystery, myth, lost love, suspense, and hurricanes.

Nearby Side Trips

Savannah National Wildlife Refuge – 694 Beech Hill Lane, Hardeeville, South Carolina 29927, 843-784-2468. *www.fws.gov/savannah. The Savannah Wildlife Visitor Center is in Jasper County, South Carolina, on U.S. 17, about 6 miles north of downtown Savannah. N32° 10. 390´ W081° 04. 570´*

Open Monday–Saturday 9:00 a.m.–4:30 p.m. Gift shop. Established in 1927, the refuge encompasses 29,000 acres of freshwater marshes, tidal rivers, creeks, and bottomland hardwoods. It is a great place to look for coastal birds and other wildlife at different times of the year.

New Ebenezer and the Jerusalem Evangelical Lutheran Church – 2966 Ebenezer Road, Rincon, Georgia, 31326, 912-754-3915. *www.newebenezer.org. From I-95 take Exit 109 to Highway 21 north for 12 miles. Then take GA 275 to the end (5 miles). N32° 22. 595´ W081° 10. 871´*

New Ebenezer is a town in Effingham County, Georgia, settled by the Salzburgers who arrived in Georgia shortly after the founding of the new colony. They left Austria to escape religious persecution and established the Jerusalem Lutheran Church in 1734. They settled on the banks of the Savannah River about thirty miles northwest of Savannah.

After the British invasion of 1778, the town was badly damaged, and it never fully recovered. The church built in 1769 still stands, and both the church and the town were placed on the National Register of Historic Places in 1974. During

**Jerusalem Evangelical Lutheran Church
in New Ebenezer**

the American Revolution the British used the church as a hospital and a stable.

The Reverend Johann Martin Boltzius was the first pastor, serving from 1734 to 1765. In spite of the enormous hardships that the new colonists faced, he encouraged the settlers to build a thriving community based on Christian principles and a strong work ethic.

National Museum of the Mighty Eighth Air Force – 175 Bourne Avenue, Pooler, Georgia, 31322, 912-748-8888. *www.mightyeighth.org.*
The museum is visible from I-95 at Exit 102, two miles south of the Savannah airport.
N32° 06. 919′ W081° 14. 149′

Open daily 9:00 a.m.–5:00 p.m. Gift shop. Pooler Crossroads Chamber of Commerce Visitor Center in the main building, 912-748-0110. The Eighth Air Force was part of the United States Army headquartered at Hunter Army Air Base during World War II. By 1944 the "Mighty Eighth" was the greatest air armada in history. On the grounds are a MIG aircraft and the Memorial Garden with a B-47. Inside are exhibits relating to the Battle of Britain and the Day of Infamy.

Fort Jackson – 1 Fort Jackson Road, 31404, 912-232-3945. *www.chsgeorgia.org. From the Historic District go east on Bay Street (which soon merges with the Islands Expressway) for 2.7 miles. Turn left at the sign.* N32° 04. 087′ W081° 03. 002′

Open daily 9:00 a.m.–5:00 p.m. Gift shop. This is the oldest fort still standing in Georgia. In 1775, during the Revolutionary War, an earthen battery was built here. The brick fort was begun in 1808 and manned during the War of 1812. Fort Jackson was most active as the headquarters for Confederate defense of the Savannah River during the Civil War. Ships entering the harbor pass the fort. Military exhibits and an audiovisual program are on display in the casemates. Cannon firings daily.

Oatland Island Wildlife Center – 711 Sandtown Road, 31410, 912-898-3980. *www.oatlandisland.org. From the Historic District go east on Bay Street (which soon merges with the Islands Expressway) for 4.5 miles. On the right is the sign for Oatland Island. N32° 03. 139' W081° 00. 845'*

Open daily 10:00 a.m.–4:00 p.m. Gift shop. Stroll the shady trails. You may see wolves, bobcats, pumas, black bears, great bald eagles, deer, and basking alligators in their natural habitats. Picnic on the boardwalk. Observe pelicans, great blue herons, woodpeckers, and long-legged egrets. In the mud you may see armies of mini-crustaceans called "fiddler crabs," so named because the male holds up its huge claw as a musician holds a fiddle. Trail maps are in the main building. Bring bug spray.

McQueen Island Bicycle and Nature Trail – *Located along the old railroad bed next to the Tybee Road (U.S. 80).*

The entrance to the trail is located just past the Bull River Bridge and before the entrance to Fort Pulaski (N32° 02. 393' W080° 56. 694'). The twenty-foot-wide trail extends for six miles. Built in 1887, the railroad carried passengers from Savannah to Tybee Island. The highway was built in 1923, making the railroad obsolete. The "rails to trails" idea put to use an unused causeway, converting it to a pleasant trail for hiking and biking. Expect to share the trail with fiddler crabs, diamondback terrapins, eastern box turtles, shore birds, and maybe an alligator.

Old Fort Jackson with Twice Daily Cannon Firings
Courtesy of the Coastal Heritage Society

Fort Pulaski National Monument and Museum – On U.S. 80, 12 miles east of Savannah, 31410, 912-786-5787. *www.nps.gov/fopu. From the Historic District go east on Bay Street (which soon merges with the Islands Expressway) for 12 miles. You'll see the sign for Fort Pulaski on the left. N32° 01. 131' W080° 53. 984'*

Open daily 9:00 a.m.–5:00 p.m. Gift shop with books. Located on Cockspur Island, this masterpiece of masonry was built for coastal defense in the early 1800s. It is named for Count Casimir Pulaski, who died in the Revolution at the Siege of Savannah. This was the first post for Lieutenant Robert E. Lee when he graduated from the U.S. Military Academy at West Point.

Beyond the moat and the portcullis, the five-sided fort encloses a two-acre parade ground. With two tiers of guns and cannon, Confederate troops felt safe and out of range of enemy artillery. The test came in 1862. Union troops on Tybee Island fired James and Parrott rifled cannon, and the projectiles crashed through the walls and came dangerously close to the powder magazine. Colonel Charles Olmstead surrendered the fort in April 1862. The area covers 537 acres and is ideal for walking or picnics.

In the distance, now surrounded by water, is the historic **Cockspur Island Lighthouse**. Constructed under the supervision of architect John Norris in 1848, the lighthouse miraculously escaped destruction as Union artillery fired over it from Tybee in the attack on Fort Pulaski. In 1881 a massive storm caused the water to rise twenty-three feet above sea level, such that it filled the lighthouse interior. It was further damaged in the great hurricane of 1893. In 1958 ownership of the

Fort Pulaski National Monument

Courtesy, Fort Pulaski National Monument

lighthouse was transferred from the United States Coast Guard to the National Park Service, which is now responsible for its maintenance and preservation.

Access to the lighthouse is limited by the tides and the terrain of the island. An overlook trail is available to visitors from Fort Pulaski. Ask for the trail guide booklet at the Visitor Center. The Lighthouse Trail is a very pleasant trail of 1.7 miles roundtrip and takes about 45 minutes to walk. There are several interesting places and lovely views of the marsh along the north channel.

There are beaches along the way as you wander through the cabbage palms and red cedars. Upon crossing a small bridge there are great views of the lighthouse and the damaged walls of Fort Pulaski. The trail will end with a close view of the Cockspur Island Lighthouse which marks the now unused south channel of the Savannah River. N32° 01. 349′ W080° 52. 962′

Cockspur Island Lighthouse

Entrance to Bonaventure Cemetery

Photographed by Charles St. Arnaud, Brig. Gen., U.S. Army, retired
Courtesy of the Bonaventure Historical Society Archives

Johnny Mercer Gravesite

Bonaventure Cemetery

Fort Screven Museum and Tybee Lighthouse – 30 Meddin Avenue, 31328, 912-786-5801. *www.tybeelighthouse.org. From the Historic District go east on Bay Street (which soon merges with the Islands Expressway) for 15 miles. Turn left at the first traffic light (Campbell Avenue) on Tybee Island, and follow the signs to the museum and lighthouse. N32° 01. 360´ W080° 50. 693´*

Open daily (except Tuesdays), 9:00 a.m.–5:30 p.m. (last ticket sold at 4:30 p.m.) Gift shop. The museum is tucked into a gun battery, a fortification built in 1875 on the site of the Union cannon that breached the walls of Fort Pulaski. Fort Screven saw service in the Spanish-American War and in both World Wars.

A World War I submarine periscope in the museum gives a sweeping view of Tybee Island and the mouth of the Savannah River. Vivid dioramas and a film tell the story of Mary Musgrove, Tybee's history under seven flags, Oglethorpe's meeting with Tomochichi, and Blackbeard the Pirate, who buried treasure on the island.

Tybee Lighthouse has 178 steps from base to beacon, and a clear view of Hilton Head, Daufuskie Island, and ships entering the channel.

Bonaventure Cemetery – 330 Bonaventure Road, 31404, 912-651-6843. *www.bonaventurehistorical.org. From the Historic District take President Street one mile to Truman Parkway. From the left lane, get on the parkway and go 2.3 miles to Victory Drive. Turn left for one mile past Skidaway Road until you see a sign on your right for Thunderbolt. Soon you will see a sign on your left at Coach's Corner for Bonaventure Cemetery. Turn left onto Downing Avenue to the dead end at Bonaventure Road. Turn right until you see the cemetery on your left. N32° 02. 707´ W081° 03. 039´*

Open daily 8:00 a.m.–5:00 p.m. In 1907 the city purchased Evergreen Cemetery, once the colonial plantation of the Tattnall family, as a burying ground. The name was changed to Bonaventure (meaning "good fortune" in Italian), the name of the plantation when it was owned earlier by John Mulryne.

The cemetery is especially lovely in the spring, when moss-draped oaks cast shadows over the many varieties of azaleas in bloom. Stop at the office for a map, or check the outside gravesite kiosk to locate family plots. Many visit the grave of Gracie Watson, daughter of the owners of the old Pulaski House, a hotel once located on Johnson Square. In 1889 she died of pneumonia at age six. Little Gracie was the darling of hotel guests. Hers is the most prominent of many Italian marble sculptures by Savannah sculptor John Walz. The John Walz Memorial Garden near the gatehouse commemorates the seventy-four sculptures he created in this cemetery.

Near the river, one of the most photographed sculptures is the stunning Italian marble in the Lawton plot. This figure of Jesus invites you to look through a grand arched gateway to the river. The central monument is in memory of Alexander

Robert Lawton, Confederate brigadier general, lawyer, and president of the railroad. The other moving sculpture is of his daughter, Corinne, who died of pneumonia at age thirty-one.

Don't miss the grave of songwriter Johnny Mercer, whose many songs include "Moon River," "Days of Wine and Roses," and "On the Atchison, Topeka and the Santa Fe." On the grave of his wife, Ginger, is inscribed "You Must Have Been a Beautiful Baby," and on his, "And the Angels Sing." Novelist and poet laureate Conrad Aiken wished for his grave to have a marble bench where visitors could sit and enjoy a martini. The bench is inscribed with the words "Cosmos Mariner, Destination Unknown."

Noble Jones, who sailed on the ship *Ann* with James Oglethorpe in 1733, and who died just before the War of Independence with his native England, is buried here. His family is remembered with a monument surrounded by an iron fence. His remains were moved here from the original burial site at his Wormsloe Plantation.

Drive past the Mongin Mausoleum decorated with Egyptian symbols and wonder at how it might have been moved here from Daufuskie Island, South Carolina, in 1873. The statue of the Bird Girl, made famous by Jack Leigh's photograph on the cover of *Midnight in the Garden of Good and Evil*, has been moved to the Telfair Museum of Art.

John Muir, founder of the Sierra Club, spent a week here sleeping among the spirits on gravestone slabs. He was intrigued with the wildlife and the foliage, and later wrote *A Thousand Mile Walk to the Gulf*, first published in 1916, reprinted by Cherokee Publishing Company.

Harry Hervey, author of *The Damned Don't Cry*, is buried in a family plot here along with his mother. Although he wasn't born in Savannah, he did live here for a time, and his book with its Savannah setting has become popular since its reprinting by Cherokee Publishing Company.

Free walking tours are offered every second Saturday afternoon at 2:00 p.m. and Sunday afternoon at 2:00 p.m., 2:30 p.m., and 3:00 p.m. by the members of the Bonaventure Historical Society. A video by Michael Jordan of Cosmos Mariner Productions, *Savannah's Historic Graveyards*, is available at most gift shops or at *www.cosmosavannah.com*.

Majestic Oak – Majestic Oak Subdivision off LaRoche Avenue, 31406. *From the Historic District take President Street one mile to Truman Parkway. From the left lane get on the parkway and go 2.3 miles to Victory Drive. Turn left, and drive 0.4 miles to Skidaway Road. Turn right and drive one mile south on Skidaway Road. Fork left onto LaRoche Avenue at Savannah State University stadium. Continue until the marsh view opens up. Look for the sign that says Majestic Oak.* N32° 00. 476´ W081° 04. 084´

The name of this area becomes obvious upon first laying eyes on this massive venerable oak tree. Given its girth of twenty-eight feet, some believe this gnarled, bearded Methuselah is three hundred years old! The Neighborhood Association maintains this giant as a historic tree. Its canopy has shaded many happy picnics, weddings, and birthday parties. Do walk under this beauty, but please don't climb on its arthritic branches.

Community of Isle of Hope – Bluff Drive, 31406. *From the Historic District take President Street one mile to Truman Parkway. From the left lane get on the parkway and go 7.4 miles to Montgomery Crossroads. Turn left. Drive 0.5 miles to Skidaway Road. Turn right and continue on Skidaway Road past the Wormsloe Historic Site. The road bends to the left. Turn right onto Rose Avenue to see Bluff Drive and the Skidaway River. N31° 59. 000´ W081° 03. 218´*

In 1736 King George II gave this high ground on the Skidaway River to three men of prominence: Noble Jones, one of the original colonists, was given five hundred acres, a tract of land that became Wormsloe Plantation; John Fallowfield, first bailiff, received the middle five hundred acres; the remaining five hundred acres were granted to the second bailiff, Henry Parker. The French Huguenots, seeking refuge during the French Revolution, called the island L'ile d'esperance (Isle of Hope). The island also served as a haven for those fleeing yellow fever in the city.

Wormsloe Historic Site – 7601 Skidaway Road, 31406, 912-353-3023. *www.gastateparks.org/wormsloe. From the Historic District take President Street one mile to Truman Parkway. From the left lane get on the parkway and go 7.4 miles to Montgomery Crossroads. Turn left and drive 0.5 miles to Skidaway Road. Turn right and continue on Skidaway Road through the traffic light to Wormsloe, on your right. N31° 58. 830´ W081° 04. 135´*

Open Tuesday–Sunday 9:00 a.m.–5:00 p.m. Gift shop. At Wormsloe, the original owner Noble Jones planted grapes and mulberry trees for silk production. He also cultivated cotton and rice and raised cattle. He cut a three-mile-long swath through the woods to the Reverend George Whitefield's orphan house, Bethesda. After centuries of single-family ownership, Wormsloe (except for the house, library, and gardens) became the property of the state of Georgia in 1973.

A stately avenue of live oaks leads to the visitor center, museum, and gift shop/ bookstore. A short film tells about life on the plantation. Walk to the ruins of Noble Jones's house, which was fortified against Indians, Spaniards, and pirates. Nearby is a small family cemetery. The remains of Noble Jones were buried here and later moved to Bonaventure Cemetery.

Wormsloe Historic Site

Courtesy of the photographer, Jeri Nokes/SnapSavannah

Bethesda Home for Boys – 9250 Ferguson Avenue, 31406, 912-351-2010. *www.bethesdaacademy.org. From the Historic District, take President Street one mile to Truman Parkway. From the left lane get onto the parkway and go 8.7 miles to Whitefield Avenue. Turn left and drive 1.4 miles to Ferguson Avenue. Turn left, and you'll see the arched entrance to Bethesda on your right.* N31° 57. 588´ W081° 05. 753´

In 1738 the Reverend George Whitefield, Church of England minister to the Georgia colony, addressed the crisis of children who had lost their parents to the yellow fever epidemic. His eloquent pleas for money tugged on many hearts and purses, including those of Lady Huntingdon, a benefactor who gave generously from her native England. Benjamin Franklin also generously contributed.

With help from his friend James Habersham, construction began on Bethesda (House of Mercy) Orphan Home, the oldest orphanage in the country in continuous operation. Bethesda opened in 1742 on 650 acres. The original buildings, destroyed by fire in 1773, have been replaced with brick buildings. The main building was built by the Union Society in 1855.

Whitefield Chapel was given by the Colonial Dames. The outdoor theater came from the Trustees Garden Club. There is a carpentry shop, an Olympic-size pool,

The Imposing Entrance to Bethesda Home for Boys

a gym and auditorium, and the creek for boating, fishing, and crabbing. Boys of school age lived in cottages with house-parents and remained at the home through high school. Through the Union Society and the Women's Board of Bethesda, funds were available for college. Many return with their fiancées to be married in Whitefield Chapel.

In 1992, Bethesda School began educating students providing a wide range of learning experiences. In April 2011, the Bethesda Home for Boys was renamed Bethesda Academy reflecting the school's new commitment to college preparatory learning for young men grades six through twelve. Bethesda has evolved over the years, and is no longer an orphanage. Most of the boys who live at Bethesda go home or to some family member on the weekends. On campus the boys live in a cottage with ten or twelve other boys and a married couple who are professionally trained to work with adolescent boys. During the week these cottage teachers provide a structured environment that fosters personal responsibility and independent living skills. In addition to attending school at Bethesda Academy, each boy is required to volunteer his time every day, working in the dining room, taking care of the animals, working in the organic garden, or volunteering as a docent in the museum. Bethesda Academy has about as many day students as those who live on the campus. The school carries on the values established in the colonial days, of spiritual formation and development as well as high academic standards. Bethesda holds a 95% graduation rate, far higher than most schools, and 87% of the students go on to college.

William H. Ford Sr. Museum and Visitor Center at Bethesda Academy – The museum is adjacent to the chapel. Exhibits tell the history of Bethesda. A large portrait of Lady Huntingdon covers one wall, and the story of Barney Diamond, who grew up here, is a highlight. Boys today are taught to raise plants and animals, among other valuable skills. The emphasis on building character and integrity is the primary focus of Bethesda's educational program.

Pin Point Heritage Museum – 9924 Pin Point Avenue, 31406, 912-667-9176. *www.chsgeorgia.org. From the Historic District take President Street one mile to Truman Parkway. From the left lane get on the parkway and go 8.7 miles to Whitefield Avenue. Turn left and drive 1.7 miles, past the traffic light at Skidaway Road, to Pin Point Road. Turn right, and you'll see the Pin Point Museum sign on your left. N31° 57. 236′ W081° 05. 426′*

Clarence Thomas, Supreme Court Justice

Open Thursday, Friday and Saturday 9:00 a.m.– 5:00 p.m. Gift shop. Pin Point was the birthplace of Clarence Thomas, Supreme Court Justice of the United States. The old oyster factory has been converted into a charming museum. It illustrates the coastal lives of people who worked the plantations on the barrier islands and earned a living from the rivers and creeks.

This museum, operated by the Coastal Heritage Society, is one of the first to focus on Gullah-Geechee heritage. The community at Pin Point

Oyster Fisherman, Pin Point, Georgia

was a strong influence on Savannah songwriter Johnny Mercer as he was growing up in Savannah. He spent time in the summers at nearby Burnside Island, within walking distance of the old oyster factory, where he heard the songs of the oyster shuckers.

Skidaway Island State Park – 52 Diamond Causeway, 31411, 912-598-2300 or 800-864-7275. *www.gastateparks.org/skidawayisland. From the Historic District, take President Street one mile to Truman Parkway. From the left lane get onto the parkway and continue for 8.7 miles to the Whitefield Avenue Exit. Turn left. Drive 1.4 miles through the traffic light. Continue straight on the Diamond Causeway. The entrance is on your left after the bridge.* N31° 56. 607′ W081° 03. 299′

Open 7:00 a.m.–10:00 p.m. daily. This 506-acre park has tent and trailer sites, a pool, picnic shelters, and restrooms with showers. The Sandpiper Nature Trail has markers identifying trees and plants. Visit the reptile room and the bird-viewing area. Children will love seeing the replica of the giant ground sloth. Its bones were dug up in the Skidaway River.

University of Georgia Marine Extension Services and Aquarium – 30 Ocean Science Circle, 31411, 912-598-2496. *www.marex.uga.edu/aquarium. From the Historic District take President Street one mile to Truman Parkway. From the left lane get onto the parkway and continue for 8.7 miles to the Whitefield Avenue Exit. Turn left. Drive 1.4 miles through the traffic light. Continue straight on the Diamond Causeway through two traffic lights to the four-way stop at McWhorter Avenue. Turn left for 4.3 miles to the aquarium. (At the fork along the way, keep left.)* N31° 59. 271′ W081° 01. 430′

Sunset Overlooking the Skidaway River
Courtesy of the University of Georgia Marine Extension Services and Aquarium

Open Monday–Friday 9:00 a.m.–4:00 p.m.; Saturday 10:00 a.m.–5:00 p.m. Gift shop. Get nose to nose with snapper, grouper, spadefish, flounder, loggerhead turtles, and saltwater wonders. One exhibit shows whale bones and bison teeth thought to be millions of years old. Hike the nature trail to see opossums, raccoons, deer, and the lowly fiddler crabs in the mud. Picnic tables overlook the Intracoastal Waterway.

Coastal Georgia Botanical Gardens and Bamboo Farm – 2 Canebrake Road, 31419, 912- 921-5460. *www.ugaextension.com/bamboo. From the Historic District take Abercorn Street south for 12 miles. At Highway 17, turn left. The entrance is on the right, one mile past Walmart and one mile before the Ogeechee River.* N31° 59. 768´ W081° 16. 076´

Open daily 8:00 a.m.–5:00 p.m., Saturday 10:00 a.m.–5:00 p.m., and Sunday noon–5:00 p.m. Before the Civil War, landowners developed rice plantations along the Ogeechee River. Dikes and canals were dug to let fresh water fill and drain the rice fields twice a day. Slaves worked the rice plantations in Chatham County, including Villambrosa, where the Bamboo Farm stands today.

After the Civil War Villambrosa was owned by a Cuban farmer who introduced giant timber bamboo imported from Japan. It grew to be fifty feet tall. In 1919 word of this large grove of bamboo, fourteen miles south of Savannah, reached Washington, D.C., and the land was leased to the U.S. Department of Agriculture. In the 1940s the USDA, in cooperation with industrialists Harvey Firestone and Henry Ford, began research into the latex composition of bamboo in hopes of producing rubber. Research stopped after the development of synthetic rubber in 1955.

ADA-Approved Nature Trail through a Maritime Forest

Courtesy of the University of Georgia Marine Extension Services and Aquarium

Several bamboo varieties were evaluated for their cancer-fighting properties, and a variety of tropical grass was studied as a source of paper and roofing material. Scientists considered water chestnut farming, but labor costs proved prohibitive. During the Vietnam War much of the bamboo was harvested for the U.S. Army and used to replicate Vietnamese villages at nearby Fort Stewart to train soldiers for combat.

In 1983 the center was deeded to the University of Georgia for research. Today the Friends of the Coastal Gardens keep the farm open to visitors. Elementary school students come to the garden to participate in the *Roots and Shoots* program. Workshops are offered for master gardeners, commercial horticulturalists, and visitors. The farm is internationally known for its one hundred–plus species of bamboo and maintains one of the most diverse collections of camellias in the United States.

Wetland Mitigation Station (Chatham County Wetland Preserve) – 912-652-7800. *Located on the Ogeechee River off U.S. Highway 17, on Chief of Love Road. N31°59.225′ W081°17.206′*

This 494-acre park has a lake, trails, gravel roads, picnic tables, and kayak access. In some areas algae-covered water surrounds the cypress trees. Open 8:00 a.m. – 8:00 p.m. No attendant.

Savannah-Ogeechee Canal and Nature Center – 681 Fort Argyle Road (Route 204), 31419, 912-748-8068. *www.savannahogeecheecanalsociety.org. From the Historic District take Abercorn Street south past I-95 where Abercorn becomes Highway 204. (From I-95 take Exit 94.) Continue on Highway 204 West away from Savannah to the canal and nature center on your left. N32° 01. 375′ W081° 18. 997′*

The museum here is open only a few days a week, but five miles of hiking trails are available anytime. The canal was constructed between 1826 and 1830 by African and Irish laborers who moved thousands of cubic yards of earth. It connected the Savannah and Ogeechee Rivers, and extended 16.5 miles with six locks. Today a museum and nature center feature canal history, archaeology, birding, reptiles, and amphibians. Hike along trails to the Ogeechee River or along the canal towpath, learn how the locks work, and enjoy the picnic area. Bring bug spray.

Explore Coastal Georgia

Fort McAllister Historic State Park – 3894 Fort McAllister Road, Richmond Hill, Georgia 31324, 912-727-2339. www.gastateparks.org/fortmcallister. N31° 53. 368´ W081° 11. 965´

Take U.S. 17 south to Richmond Hill, fifteen miles south of Savannah. Turn left on GA 144. Go eight miles. The sign for the fort is on your left.

Open daily 8:00 a.m.–5:00 p.m. Gift shop, including books. Fort McAllister on the Ogeechee River was attacked seven times by Union ironclads, but it did not fall until General Sherman approached from the west on his March to the Sea in December of 1864. Explore the cannons, the barracks, and the best-preserved earthwork fortification of the Confederacy. The shaded campground is bordered by a tidal creek. The dock and boats are available for fishing or picnics. Nature hikes and soldiering programs are offered during the week, and there are special programs on the weekends.

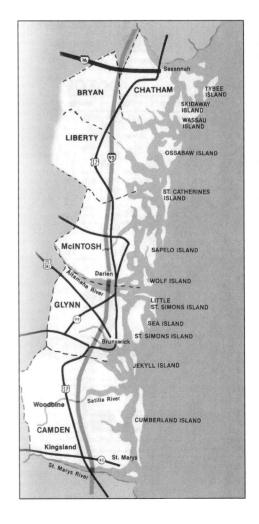

Midway Church

Historic Midway – Thirty miles south of Savannah.

 From Savannah take U.S. 17 or I-95.

Here is the home and burial ground of the Reverend Charles Colcock Jones, whose family letters from 1860 through 1868 provided the source material for Robert Manson Myers's book *Children of Pride.*

Midway Church is situated on U.S. 17, in Midway, Georgia 31320. *www.discoverlibertyga.com.* N31° 48. 352´ W081° 25. 820´

In 1754 immigrants organized a New England Congregational church that was burned by the British in 1778. The one now standing was constructed in 1792. The church produced two signers of the Declaration of Independence, Button Gwinnett and Lyman Hall; eighty-six ministers of the gospel; and seven missionaries to foreign lands.

Midway Museum – 491 North Coastal Highway (U.S. 17), 31320, 912-884-5837. *www.themidwaymuseum.com.* N31° 48. 419´ W081° 25. 816´

Open Tuesday–Saturday 10:00 a.m.–4:00 p.m. Gift shop. Here is an authentic reproduction of an eighteenth-century home. Well worth the admission, the home is built of old heart pine and furnished with period furniture. The collection of heirloom furnishings includes paintings and artifacts used in colonial homes, as well as historical books and documents.

Midway Cemetery – Across the street from Midway Church. N31° 48. 338´ W081° 25. 856´

The headstones are inscribed with the names of many early Georgia families. The road that separates the church and the cemetery is one of the oldest in the state. It was laid out by James Oglethorpe to connect Savannah with the Scottish settlement at Darien. The Indian chief Tomochichi furnished guides to aid the settlers in establishing trails through the marshes and swamps inhabited by alligators.

Students of Dorchester Academy, 1919

Courtesy, Georgia Department of Archives and History

Dorchester Academy – 8787 East Oglethorpe Highway, Midway, Georgia 31320, 912-884-2347. *www.dorchesteracademy.com.* N31° 48. 102´ W081° 27. 900´

In 1868, soon after the end of the Civil War, the American Missionary Association started a primary school for black children and a Congregational church three miles west of the old Midway Church. Blacks and whites had worshiped together in this old church since 1752, with blacks seated in the gallery and whites in the pews below. However, black children had not been taught to read or write. The request for a teacher was for a young man of good moral character, southern-born and colored, and a preacher, if possible. Eliza Ann Ward, an abolitionist from Massachusetts, was the first teacher.

Cay Creek Wetlands Interpretive Center – 189 Charlie Butler Road, Midway, Georgia 31320, 912-884-3344. *www.libertycounty.org.* N31° 47. 117′ W 081° 23. 696′

Walk along the boardwalk and observe the rich diversity of coastal plants and animals. The earthen berms are the remains of dikes used for growing rice. The gardens were designed by Thomas Angell of Verdant Enterprises, using native plants and natural elements found in coastal wetlands. *www.verdantenterprises.com.*

Dorchester Presbyterian Church

Dorchester Presbyterian Church – 336 Brigdon Road, 5.3 miles east of Midway, Georgia 31320, N 31° 45. 543 W 081° 21. 293

In 1843 a group of coastal Georgians settled at Dorchester, a site about halfway between Midway and Sunbury. Some of the houses at Sunbury were dismantled and reassembled at the new location. The church was erected between 1852 and 1854 and still stands today. The ties between Midway and Sunbury can be seen through artifacts at the church. The marble baptismal font at Dorchester was originally at Midway, and the bell in the cupola was originally at Sunbury, where it rang to announce church, school, and other events. Sunday services are held here once a month.

Melon Bluff Heritage and Nature Reserve – 2999 Islands Highway, Midway, Georgia 31320, 912-884-5779.

 Take Exit 76 from I-95 and go three miles east.

Privately owned, this site is available for special groups or environmental education programs. Twenty-two hundred acres of sustainable forests, pine uplands, blackwater swamp, salt marsh, fields, lakes, and the North Newport River are all available for hiking, biking, and horseback riding.

Seabrook Village – 660 Trade Hill Road, Midway, Georgia 31320, 912-884-7008. N31° 44. 654´ W081° 16. 179´

Open Tuesday–Saturday 10:00 a.m.– 4:00 p.m. Eight buildings, including a one-room schoolhouse, make up the African American living history museum. The Seabrook community was established through General Sherman's Field Order 15, giving forty acres and a mule to newly freed people. Families established farms on the same land they had worked as captives. Visit the museum and try your hand at grinding corn into meal or grits, or washing clothes on a scrub board.

Fort Morris State Historic Site – 2559 Fort Morris Road, Midway, Georgia 31320, 912-884-5999. *www.gastateparks.org/Fortmorris.* N31° 45. 696´ W081° 16. 918´

Open Thursday–Sunday 9:00 a.m.–5:00 p.m. Gift shop. Located on a low bluff on the Medway River at Sunbury, the fort was constructed to protect the colonists from the British in 1776. It was captured by the British in 1779 and used against them in the War of 1812. Today visitors can stand within the earthwork remains and look across St. Catherines Sound. A museum and film describe the colonial port of Sunbury and the area's history. The site does not offer overnight camping. Visitors may borrow binoculars and a field guide to go birding. Downy and pileated woodpeckers, goldfinches, wood storks, painted buntings, egrets, and other species may be seen here.

Sunbury and Sunbury Cemetery – A short drive from Fort Morris. N31° 46. 192´ W081° 17. 023´

There's not much left of Sunbury today. Founded soon after Midway in 1758, Sunbury rivaled Savannah as Georgia's main ocean port. Lumber, rice, indigo, slaves, and corn went in and out of the port. Sunbury was the scene of much fighting during the American Revolution, from 1776 through 1779. Unable to survive the British assault of 1779, it never recovered as a thriving community. By 1848 not much remained of the old town except the cemetery, which can be seen today. Here are buried men and women whose lives contributed much to the early history of Georgia. The earliest burials date back to colonial and revolutionary days.

Leconte-Woodmanston Rice Plantation and Botanical Garden –
4918 Barrington Ferry Road, Riceboro, Georgia 31323, 912-884-6500.
www.leconte-woodmanston.org. N31° 42. 146′ W081° 28. 632′

Open daily for hiking, picnicking, and self-guided garden tours. Cars not allowed inside. Guided tours by appointment, $5.00 per person. In 1760 John Leconte established Woodmanston, a swamp rice plantation along the headwaters of the South Newport River. His son, Louis Leconte, moved into the family's hunting lodge in 1811 and established Georgia's first botanical garden. He cultivated rare plants from all parts of the world. His sons, John and Joseph, were two of the most distinguished scientific scholars of the nineteenth century. John published many scientific papers and was president of the University of California from 1869 to 1881. The family is responsible for the tasty Leconte pears. Walk along the Avenue of Oaks, see the foundations of Louis's home, view a replica of a slave cabin, and hike the interactive mile-long trail along earthen rice dikes.

Geechee Kunda – 622 Ways Temple Road, Riceboro, Georgia 31323, 912-884-4440. *www.geecheekunda.com.* N31° 41. 684′ W081° 24. 385′

 Take I-95 to Exit 67, then U.S. 17 south for three miles.

Located on the site of a former plantation where enslaved Africans worked for generations, Geechee Kunda is a spiritual reminder of suffering and survival. Created to preserve and perpetuate African culture and traditions, the center educates and inspires those interested in African American heritage. Visitors come for weddings, reunions, meetings, or to browse African artifacts in the gift shop or museum. Geechee Kunda is the official home of Jamal Touré, the African spirit of Day Clean. Day Clean Journeys in Savannah can be reached at 912-220-5966. *www.daycleansoul.com.*

Harris Neck National Wildlife Refuge – 5000 Wildlife Drive, NE, Townsend, Georgia 31331, 912-832-4608. *www.fws.gov/harrisneck.* N31° 37. 793′ W081° 17. 146′

This wildlife refuge is fifty miles south of Savannah, in McIntosh County, Georgia. Take Exit 67 from I-95, travel one mile south on U.S. 17, then seven miles east on Harris Neck Road.

Open daily, sunrise to sunset. Visitor Center, Monday–Friday 8:00 a.m.–4:30 p.m. This refuge was established in 1962, when federal lands were transferred from the FAA, which acquired the land in World War II for an airfield. It serves as an important link in the chain of refuges along the Atlantic Seaboard for migrating birds.

Harris Neck's 2,762 acres provide a variety of habitats, including salt marsh, grassland, deciduous woods, and cropland. Many species of birds are attracted to these diverse habitats. In 1865 Harris Neck was deeded by a plantation owner to a former slave. Black families who settled there built houses and boats and started crab and oyster houses. In 1942 the land was taken by the federal government, to be used as an airstrip, displacing many families.

Today there is a struggle between the Fish and Wildlife Service, interested in maintaining a rookery for the endangered wood storks, and the families and their descendants who felt their land was taken unfairly. The families are Gullah/Geechee people, descendants of West African slaves, who became some of the nation's first black land owners. They have asked Congress to return the land.

Sapelo Island Visitor Center – 1766 Landing Road SE, Darien, Georgia 31305, 912-437-3224. *www.gastateparks.org/sapelo.* N31° 27. 283′ W081° 21. 915′

Open Tuesday–Saturday 7:30 a.m.–5:30 p.m. Museum and gift shops located in both the visitor center and at the Reynolds Mansion. A trip to the island is a thirty-minute ferry ride. Purchase a ticket here. Reservations are required for a guided tour of the island. Visitors to Sapelo can see every facet of a barrier island's natural community, from the forested uplands to the vast salt marsh and the complex beach and dune systems. Sapelo offers rooms at the historic Reynolds Mansion for groups. Some families in the old African American community of Hog Hammock rent out rooms with breakfast in their small oceanside homes. If you're lucky, you may get a supper of fish or barbecue. A treat might be to hear Cornelia Walker Bailey telling stories on her porch, or to watch Stanley Walker knitting a cast-net for catching shrimp.

Fort King George Historic Site – 302 McIntosh Road SE, Darien Georgia, 31305, 912-437-4770. *www.gastateparks.org/FortKingGeorge.* N31° 21. 895′ W081° 25. 031′

Open Tuesday–Saturday 9:00 a.m.–5:00 p.m.; Sunday 2:00 p.m.–5:30 p.m. Gift shop. This is the oldest English fort remaining on the Georgia coast. Constructed in 1721, it consisted of a cypress blockhouse, barracks, and a palisaded earthen fort. The museum and film discuss the Guale Indians and history of Darien. The site is on the Colonial Coast Birding Trail on the Altamaha River.

Hofwyl-Broadfield Plantation – 5556 U.S. 17, Brunswick, Georgia 31525, 912-264-7333. *www.gastateparks.org/HofwylBroadfield.* N31° 18. 429′ W081° 27. 470′

Open Thursday-Saturday 9:00 a.m.–5:00 p.m. Gift shop. This plantation on the Altamaha River represents the history of the rice-growing culture on the Georgia coast. Although rice cultivation declined after the Civil War, the family continued to grow rice here until 1913. The last generation left the home to the state of Georgia in 1973. The museum features family heirlooms and silver. Visitors can see a short film on the plantation's history and take an easy walk to the antebellum home for a guided tour. Herons, egrets, ibis, and painted buntings may be seen on the Colonial Coastal Birding Trail.

Fort Frederica National Park – 6515 Frederica Road, Saint Simons Island, Georgia 31522, 912-638-3639. *www.nps.gov.* N31° 13. 390′ W081° 23. 347′

 Take U.S. 17 and the Brunswick–Saint Simons Causeway to St. Simons Island.

Open daily 9:00 a.m.–5:00 p.m. Gift shop. Fort Frederica was established by James Oglethorpe to guard the fledgling colony of Georgia from attacks by the Spaniards to the south. In 1742 the Spaniards lunched and lounged in a clearing on St. Simons Island. Oglethorpe and troops ambushed them and made the salt water run red with the blood of Spanish casualties. The Spaniards retreated, and King George II awarded the rank of brigadier general to James Oglethorpe. The Battle of Bloody Marsh was Oglethorpe's most significant defeat of the Spanish, claiming Georgia for England.

Visit the ruins of the tabby fort, the barracks, the moat, and the walls. A video in the visitor center tells about the excavation of this site in the 1940s.

St. Simons Lighthouse and the Museum of Coastal History – 610 Beachview Drive, St. Simons Island, Georgia 31522, 912-638-4666. *www.saintsimonslighthouse.org.* N31° 08. 051′ W081° 23. 577′

 From U.S. 17 in Brunswick, take the FJ Torras Causeway to St. Simons Island. After the bridge over the Frederica River, turn right onto King's Way, pass the blinking light at Sea Island Causeway, and continue through the traffic signal at Frederica Road (airport will be on the left). At the next signal, turn right onto Mallery Street, one block to Beachview Drive, then left for a quarter mile to Twelfth Street. The parking lot is on the right.

Monday–Saturday 10:00 a.m.–5:00 p.m.; Sunday 1:30 p.m.–5:00 p.m. Last climb: 4:30 p.m. Gift shop. The original lighthouse was built in 1810. It was seventy-five feet tall and topped with an oil-burning light. During the Civil War, U.S. military forces maintained a naval blockade along the coast. Union troops forced the Confederate soldiers to flee. Retreating men destroyed the lighthouse to prevent it from aiding the navigation of Union warships. A new 104-foot-tall lighthouse replaced it in 1872, with a biconvex Fresnel lens. A spiral staircase with 129 steps leads to the galley. The lighthouse keeper's dwelling at the base is now a museum.

Maritime Center at the Historic Coast Guard Station – 4201 First Street, St. Simons Island, Georgia 31522, 912-638-4666. *www.saintsimonslighthouse.org.* N31° 08. 733′ W081° 22. 378′

Gift shop. Maritime military and natural history are explored in seven galleries highlighting the importance of the seafaring community and the coastal ecosystem. Hands-on exhibits and activities.

Tidelands Nature Center – 100 South Riverview Drive, Jekyll Island, Georgia 31527, 912-635-5032. *www.tidelands4h.org.* N31° 02. 332´ W081° 25. 137´

Gift shop. The University of Georgia's 4-H program offers hands-on marine science programs for visitors and school groups. Visit the nature center and observe sea turtles, snakes, sharks, sting rays, hermit crabs, whelks, alligators, and other residents of the natural land and sea environments. Take a three-hour kayak tour of Jekyll Creek.

Jekyll Island Museum – 100 Stable Road, Jekyll Island, Georgia 31527, 912-635-4036. *www.jekyllisland.com.* N31° 03. 49´ W081° 25. 099´

Open daily 9:00 a.m.–5:00 p.m. Gift shop. Located in the former Club Stables, the museum is a history center in the historic district of Jekyll Island. The center includes a natural history and archaeological exhibit, an exhibit on the history of the island, and an eight-minute video on the history of Jekyll Island. A self-guided multimedia tour allows guests a virtual tour of the historic district at a leisurely pace. See for yourself the natural beauty that has long drawn visitors to its barrier shores, from the Native Americans and French settlers to the Jekyll Island Club millionaires and thousands of visitors who arrive today. Take a guided tram tour of the entire historic district, with entry into two of the restored cottages.

Jekyll Island Landmark Historic District (Millionaires' Village) – On Jekyll Island. N31° 03. 611´ W081° 25. 239´

In 1886 the Jekyll Island Club consisted of one hundred of America's wealthiest families—Astors, Vanderbilts, Pulitzers, Morgans, McCormicks, Cranes, and others. The main clubhouse was a Victorian mansion with towers and verandas, and the families built their "cottages" nearby. Visitors can stay at the Jekyll Island Club Hotel and walk along tabby walkways under massive live oaks to shops and restaurants.

Georgia Sea Turtle Center – 214 Stable Road, Jekyll Island, Georgia 31527, 912-635-4444. *georgiaseaturtlecenter.org.* N31° 03. 584´ W081° 25. 171´

Open Tuesday–Sunday, 9:00 a.m.–5:00 p.m. Gift shop. The center provides research, education, and rehabilitation for injured sea turtles and encourages the preservation of our natural environment. Visitors see live turtles being cared for before release into the ocean. Explore interactive exhibits on sea turtle biology, conservation, rehabilitation, and the sea turtle's amazing journey from egg to adulthood.

Crooked River State Park – 6222 Charlie Smith Sr. Highway, St. Marys, Georgia 31558, 912-882-5256. *www.gastateparks.org.* N30° 50. 598´ W081° 33. 491´

Open daily 8:00 a.m.–10:00 p.m. Gift shop. This scenic park is on Eliot's Bluff on the banks of the Crooked River. Camping facilities and comfortable cabins are available. The park's nature center offers personal encounters with fish, snakes, turtles, and animals native to coastal Georgia.

St. Marys Submarine Museum – 102 St. Marys Street, West, St. Marys, Georgia, 31558, 912-882-2782. *www.stmaryssubmuseum.com.* N30° 43. 236´ W081° 32. 958´

Open Tuesday–Saturday 10:00 a.m.–4:00 p.m. Gift shop. St. Marys is the home of Kings Bay Naval Submarine Base, one of two Trident submarine bases in the world. Explore submarine memorabilia, artifacts, and photos. Children can peer through a periscope to see across the state line to Florida.

Cumberland Island Visitor Center – 113 St. Marys Street West, St. Marys, Georgia 31558, 912-882-4335. *www.nps.gov/cuis.* N30° 43. 227´ W081° 32. 976´

Brush up on coastal ecology and decide whether you want to visit Cumberland Island National Seashore. Access is via a thirty-minute ferry ride across the sound to the island. Plan ahead and take food and drink along. There are no stores on the island. The trails and unspoiled beaches are pristine.

Find the ruins of Dungeness, the family mansion, built by Thomas and Lucy Carnegie on the site of an earlier home built by Catherine Greene, widow of General Nathanael Greene. See the little chapel where John F. Kennedy Jr. was married. Plum Orchard is a thirty-room mansion built by Lucy Carnegie in 1898 as a wedding present for her son George L. Carnegie and his wife Margaret. Don't miss the return ferry, which usually makes only one trip a day. Overnight camping is allowed for up to seven days with a reservation. Sixteen miles of white sandy beaches have remained undisturbed. Rows of dunes as high as forty feet, dotted with sea oats, line the beach. Herds of wild horses graze and frolic on the beaches. Many types of sea birds nest on the island. Loggerhead sea turtles come ashore to lay their eggs.

The National Park Service offers a rugged six-hour motorized tour to the historic sites on the north end of the island. Overnight accommodations are available at the Greyfield Inn, P.O. Box 900, Fernandina Beach, FL, 32035, 800-717-0821 or 904-261-6408. *www.greyfieldinn.com.* Accessible by boat from Fernandina Beach.

Greyfield was built in 1901 as a home for Lucy and Thomas Carnegie's daughter, Margaret Ricketson. In 1962 Greyfield was opened as an inn by Margaret's daughter, Lucy Ferguson, and her family. Greyfield is furnished as it was at the turn of the century, providing guests with a link to the past. Guests are treated as family—they are afforded casual elegance and gourmet dining. Natural history/ wildlife tours are offered daily. Other activities include birding, shelling, fishing, biking, swimming, beachcombing, and hunting for sharks' teeth.

Georgia Radio Museum and Hall of Fame – 400 Osborne Street, St. Marys, Georgia 31558, 912-882-4000 or 800-868-8687. *www.grhof.com.* N30° 43. 485′ W081° 32. 845′

This museum includes a large collection of antique radios, vintage microphones, electronic equipment, turntables, reel-to-reel recorders, audio processors, vinyl records, and radio station promotional items, as well as books and photos.

Orange Hall House Museum – 311 Osborne Street, St. Marys, Georgia 31558. *www.orangehall.org.* N30° 43. 464′ W081° 32. 857′

Orange Hall offers an extraordinary peek at antebellum life in a three-story Greek Revival–style house built in the early 1800s. It is filled with artifacts from the era and offers tours seven days a week. Open daily.

Cumberland Island National Seashore Museum – 129 Osborne Street, St. Marys, Georgia 31558, 912-822-4336 or 888-817-3421. *www.stmaryswelcome.com.* N30° 43. 228′ W081° 32. 905′

This museum houses a collection of artifacts that capture the rich history of Cumberland Island, from both the famed Carnegie family and the Timucuan Indians who once inhabited the island. It includes an exhibit focusing on one of the last battles of the War of 1812. Open afternoons, Monday–Saturday.

St. Marys Railroad Company – 1000 Osborne Street, St. Marys, Georgia 31558, 912-200-6235. *www.stmarysrailroad.com.* N30° 44. 099′ W081° 32. 673′

Immerse yourself in history, fun, and adventure on the St. Marys Express, which will take you through St. Marys' scenic woodlands and marshlands. The excursion, lasting an hour and fifteen minutes, will bring you face to face with the historic past, the world of nature, and some great entertainment. The railroad operates seasonally with a variety of excursions. Toot toot!

St. Marys Convention and Visitors Bureau/St. Marys Welcome Center – 400 Osborne Street, St. Marys, Georgia 31558, 912-882-4000 or 800-868-8687. *www.visitstmarys.com.* N30° 43. 485′ W081° 32. 845′

Historic St. Marys offers picturesque streets lined with centuries-old live oaks and the tranquil beauty of waterways and marshes. Once home to pirates, smugglers, and a robust shipping industry, today the city prides itself on preserving its rich and varied history. The welcome center offers up-to-date information about the area and its attractions.

Area Hotel

Riverview Hotel – 105 Osborne Street, St. Marys, Georgia 31558, 912-882-3242. *www.riverviewhotelstmarys.com.*

Built in 1916, this hotel has been family-owned and -operated since the 1920s. The veranda overlooks the St. Marys River. Charming period rooms. A unique experience.

Area Bookstores

Beachview Books – 215 Mallery Street, St. Simons Island, Georgia 31522, 912-638-7282. Books of local interest, used books, out-of-print books, and some rare books.

G. J. Ford Bookshop – 600 Sea Island Road (The Shops at Sea Island), St. Simons Island, Georgia 31522, 912-634-6168. *www.gjfordbookshop.com.*

An independent bookshop offering books of local and regional interest and more. Children's books, audiobooks, classical CDs, and cards. Out-of-print searches and special orders.

Hattie's Books – 1531 Newcastle Street, Brunswick, Georgia 31520, 912-554-8677. *www.hattiesbooks.net.*

A friendly, warm, quaint, and quirky independent bookstore located in downtown Brunswick. The latest national best sellers are available here, along with local history, children's books, nonfiction, romance, and a few beach reads.

Jekyll Books – 101 Old Plantation Road (The Shoppes at the Old Infirmary), Jekyll Island, Georgia 31527.

The former cottage of Joseph Pulitzer is divided into fourteen themed rooms that feature books, gifts, and apparel related to each theme. The themes range from coastal and southern life to regional cooking, children's items, nature, humor, and more.

Once Upon a Bookseller – 207 Osborne Street, St. Marys, Georgia 31558, 912-882-7350. *www.onceuponabookseller.com.*

Selections range from a guide through local history or through the local flora and fauna of the coastal barrier islands to the newest paperback novels. You'll find southern literature, reference books, military nonfiction, science fiction, children's books, cookbooks, poetry, romance, and self-help.

Georgia's Barrier Islands

Georgia's coast extends for only a hundred miles, but because salt water meanders in and out of the coastal marsh, there are hundreds more miles of coast to be enjoyed. Georgia's barrier islands stand between the coast and the Atlantic Ocean, offering protection and scenic natural environments to be explored. Behind the barrier islands, and sheltered from the forces of the Atlantic Ocean, are estuaries—places where salt water and fresh water meet. The salt marshes lie along the edges of the nutrient-rich estuaries. The marshlands serve as a nursery for many species of sea life essential to the ecology, recreation, and economy of coastal Georgia.

Georgia's coast is at the center of a long gradual bend of the eastern United States that forms a large open bay called the South Atlantic Bight. Beyond the barrier islands is a submerged portion of the lower coastal plain—the continental shelf. The Gulf Stream is the river of water that flows just beyond the continental shelf. The barrier islands are just one part of the coastal environment. Of all the barrier islands, only four have been developed with bridges and causeways, and the others are accessible by boat.

Tybee

Tybee is the northernmost barrier island, accessible by bridge and causeway. One of the four developed islands, Tybee has been enjoyed as a popular playground for over a hundred years. From the History Museum across from the lighthouse to the Beach Bum Parade, visitors enjoy its white sandy beaches and casual lifestyle. The Visitor Center is located on U.S. 80 (802 First Street), Tybee Island, Georgia 31328, 912-786-5444. *www.visittybee.com.* N32° 00. 967′ W081° 50. 932′

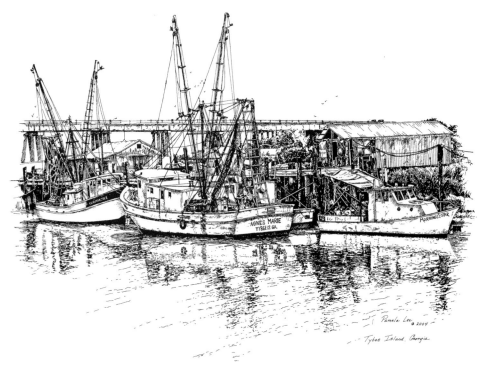

Tybee Island Marina
Courtesy of the artist, Pamela Lee

Wassaw Island

Wassaw Island is the next down the coast, owned by the state of Georgia and accessible only by boat. Although Native Americans lived on the island for hundreds of years, the first owner and inhabitant of the island in the nineteenth century was Anthony Odingsell, a freed slave who was given the land by his master. Anthony Odingsell was the wealthiest free person of color in Georgia for many years.

In 1866 a New England businessman, George Parsons, bought the island for hunting and for his family's enjoyment. We can appreciate today the wealthy Yankees who purchased these islands, saving them from development. In 1969 the Parsons family conveyed the land to the Nature Conservancy of Georgia, protecting it for future generations. Today the island is managed by the U.S. Fish and Wildlife Service, and day-trippers are allowed to visit by boat. Contact Wassaw Island National Wildlife Refuge, 843-784-2468. *www.fws.gov/wassaw.* N31° 52. 712´ W080° 58. 940´

Ossabaw Island

Ossabaw Island is located approximately twenty miles south of Savannah, by water. The third-largest of Georgia's barrier islands, Ossabaw still yields evidence of its early Native American inhabitants. Spanish Jesuits visited the island in 1568, followed by Franciscans, who established missions along the coast. John Morel purchased Ossabaw in 1760, and his family owned most of it for over a hundred years. After the Civil War, freed slaves lived on the island, and their tabby cabins are being restored. Their community centered around the Hinder Me Not Church on the island.

When hurricanes in the 1890s damaged the island, many former slaves moved to the mainland and settled at Pin Point, where the Heritage Museum tells their story. In 1924 Dr. Henry Torrey and his family bought the island and built a large house on the north end. The Torreys developed roads and built a beach house and hunting lodges. Formal gardens were laid out at the main house. At the time of this writing, Dr. Torrey's daughter, Eleanor West, was still living there at age 102.

Most of Ossabaw is owned by the state of Georgia, and educational projects and programs operate continuously. As the state's first heritage preserve, it conducts scientific and cultural research and environmental preservation. The Ossabaw Island Foundation is located at 305 Fahm Street, Savannah, Georgia 31401, 912-233-5104. *www.ossabawisland.org.*

Saint Catherines Island

Saint Catherines Island was inhabited for over 3,500 years by the Guale Indians and later by the Spanish, who built the Santa de Guale mission on the island. The mission disappeared over time but was rediscovered in 1982 by Dr. David Hurst Thomas of the American Museum of Natural History. In the eighteenth century the island was home to Button Gwinnett, one of Georgia's three signers of the Declaration of Independence. In 1943 Edward John Noble, who made a fortune in Life Savers, bought the island. The E. J. Noble Foundation now supports the St. Catherines Island Foundation, which now owns the island and uses it for research, conservation, and education. For many years anyone passing by in a sailboat might see an oryx grazing. Only lemurs remain, doing as well as they did in their native Madagascar. This island is accessible only by boat, and permission to visit it can be difficult to arrange. Contact St. Catherines Island Foundation, 182 Camellia Road, Midway, Georgia 31320, 912-884-5005.

Blackbeard Island

Blackbeard Island is named for the pirate Edward Teach, who conducted raids on ships in the area in the early eighteenth century. The legend that pirate treasure was buried on the island has persisted, although no one has ever dug up any loot. This island, like St. Catherines, Wassaw, and Ossabaw, is undeveloped. It is two miles wide and six miles long. In 1800 the United States War Department bought the island to harvest timber for shipbuilding. Later the government used it as a quarantine station for yellow fever victims. The yellow fever epidemic of 1876 claimed over a thousand lives in Savannah alone. On the south end of the island are the remains of a brick crematory built in 1904.

The Blackbeard quarantine station was closed in 1909 after vaccines developed by Walter Reed and others had practically eliminated yellow fever. In 1914 President Wilson made the island a wildlife preserve. Accessible only by boat and for daytime use only, the island is administered by the U.S. Fish and Wildlife Service. Contact Blackbeard Island National Wildlife Refuge, 843-784-2468. *www.fws.gov/blackbeardisland*. N31° 29. 350´ W081° 12. 571´

Sapelo Island

Sapelo Island is a great place to visit if you can live without some modern conveniences. The island is owned and managed by the state of Georgia, with the exception of Hog Hammock, the African American community made up of descendants of slaves who lived and worked there. Thomas Spalding bought most of the island and cultivated cotton, making Sea Island cotton known the world over. He built a sugar mill out of tabby, and with his many slaves cut down live oaks for building ships. He was known for his humane treatment of slaves, always using a black overseer who allowed the workers to earn free time. He cultivated rice in the estuaries near the island, and bought Hutchinson Island across the river from Savannah for growing rice and sugarcane.

To visit the island, contact the Sapelo Island Visitor Center, 1766 Landing Road SE, Darien, Georgia 31305, 912-437-3224. *www.sapelonerr.org*. N31° 27. 283´ W081° 21. 915´

Wolf Island National Wildlife Refuge

Wolf Island National Wildlife Refuge is one of seven wildlife refuges administered by the Savannah Wildlife Refuge in Hardeeville, South Carolina. These refuges extend from Pinckney Island near Hilton Head, South Carolina, through Wolf Island near Darien, Georgia. In addition to these three, the seven include Tybee, Wassaw, Harris Neck, and Blackbeard. Over 75 percent of Wolf

Island's five thousand acres consist of salt marsh. The island was designated a national wilderness area in 1975. Beach, marsh, and upland areas are closed to visitors. 843-784-2468. N31° 21. 100′ W081° 18. 138′

Little Saint Simons Island

Little Saint Simons Island is accessible only by boat. It was acquired by Major Pierce Butler in 1774. Not noted for treating his slaves kindly, he owned more slaves than any other slaveholder in Georgia. Major Butler's grandson married Fanny Kemble, an English Shakespearean actress who was shocked by the conditions on the island. In 1906 it was sold by the Butler family to O. F. Chichester of the Eagle Pencil Company. Red cedar trees on the island made good pencils. Little Saint Simons is Georgia's only remaining family-owned island. The old hunting lodge is now an inn for guests. The Lodge is limited to thirty-two guests, and provides a naturalist to lead your tour of the island. Activities range from interpretive natural history programs to boating, bicycling, canoeing, kayaking, or just walking the island's seven miles of pristine beach. Exploring the island offers the opportunity to observe the area's wildlife in its natural habitat. The rich and varied wilderness encourages exploration and relaxation, interspersed with sightings of American alligator, armadillos, dolphins, and a variety of birds.

The Lodge – 866-855-0738. E-mail: lodge@littlestsimonsisland, or visit *www.littleSSI.com.*

St. Simons Island

St. Simons Island is the second-largest and most developed of Georgia's barrier islands. The island is accessible by bridge and causeway. It has beautiful big live oaks, and over two hundred species of birds visit the island each year. Its forests have never been harvested for timber. In 1736 James Oglethorpe came here, soon after founding the city of Savannah, and he established Fort Frederica. Major Butler's plantation, Hampton Point, was on the north end of the island. The center of religious life during the plantation era was Christ Church Frederica, the second-oldest Episcopal church in Georgia (after Christ Church Savannah). The earliest services for this congregation were led by John Wesley, who traveled down from Savannah. By the 1880s the island's tourist industry was thriving, and it has continued to do so into the twenty-first century.

St. Simons Island Visitor Center, 530-B Beachview Drive, St. Simons Island, Georgia 31522, 800-933-2627. *www.explorestsimonsisland.com.*

Sea Island lies just east of St. Simons Island along the causeway. The island was largely uninhabited until the 1920s. When William Coffin bought it in 1928, he built a stately hotel called The Cloister. Mr. Coffin's cousin, Alfred W. Jones, managed the company through the depression. Over the years The Cloister has been enlarged from 46 to 286 rooms. 100 Cloister Drive, Sea Island, Georgia 31561, 855-714-9201. *www.seaisland.com.*

Jekyll Island

Jekyll Island is the smallest of Georgia's barrier islands, and it is accessible by causeway. In 1886 a group of wealthy businessmen, including the Rockefellers, J. P. Morgan, the Pulitzers, the Vanderbilts, and others built the Jekyll Island Club. A handsome Victorian structure with large porches, turrets and towers, it was a vacation spot for hunting and fishing. Families built "cottages" nearby, which were spacious homes. The island has twenty miles of trails for hikers and bikers. In 1947 the state of Georgia ruled that 65 percent of the island must remain undeveloped. In 1858 the ship *Wanderer* unloaded 490 slaves here, the last to be imported into America. Tabby ruins of original structures remain today.

Jekyll Island Welcome Center, 901 Downing Musgrove Causeway, Jekyll Island, Georgia 31527, 877-453-5955. *www.jekyllisland.com.*

Cumberland Island

Cumberland Island is the largest and the southernmost barrier island. For thousands of years humans lived here without disturbing it. With eighteen miles of shoreline, there is plenty of unspoiled beach, as well as large sand dunes, some forty feet high. Oak trees are the heart of this maritime forest. Revolutionary War hero Nathanael Greene purchased land on the island in 1783 to harvest live oaks for shipbuilding. Wood from the island was used to build the *USS Constitution*, also known as Old Ironsides. His widow, Caty, built a mansion, which she called Dungeness, named after Oglethorpe's hunting lodge. Although trees were cut for shipbuilding and cotton fields were cleared, the island has returned to its natural state. Horses have grazed and galloped on the island since the 1500s. The Carnegie family bought it in the 1880s, and the National Park was established in 1972. At one time there were 348 slaves on the island. Dungeness, with its fifty-nine rooms, burned down in 1959. The ruins remain. There is no bridge to the island. Catch the ferry at St. Marys, Georgia. The Park Service allows three hundred visitors a day. Visitors can either camp out or spend the night in the charming Greyfield Inn. Greyfield Inn, 904-261-6408 or 888-806-6408. *www.greyfieldinn.com.*

Cumberland Island Visitor Center, 113 St. Marys Street, St. Marys, Georgia 31558, 912-882-4335. *www.nps/cuis.gov.* N30° 43. 227′ W 081° 32. 976.′

Little Cumberland Island

Little Cumberland Island is part of the Cumberland Island National Seashore. It is separated from Cumberland by Christmas and Brockington Creeks. Some homes have been built here, but the island is private and not open to visitors.

Gray's Reef National Marine Sanctuary

Gray's Reef National Marine Sanctuary is one of America's ocean treasures. Twenty miles offshore and seventy feet underwater, it is accessible only by boat. Independent boat operators run fishing and diving trips to the sanctuary. Educators use the reef as a living classroom, and scientists use it as a living laboratory for marine research. It is managed by the National Oceanic and Atmospheric Administration (NOAA). The reef is comprised of rock outcroppings that stand above the shifting sands of the continental shelf. It supports invertebrates, soft corals and sponges, and reef and pelagic fishes. *www.graysreef.noaa.gov.* 912-598-2345.

Gullah Geechee Cultural Heritage Corridor

Gullah Geechee Cultural Heritage Corridor – Signs are being erected to direct visitors to sites important to the culture of slave descendants along the sea islands of the east coast. The Gullah Geechee Heritage Corridor Commission is placing fifty-four signs along the corridor from Jacksonville, North Carolina, south to Jacksonville, Florida. The signs are either on U.S. 17 or along Florida Route A1A. The culture known as Gullah in the Carolinas and Geechee in Georgia and Florida survived for decades because of the isolation of the area's sea islands. The signs are an effort to call attention to a culture that has been threatened by rapid coastal development.

Shopping

Welcome to the "Shopping" chapter of the *Savannah Guidebook*. Savannah's Historic District has been the site of three centuries of commerce, and new shops open and others close on a regular basis. If you need an updated listing of recent additions or closings, check our website at *www.savannahguidebook.net*.

Broughton Street

For most of the past century Broughton Street was the place to go for shopping. The city's nicest stores were found on both sides of the street, and the streetcar ran down the middle. In the 1960s, however, Broughton Street suffered a decline. Adler's, the largest department store, was destroyed in a devastating fire in 1958, and in 1969 the Oglethorpe Mall was built on the south side of town. The mall was popular, and shopping in an air-conditioned environment was appealing. Broughton Street nearly dried up. A few stores, such as Fine's, Levy's, and Globe Shoe Company, kept their doors open for faithful customers, but even then, business was not booming.

Today the Savannah Development and Renewal Authority has revitalized this now humming street. Loft apartments are in demand from students and shop owners, and many large anchor stores (Gap, Banana Republic, J. Crew, Marc Jacobs) have put down roots. Ethnic and local restaurants and high-fashion boutiques line the street. Shopping on Broughton Street is once again an adventure. The street runs east and west across the northern part of the Historic District.

The neon glow of Leopold's Ice Cream and the
Savannah College of Art and Design at night

 Begin your exploration with an ice cream cone at **Leopold's Ice Cream** *at 212 East Broughton Street, and walk west.*

Den's Men and Boys Shop
128 East Broughton Street, 31401, 912-233-3356.
A large selection of casual men's clothing.

24 E Design Company
24 East Broughton Street, 31401, 912-233-2274. *www.24estyle.com.*
Modern furniture, commercial chairs, and custom designs.

Globe Shoe Company
17 East Broughton Street, 31401, 912-232-8161.
A Savannah tradition, fitting men and women since 1892. Here you'll find Ecco, Mephisto, Stuart, Weitzman, Cole Haan, Munro, and Ugg, among other brands.

Half Moon Outfitters

15 East Broughton Street, 31401, 912-201-9393. *www.halfmoonoutfitters.com.*
Gear for outdoors—paddle-boarding, kayaking, rock climbing, and surfing.

Milan Day Spa

10 East Broughton Street, 31401, 912-236-4900. *www.milandayspabroughton.com.*
Stop by for a hot stone massage or pedicure.

Levy Jewelers

2 East Broughton Street, 31401, 912-233-1163. Savannah's fourth-generation family
jewelry business, exemplifying a long tradition of fine jewelry.

Like Accessorize It

2 West Broughton Street, 31401, 912-232-4182. Jewelry, purses, and more.

FedEx Office Print and Ship Center

5 West Broughton Street, 31401, 912-443-1901. *www.local.fedex.com.*
Offers printing services and shipping via FedEx.

Low Country Gourmet Foods

10 West Broughton Street, 31401, 912-233-7500.
www.shop.lowcountrygourmetfoods.com.
Extra virgin olive oils, aged balsamic vinegars, and gourmet seasonings.

The Spice and Tea Exchange of Savannah

14 West Broughton Street, 31401, 912-790-1669. *www.spiceandtea.com.*
Spices, olive oils and blends, samplers, sugars, and gift boxes.

Loft

15 West Broughton Street, 31401, 912-234-7941. *www.loft.com.*
Women's apparel in contemporary styles.

New York Boutique

19 West Broughton Street, 31401, 912-232-9057. Men's clothing and shoes.

J. Parker Ltd.

20 West Broughton Street, 31401, 912-234-0004. *www.jparkerltd.com.*
Suiting Savannah since 1972 in traditional southern style.
A complete men's store, from casual to formal.

Copper Penny/Shooz

22 West Broughton Street, 31401, 912-629-6800. *www.shopcopperpenny.com.*
A stylish collection of clothing, shoes, and accessories.

The Paris Market and Brocante
36 West Broughton Street, 31401, 912-232-1500. *www.theparismarket.com.*
Jewelry, bath and beauty products, candles, furniture,
lighting, garden, baby things, and kitchen items.

L'Occitane
101 West Broughton Street, 31401, 912-236-7514. *www.loccitane.com.*
Perfumes from Provence.

Savannah Bee Company
104 West Broughton Street, 31401, 912-233-7873. *www.savannahbee.com.*
Honey-sweetened drinks, a video of beekeeping, and a children's play skep.
There is a second shop at 1 West River Street.

Go Fish
106 West Broughton Street, 31401, 912-231-0609. *www.savannah.gofishretail.com.*
Clothing, jewelry, shoes, and accessories from around
the world, including batiks from Indonesia.

Villa Savannah
109 West Broughton Street, 31401, 800-955-2871. *www.shopvillasavannah.com.*
Fashion, jewelry, candles, botanicals, pillows, and rugs.

Banana Republic
121 West Broughton Street, 31401, 912-447-8473. *www.bananarepublic.com.*
Classic clothing for men and women in the 1849 Telfair Building,
which used to be Hogan's.

Gap
122 West Broughton Street, 31401, 912-790-0977. *www.gap.com.*
Clothes for men, women, and children in the old Kress building.

J. Crew
201 West Broughton Street, 31401, 912-233-4368. *www.jcrew.com.*
Women's and men's clothes, shoes, and formal wear.

Nourish
202 West Broughton Street, 31401, 912-232-3213. *www.handcraftedsoap.com.* Bath
products. Second location at 7360 Skidaway Road in Sandfly, 31406, 912-777-5479.

The Ancient Olive
204 West Broughton Street, 31401, 912-495-5339. Specialty grocery store and gift
shop. Offering gourmet foods and fine art.

Modern Sylvester & Company
205 West Broughton Street, 31401, 912-236-1150. *www.sylvesterandco.com.*
Home furnishings, gifts. Dreamy iced coffee and cookies.

Savannah Rae's Gourmet Popcorn
206 West Broughton Street, 31401, 912-495-5015. *www.savannahraes.com.*
All kinds of gourmet popcorn.

Free People
217 West Broughton Street, 31401, 912-234-1678. *www.freepeople.com.*
Boutique with boho-chic clothing. Whimsical dresses, tops, and skirts.

Urban Outfitters
221 West Broughton Street, 31401, 912-238-5606. *www.urbanoutfitters.com.*
Clothing and accessories for men and women.

Palm Avenue
223 West Broughton Street, 31401. *www.shoppalmavenue.com.* Lilly Pulitzer dresses.

Goorin Brothers Hat Shop
228 West Broughton Street, 31401, 912-238-4288. *www.goorin.com.*
Fine felt hats, hand-woven straws, cloth caps and others. Established 1895.

Cardeologie
312 West Broughton Street, 31401, 912-234-3009. *www.cardeologie.net.*
Greeting cards, gifts, and curiosities. Artwork by Pamela Lee is available here.

Shopping on Broughton Street in the Good Ole Days

Fab'rik Savannah
318 West Broughton Street, 31401, 912-234-8740. *www.fabriksavannah.com.*
Boutique, shoes.

Kate Spade
319 West Broughton Street, 31401, 912-495-6505. *www.katespade.com.*
Bold and stylish women's clothing.

Prospector Company
320 West Broughton Street, 31401, 912-234-1175. *www.prospectorco.com.*
Clothing and accessories, home goods. Wares with a purpose.

Lucy-Lu's
321 West Broughton Street, 31401, 912-384-5829.
Designer denim and fashion shopping. Gifts for girls.

Marc by Marc Jacobs
322 West Broughton Street, 31401, 912-234-2800. *www.marcjacobs.com.*
Men's, women's, and children's clothing and accessories.

Chocolat by Adam
323 West Broughton Street, 31401, 912-335-2914. *www.chocolatat.com.*
Chocolates, as well as classes in making classic truffles and mendiants.

Zia Boutique
325 West Broughton Street, 31401, 912-233-3237. *www.ziaboutique.com.*
Sterling silver and reasonably priced jewelry.

 Walk one block north on Montgomery Street to …

Anthropologie
38 Montgomery Street, 31401, 912-944-6113. *www.anthropologie.com.*
Women's clothes, shoes, and accessories.

 You are now at Franklin Square. Walk through the square and enter City Market.

City Market

Franklin Ward South has shops opening onto the courtyard. Inside are working artists, upstairs and down. At street level are ...

Signature Gallery
303 West St. Julian Street, 31401, 912-233-3082. *www.signaturegallerysavannah.com.*
Paintings, jewelry, photography, stained and blown glass,
metal sculptures, wood, pottery, and etchings.

All Things Georgia
305 West St. Julian Street, 31401, 912-233-7017. Handsome quilts, preserves,
Bird Girl jewelry, shell ornaments, aprons, local coffees, loose teas.

Alix Baptiste's Art Gallery
307 West St. Julian Street, 31401, 912-441-0845. *www.alixbaptiste.com.*
Colorful original and limited editions of Caribbean paintings by this Haitian artist.

Cinnamon Bear Country Store
309 West St. Julian Street, 31401, 912-232-2888. *www.cinnamonbearstores.com.*
Fruit jellies, jams, peach pecan amaretto preserves, souvenirs, and mustard dips.

Raffine Gallerie
306 West Congress Street, 31401, 912-232-6400. *www.rafinegallerie.com.*
Featuring paintings by Vicci Waits. Local art, jewelry, and pottery.

Twinkle
33 Jefferson Street, 31401, 912-234-1001. Jewelry, scarves, watches, and purses.

Shopping for Produce at the City Market

Savannah Cigars

309 West Congress Street, 31401, 888-310-8331. *www.savannahcigarsinc.com.*
Offering their own brand of Savannah cigars, as well as humidors stocked with
handmade stogies, pipes, and imported cigarettes.

Studio 1, Dottie Farrell and Bess Ramsey

Upstairs, 309 West St. Julian Street, 31401, 912-341-0122. Two Savannah artists
capture Low Country flavor. Outstanding dog portraits.

Studio 1-A, Samantha Claar

309 West St. Julian Street, 31401, 912-786-4351. Gullah paintings, jewelry, and rugs.

Gallery 2, The Savannah Gallery

Upstairs, 309 West St. Julian Street, 31401, 912-667-4378.
Local artists offer paintings, pottery, weaving, and stained glass.

Gallery 3, Carrie Kellogg, landscape photographer

Upstairs, 309 West St. Julian Street, 31401, 912-441-2093. *www.carriekellog.com.*

Gallery 4, Jonathan Keller

309 West St. Julian Street, 31401, 912-495-5480.
Abstract paintings and Gullah artists.

Gallery 5, Kira Kira

Upstairs, 309 West St. Julian Street. 31401, 912-713-8601.
Paintings by four local artists.

Studio 6, Susie Chisholm, Sculptor

Upstairs, 309 West St. Julian Street, 31401, 912-441-6261. *www.susiechisholm.com.*
Sculptures for collectors, and public art. The bronze sculpture of Johnny Mercer, on
the west side of Ellis Square, is one example of her work.

Studio 7, Luba Lowry

Upstairs, 309 West St. Julian Street, 31401, 651-894-3053. *www.lubalowry.com.*
Unveiling the human mystery through portraiture.

Studio 8, Dan Cole and William Kwamena-Poh

Upstairs, 309 West St. Julian Street, 31401, 912-201-9009. *www.williamkfineart.com.*
Watercolors from Ghana, West Africa.

Gallery 9, Upstairs, Sue Gouse Inspirations

309 West St. Julian Street, 31401, 912-667-4378. *www.suegouseinspirations.com.*
Savannah scenes, oil on canvas. Giclee prints of original oil paintings.

Gallery 10, Pamela Dykema and Andrea Stark

Upstairs, 309 West St. Julian Street, 31401, 912-429-5326. Watercolors of local
scenes, as well as acrylics and oils.

Gallery 11

Upstairs, 309 West St. Julian Street. 31401, 912-247-0389. Fifteen local artists display
their paintings, ceramics, and jewelry.

 Cross the courtyard to Franklin Ward North. Downstairs you'll find …

Savannah's Candy Kitchen

318 West St. Julian Street, 31401, 912-201-9501. *www.savannahcandy.com.*
Pecan pralines, chocolate fudge, and samples.

Christmas on the Market

307 West Bryan Street, 31401, 912-234-5324. Christmas ornaments and decorations.

Silver Silk and Beads

310 West St. Julian Street, 31401, 912-236-2890. *www.ssbsavannah.ning.com.*
Sterling silver jewelry, handmade beads.

September

306 West St. Julian Street, 31401, 912-232-0013. New styles
with a southern edge, in the heart of City Market.

Stephen Kasun and Dusty Vollmer Gallery

305-B West Bryan Street, 31401, 407-474-0411. *www.kasunstudio.com.*
Original oil paintings, photography.

A. T. Hun Art Gallery

302 West St. Julian Street, 31401, 912-233-2060 or 912-604-6148.
www.athun.com. Come in for some Hun fun. This gallery
is eclectic, bold, nostalgic, and adventurous.

 Upstairs you'll find …

Wayne Chambers Gallery

308 West St. Julian Street, #104, 31401, 912-234-6899.
Fine watercolors and giclee prints.

Mr and Mrs Robert Groves driving the cart of "watermelons" to the City Market for the grand ball before the Market was torn down in 1954.

*John and Maitie McGowan, Dick and Marjorie Schley, and Kass and
Reuben Clark are dressed up as the "watermelons" sold in the City Market.*

Brian MacGregor Gallery
308 West St. Julian Street, #103, 912-596-2201.

Portraits by Tisha
309 West St. Julian Street, 31401, 912-484-1496. *www.portraitsbytisha.com.*
Tisha paints in oil on linen.

King David
308 West St. Julian Street, #107, 31401, 912-441-9040.
Jewelry fashioned from spoons and forks.

Albert Seidl Fine Art
308 West St. Julian Street, #110, 31401, 912-665-1485. *www.albertseidl.com.*
Nautical themes, mermaids, jazz and sports prints, and original work.

 Cross Jefferson Street to Decker Ward in the next courtyard. In Decker Ward South you'll find …

Trolley Stop Gifts
217 West St. Julian Street, 31401, 912-233-5604. *www.trolleytours.com.* Kitchenware,
souvenirs, and a wall of local books. Prints and cards by Pamela Lee sold here.

Byrd Cookie Company
213 West St. Julian Street, 31401, 912-233-8816. Home-baked cookies, free samples,
Sandfly barbecue sauce, and other Savannah products. Will ship anywhere.

Thomas Kinkade Gallery
211 West St. Julian Street. 31401, 912-447-4660. *www.thomaskinkade.com.*
Limited edition canvases and gifts.

September's Loft
209 West St. Julian Street, 31401, 912-495-5681.
New styles with a southern edge in the heart of City Market.

 In Decker Ward North you'll find …

Bozena's/Something for Everyone Gifts
230A West St. Julian Street. 31401, 912-234-0086. European antiques, jewelry,
English and French soaps, linens, and fancy umbrellas.

Woof Gang Bakery
202 West St. Julian Street, 31401, 912-495-5806. *www.woofgangbakery.com.*
Dog treats and grooming. Your neighborhood pet store.

Ellis Square

Ellis Square was once the site of the old City Market. The market building, built in 1872, housed a colorful array of seafood vendors, basket weavers, and farmers selling fresh produce, accompanied by the happy sounds of laughter and bargaining. Mules hauled wagons loaded with peaches, persimmons, scuppernongs, melons, and sugarcane to the market stalls. Streetcars discharged eager shoppers. This bustling scene vanished overnight when the building was torn down in 1954. An ugly multilevel parking garage arose in its place.

Just before the market was torn down, Savannahians held a grand ball in the market building. Everyone came dressed like items sold in the market—fish, okra, squash, and carrots, among other things. Evelyn and Robert Groves drove a mule hitched to a wagon with a load of hay, and friends dressed as watermelons.

After the destruction of the City Market, people in Savannah began to appreciate the value of the city's historic buildings. When other structures were threatened, the seven Savannah ladies to whom this book is dedicated were stirred to action, and the historic preservation movement began. Citizens recognized the value of the original city plan with its streets, squares, and historic homes. Historic Savannah, Inc., was created, and its revolving fund saved many valuable buildings from destruction.

After fifty years, the lease for the parking garage expired. The structure was torn down, and an open pedestrian park was created with an information center, an interactive fountain, benches under shady live oaks, and a statue of Johnny Mercer.

There is parking underneath the square with an entrance on Whitaker Street and elevators up to the Visitor Information Center. The management office is located at 219 West Bryan Street, 31401, 912-232-4903. *www.savannahcitymarket.com.*

 Shopping continues from City Market to …

Corner Store
19 Barnard Street, 31401. Next door to Woof Gang Bakery, 912-232-2152.
Souvenirs, gift shop.

 Then cross back toward Broughton Street to the neighborhood south of Ellis Square …

Like Accessorize It
31 Barnard Street, 31401, 912-236-0560. Women's fashion accessories.

Compass Prints, Inc., Ray Ellis Gallery
205 West Congress Street, 31401, 912-234-3537. *www.rayellis.com.*
Original Low Country scenes, prints, and note cards.

Corner Store
30 Barnard Street, 31401, 912-232-2152. Congress and Barnard Streets.
Souvenirs, gift shop.

Terra Cotta
34 Barnard Street, 31401, 912-236-6150. *www.terracottasavannah.com.*
New and vintage-style clothing, soaps.

Kitchens on the Square
38 Barnard Street, 31401, 912-236-0100. *www.kitchensonthesquare.com.*
Cookware, gadgets, and tableware.

Salt Table
51 Barnard Street, 31401, 912-447-0200. *www.salttable.com.*
Salts, teas, seasonings, sugars, and popcorn.

Kobo Gallery
33 Barnard Street, 31401, 912-201-0304. *www.kobogallery.com.*
Lots of talented local artists.

Paula Deen Store
108 West Congress Street, 31401, 912-232-1579. *www.pauladeen.com.*
Books and kitchenware. Souvenirs of the famous chef.

Metals and Paint
107 West Congress Street, 31401, 912-234-7744.
Silver jewelry, glass beads, gemstone rings, pearls.

Tervis
111 West Congress Street, 31401, 912-233-7986. A variety of colorful insulated cups,
glasses, and tumblers. The many designs feature popular destinations and college logos.

 Cross Whitaker Street to ...

Mack's 5 & 10
31 West Congress Street, 31401, 912-944-0108.
Souvenirs, gifts, toys, T-shirts, local Savannah books. In business since 1946.

Scents for Cents
31 West Congress Street, 31401, 912-659-3990. *www.savannahscentsforcents.com.*
Candles, tarts, fragrance oils, and warmers.

Wicked Cakes
38 Whitaker Street, 31401, 912-298-0040.
Try a wild turkey honey cupcake topped with bacon.

River Street

These multistoried buildings were once cotton warehouses. Factors (merchants) stood on the iron balconies to watch cotton loaded onto ships for export overseas. Ballast stones used for weight in the hulls of trading ships were later used to construct parts of the River Street ramps and walls. River Street now offers an eclectic mix of shops and restaurants, and its candy stores offer free samples of pecan pralines and goober brittle.

Village Craftsmen
223 West River Street, 31401, 912-236-7280. *www.thevillagecraftsmen.com.*
Pottery, paintings, jewelry, woodwork, by local artists.

Christmas on the River
219 West River Street, 31401, 912-236-8918.
Decorations, lights, manger scenes, and Christmas villages.

Earthbound Trading Co.
215 West River Street, 31401, 912-231-0804. A safari atmosphere. Items from Bali, Nepal, India, and other faraway countries.

Black Dog
211 West River Street, 31401, 912-335-7472. *www.theblackdog.com.*
Men's, women's and children's clothes from Martha's Vineyard.

Land and Sea Wear
209 West River Street, 31401, 912-232-2830. Casual and holiday clothing.

Scarlett's
205 West River Street, 31401, 912-236-6064. Sandals, scarves, purses, and hats.

Loafer's Loft
121 West Upper Factors Walk, 31401, 912-232-6006. T-shirts and gift items.

Fine Things under $20
121 West River Street, 31401, 912-230-1995. Jewelry, watches, and handbags.

Missing Pieces
5 West River Street, 31401, 912-232-9922. A clothing store and so much more, located under the Hyatt Hotel.

Savannah Bee Company
1 West River Street, 31401, 912-234-7088. *www.savannahbee.com.*
Honey-sweetened drinks, a video of beekeeping, children's play skep.

River Street Sweets
13 East River Street, 31401, 912-234-4608. *www.riverstreetsweets.com.*
Pralines, delightful candy, samples, catalog.
Additional location at 4515 Habersham Street, 31405.

Sona Gifts
17 East River Street, 31401, 912-234-1990. Clothing, souvenirs.

Arts and Crafts Emporium
40 East Factors Walk (upstairs), 31401, 912-238-9148.
www.artsandcraftsemporium.com. A marketplace for American crafters.
Note cards by Pamela Lee sold here.

True Grits
107 East River Street, 31401, 912-234-8006.
Local prints, cookbooks, lighthouses, nautical gifts, Sheila pieces.

The Mad Hatter
123 East River Street, 31401, 912-232-7566. Hats and more hats!

Cinnamon Bear Country Store
205 East River Street, 31401, 912-233-0871. Jellies, jams, and souvenirs.

Fabulous Finds under $20
207 East River Street, 31401, 912-447-6666. *www.fabulousfindsunder20.com.*
Jewelry, sunglasses, and handbags.

Gallery 209
209 East River Street, 31401, 912-236-4583. *www.gallery209savannah.com.*
A co-op with pottery, paintings, jewelry, and woodwork by local artists.

Savannah Candy Kitchen
225 East River Street, 31401, 912-233-8411. *www.savannahcandy.com.*
Gift baskets, southern pralines, fudge, and pecan pies.

Gift Shack
2 North Lincoln, 31401, 912-238-5250. Sea shells, coral, hand-painted shoes, Woodie's sandals, purses, and costume jewelry.

Simply Savannah
301 East River Street, 31401, 912-443-0272. Magnolia, pineapple, *Gone With the Wind*, and Civil War items. Southern foods, hats, and accessories. Prints and note cards by Pamela Lee sold here.

Fannie's Your Aunt, Bob's Your Uncle
305 East River Street, 31401, 912-232-4546. Books, souvenirs, and "Life is good" items. Salt Life and dog items, as well as books about Savannah.

The Peanut Shop
407 East River Street, 31401, 912-232-8612. *www.thepeanutshop.com.* Virginia peanuts, cashews, almonds, peanut brittle, pecans, and pistachios.

Five and Dime General Store
411 East River Street, 31401, 912-349-2059. Souvenirs, cold drinks, band-aids, sunglasses, snacks, toys, and sunscreen.

Artsy's Gallery
427 East River Street, 31401, 912-341-8899. *www.artsygallery.com.* Local and national prints, as well as reasonably priced framing.

Savannah Tees Outlet
429 East River Street, 31401, 912-234-2343. Inexpensive clothing, catering to tourists.

Something for Everyone Gifts
502 East River Street, 31401, 912-843-683-9991. A wide assortment of specialized gifts.

Something Different
505 East River Street, 31401, 912-441-2664. *www.yourpersonalgift.com.* Jewelry, toys, pirates' plunder, and swords. Primarily a "fair trade" store.

Travel House
508 East River Street, 31401, 912-944-6100. Souvenir shop.

 At the East end of River Street are two open sheds with booths offering a variety of interesting merchandise. Enjoy exploring for yourself.

Bay Street Along Factors' Walk

Here you'll find old cotton warehouses converted into shops, restaurants, and hotels. Constructed in the first half of the nineteenth century, after the invention of the cotton gin (short for engine), these buildings serve as a reminder of the days of "King Cotton," when merchants prospered and built grand mansions throughout the Historic District.

RMC Boutique

316 East Bay Street, 31401, 912-335-2389. *www.rmcboutique.com.* Jewelry, apparel, and gifts. "Your husband called and said buy anything you like."

Exit Strategy

310 East Bay Street, 31401. Ice cream, espresso, hot chocolate.
Craft beer, frozen custard.

Golden Realm Antiques

306 East Bay Street, 31401, 912-335-8623. Antiques and oddities.
Costume jewelry and art.

Southern Gents Antiques

208 East Bay Street, 31401, 912-232-9122. Victorian antiques, antique estate jewelry, oil paintings, watercolors, and in-store gourmet food shop.

Savannah Belle

206 East Bay Street, 31401, 912-232-4833. Boutique and gallery, local art.

Factor's Cottage

204 East Bay Street, 31401, 912-443-9337. *www.factorscottage.com.* Funny coasters, sleep shirts, effusion lamps, regal rugs, and Savannah cookbooks.

Laurel Canyon

202 East Bay Street, 31401, 912-721-7689. *www.laurelcanyongifts.com.*
Gifts for the body and soul.

Verdery's

130 East Bay Street, 31401, 912-236-9384. Lamps, as well as Ye Ole Tobacco Shop.

Savannah Rose

126 East Bay Street, 31401, 912-232-9449. A boutique with an attitude, offering Franz pottery, estate jewelry, and more.

Matter of Factors

120 East Bay Street, 31401, 912-231-2100. Wine, gifts, and local books, including the popular title *Savannah Then and Now.*

Cool Savannah Tours and Gifts
42 East Bay Street, 31401, 912-233-3667. *www.coolsavannahgifts.com.*
Rare Savannah treasures, grand lighting, antiques, fine art, significant signatures,
and Persian rugs. You can book tours here for children and adults.

Travel Traders
2 West Bay Street, 31401 (inside the Hyatt), 912-238-1234.
Souvenirs, gifts, and local books.

Goldon House Gallery
220 West Bay Street, 31401, 912-238-0220.
Authentic Asian antiques in an historic building.

Books on Bay
224 West Bay Street, lower level. 31401, 912-236-7115. *www.booksonbay.com.*
Vintage (1600s–1900s), rare, and collectible books. Remember Nancy Drew,
the Hardy Boys, Tom Swift, the Bobbsey Twins, the Lone Ranger, Zane Grey,
Shakespeare, the Wizard of Oz, and Uncle Remus? They're all here.

Fiesta and More
224 West Bay Street, lower level, 31401, 912-238-1060. *www.fiestaandmore.com.*
Fiesta, depression glass, and collectibles.

The Attic Antiques
224 West Bay Street, upper level, 31401, 912-236-4879. Antiques and collectibles.

Jere's Antiques
9 North Jefferson Street, 31401 (Bay Street and Jefferson), 912-236-2815.
www.jeresantiques.com. Antique furniture. English pub bars, pianos,
wardrobes, and stained glass. Will ship.

Historic Houses and Museum Gift Shops

Andrew Low House Gift Shop

329 Abercorn Street, 31401, 912-233-6854. *www.andrewlowhouse.com.*
Mugs, serving sets, Tervis tumblers, hand-painted hand fans, and local books,
including *Savannah Safari Walking Adventure* and *Naughty Grandmother*, plus
cookbooks. Savannah pen-and-ink drawings by talented artist Pamela Lee and
African American Journey by Jamal Touré are sold here.

Beach Institute Gift Shop

502 East Harris Street, 31401, 912-234-8000. *www.kingtisdell.org.*
African American history books by local authors, jewelry, catalogues and posters
of carvings by Ulysses Davis, handmade quilts. *African American Journey* by Jamal
Touré and note cards by Dan Kaufman are sold here.

Davenport House Museum Gift Shop

324 East State Street, 31401, 912-236-8097. *www.davenporthousemuseum.org.*
Georgia peach preserves, not-so-hot fans, Davenport Christmas ornaments,
and local books, including *The Savannah Cookbook*, 1933 edition, *Savannah
Specters*, *Savannah Sampler Cookbook*, and *Savannah Then and Now.* Pen-and-ink
illustrations of Savannah scenes and buildings by local artist Pamela Lee.
Prints and note cards by Dan Kaufman.

Georgia State Railroad Museum Gift Shop

655 Louisville Road, 31401, 912-651-6823. *www.historicrailroadshops.org.*
Images of America books, Thomas the Tank Engine and Chuggington products,
coffee-table train books, and children's toys.

Jepson Museum Gift Shop

207 West York Street, 31401, 912-651-9654. *www.telfair.org.*
Handbags and accessories, Bird Girl statues, local books, coiled cloth bowls,
"dropped" glass vases, clay nesting bowls. Pen-and-ink illustrations of Savannah
scenes and buildings by Pamela Lee. Prints and note cards by Dan Kaufman.

Juliette Gordon Low Girl Scout Center Gift Shop

142 Bull Street, 31401, 912-233-4501. *www.juliettegordonlowbirthplace.org.*
Fun patches, official Birthplace pins, copies of Victorian toys, scarves and
totes, porcelain dolls, and teapots and teacups. Pen-and-ink illustrations of
Savannah scenes and buildings by Pamela Lee.

Massie Heritage Interpretation Center Gift Shop

207 East Gordon Street, 31401, 912-201-5070. *www.massieschool.com.*
Twig pencils, woven fans, Victorian, colonial, and tricorn-style hats, plus
Early American stencil books, tea sets, and imitation arrowheads.

National Museum of the Mighty Eighth Air Force Gift Shop

175 Bourne Avenue, Pooler, Georgia, 31322, 912-748-8888. *www.mightyeighth.org.*
Wooden propellers, A-2 leather jackets, aviator and bomber
jackets for children, airplane clocks, globes, and books.

Owens Thomas House Store

124 Abercorn Street, 31401, 912-233-9743. www.telfair.org.
Bird Girl statues, stationery, children's gifts, garden décor, ceramics, cookbooks,
and local books, including *Savannah Then and Now.* Work by local
artist Pamela Lee and photographer Dan Kaufman.

Ralph Mark Gilbert Civil Rights Museum Gift Shop

460 Martin Luther King Jr. Blvd., 31401, 912-231-8900. Books, souvenirs. Tours.
African American Journey by Jamal Touré sold here.

Savannah History Museum Gift Shops

303 Martin Luther King Jr. Blvd., 31401, 912-238-1779. *www.chsgeorgia.org.*
Bird Girl statues, Byrd cookies, Victorian-style jewelry, broaches,
quilted handbags, and local books. Savannah ornaments, t-shirts, mugs, hats, and
souvenirs. Train merchandise, military commemorative gifts, and blacksmith items.
Food, teas, jelly, syrups, and jams from local companies. Puzzles, Southern fans and
scarves and paper doll books.

Savannah Visitor Center Gift Shop

301 Martin Luther King Jr. Blvd., 31401, 912-944-0455. Savannah souvenirs,
T-shirts, mugs, books, maps, and hats.

SCAD Museum of Art

601 Turner Blvd., 31401, 912-525-7191. *www.scadmoa.org.* A small café, fine art
books, postcards, T-shirts, bags, journals, and sketch pads designed by students.

Ships of the Sea Museum Gift Shop

41 Martin Luther King Jr. Blvd., 31401, 912-232-1511. *www.shipsofthesea.org.*
Posters showing an 1871 bird's-eye view of Savannah and the Ocean
Steamship Savannah Line, children's books, build-your-own-ship kits,
online store. Note cards by Dan Kaufman sold here.

Bull Street Corridor

Bull Street was named for Colonel William Bull of South Carolina, surveyor and friend of James Oglethorpe in 1733. Colonel Bull helped choose a site on a high bluff, fifteen miles upriver from the Atlantic Ocean, for the new town of Savannah. Bull Street, with its five squares (Johnson, Wright, Chippewa, Madison, and Monterey), runs north and south through the Historic District, stops at Forsyth Park, and picks up again at the south end of the park.

Flip Flop Shop
100 Bull Street, 31401, 912-480-9831. *www.flipflopshops.com.*
"Free your toes!" Great variety of flip flops from $19.00 and up.

Harper
118 Bull Street, 31401, 912-235-5172. *www.harpersavannah.com.*
This gift shop exemplifies modern sophistication.

Savannah Memories
135 Bull Street, 31401, 912-232-8011.
A souvenir gift shop with local books and an enormous variety of T-shirts.

Magnolia's of Savannah
137 Bull Street, 31401, 912-236-1004. www.*magnoliasofsavannahonline.com.*
Home décor, holiday items, and bath products.

Jewelry Consignment Network
139 Bull Street, 31401, 912-234-0207. *www.jewelryconsignment.com.*
A full-service jewelry store specializing in consignments of estate jewelry.

Gallery Espresso
234 Bull Street, 31401, 912-233-5348. *www.galleryespresso.com.*
Coffee beans, French presses, art, wine, and desserts. Pet-friendly.

Simply Silver
236 Bull Street, 31401, 912-238-3652. *www.angevinesfinesilver.com.* Fine silver gifts.
Baby items, charms, antique flatware, Christmas ornaments and jewelry.

Perry Rubber Bike Shop
240 Bull Street, 31401, 912-236-9929. *www.perryrubberbikeshop.com.*
A full-service bike shop.

Red Clover
244 Bull Street, 31401, 912-236-4053. *www.shopredclover.com.*
Ladies' apparel.

Southern Charm Antiques
250 Bull Street, 31401, 912-233-9797 or 866-socharm.
www.southerncharmantiques.com.

Porcelain, crystal, objets d'art, silver, rugs, books, and chandeliers.

Gaucho Too
251 Bull Street, 31401, 912-232-7414. *www.gauchosavannah.com.*
Ladies' apparel. A classic Savannah look.

The Christmas Shop
307 Bull Street, 31401, 912-234-5343. *www.the-christmas-shop.com.*
Nativity scenes, decorations for all seasons, children's clothing, and jewelry.

Saints & Shamrocks
309 Bull Street, 31401, 912-233-8858. *www.saintsandshamrocks.com.*
Religious merchandise, along with Irish and fair trade gifts.

E. Shaver Booksellers
326 Bull Street, 31401, 912-234-7257.
Twelve rooms of books, featuring national and local titles, including *The Damned
Don't Cry*, Savannah's first scandalous novel. Pen-and-ink drawings by Pamela Lee
and *African American Journey* by Jamal Touré sold here.

Shopscad
340 Bull Street, 31401, 912-525-5180. *shopscad.blogspot.com.*
Student and faculty artwork.

Arthur Smith Antiques
402 Bull Street, 31401, 912-236-9701. *www.arthursmithantiques.com.*
Art, chandeliers, sconces, case pieces, rugs, and silver.

George Davis Antiques and Interiors
408 Bull Street, 31401, 912-232-6603. *www.georgedavisantiques.com.*
Eighteenth- and nineteenth-century French and English furniture and accessories.

Frieze Savannah
1 West Jones Street, 31401, 912-335-7434. *www.friezesavannah.com.*
A rare and varied collection of gifts and home accents from exotic locales.

Folklorico
440 Bull Street, 31401, 912-232-9300. *folklorico.sav@gmail.com.*
Fair trade gifts. Jewelry, handbags, iconography, crosses, hand-loomed silks, steel
sculptures, pottery, basketry, textiles, carving, folk art, and crafts from many countries.

Alex Raskin Antiques

441 Bull Street, 31401, 912-232-8205. *www.alexraskinantiques.com*. Wander through four floors of treasures in the historic Noble Hardee mansion on Monterey Square.

Just a Hop and a Skip Off the Bull Street Corridor

Savannah Galleries

30 East Bryan Street, 31401, 912-232-1234. *www.savannahgalleries.com*. American and English antiques, paintings, porcelains, silver, and rugs.

Rivers and Glen Trading Company

24 Drayton Street, 31401, 912-349-2352. *www.riversandglen.com*.
Classic outdoor attire.

Reynolds Square Fine Art Gallery

31 Abercorn Street, 31401, 912-236-9797. *www.reynoldssquarefineart.com*.
Traditional oil paintings by Joe Saffold, paintings by Irene Mayo, and bronze sculptures by Susie Chisholm.

The Frayed Knot

6 West State Street, 31401, 912-233-1240. *www.thefrayedknotsav.com*.
A yarn emporium.

Wright Square Antique Mall

14 West State Street, 31401, 912-234-6700. *www.wrightsquareantiquemall.com*.
Antiques, collectibles, repurposed items.

Antiquities

20 West State Street, 31401, 912-234-3733. *www.antiquitiessavannah.com*.
Vintage purses and toys. Jewelry, hats, china, paintings, old cameras. Will ship.

Friedman's Fine Arts

28 West State Street, 31401, 912-234-1322. *www.info@friedmansfineart.com*.
In business for over a hundred years, Friedman's is a great
venue for purchasing/investing in fine art.

Liquid Sands Glass Gallery

5 West York Street, 31401, 912-232-3600. *www.liquidsandsglassgallery.com*.
Vases, sculpture, and jewelry from many American glass studios.
Museum-quality glass.

Shoe Bedo
7 West York Street, 31401, 912-495-5076.
You will want to buy every shoe in this store!

Oliver Bentley's Barking Bakery
13 West York Street, 31401, 912-395-2275. *www.oliverbentleys.com*.
Offers premium dog treats, free of gluten, wheat, corn, or soy.
No sugar, salt, or fillers. Gift boxes. Botanical bath products.

Yves Delorme
134 Whitaker Street, 31401, 912-232-3563. *www.yvesdelorme.com*.
French linens for bed, bath, and table. Furniture, decorative
accessories, lighting, soaps, fragrances, lingerie, gifts.

Atelier Gallerie
150 Abercorn Street, 31401, 912-233-3140. *www.agsavannah.com*.
Artisan-created fine jewelry and costume jewelry.

Michael V. deCook Antiques
20 West Hull Street (on Chippewa Square), 31401, 912-232-7149. Eighteenth- and
nineteenth-century furniture and accessories in a classic 1853 townhouse.

Parker's Market
222 Drayton Street, 31401, 912-233-1000. *www.parkersav.com*.
Gourmet takeout, groceries, and wine.

The Book Lady Bookstore
6 East Liberty Street, 31401, 912-233-3628. *www.thebookladybookstore.com*.
Fifty thousand books in forty genres, new and used. Offering a search
service, appraisals, out-of-print and first editions, author events.

Stitch
6 East Liberty Street, 31401, 912-856-6159. Clothing design and fine alterations.

The Artful Kitchen
6 East Liberty Street, 31401, 912-677-2845.
Local handcrafted foods, beverages, and pottery.

Roots Up Gallery
6 East Liberty Street, 31401, 912-677-2845. *www.rootsupgallery.com*.
Southern folk art created by legacy and contemporary artists.

Satchel
4 East Liberty Street, 31401, 912-233-1008. *www.shopsatchel.com*.
Handbags and leather goods made in Savannah.

Fabrika
2 East Liberty Street, 31401, 912-236-1122. Fine fabrics.

Everett and Cobb Antiques and Interiors
12 West Harris Street, 31401, 912-232-3000. *www.everettandcobb.com*
Eighteenth-, nineteenth- and early-twentieth-century American,
English, and European furniture and accessories.

C. H. Brown Antiques and Fine Silver
14 West Jones Street, 31401, 912-236-0732.
American, English, and continental silver. Porcelain, artwork, and furniture.

V and J Duncan Antique Maps, Books, and Prints
12 East Taylor Street, 31401, 912-232-0338. *www.vjduncan.com.*
Old engravings, mezzotints, lithographs, and photographs, plus old and new
Savannah books. Prints of architectural interest, birds, animals, and botanicals.
Thousands of portraits and maps.

Pomegranate at Taylor House
10 West Taylor, 31401, 912-234-5520. *www.taylor-galleries.com.*
Art, gifts, silver, and antiques. Elegant flatware, dinnerware, glassware,
fine china, and fine table accessories.

Johnnie Ganem's Package Shop & Winery
501 Habersham Street, 31401, 912-233-3032. *www.johnnieganem.com.*
Wine, beer, and liquor.

Whitaker Street

Whitaker Street is one way, running south. Several small shops are clustered
within an easy walk south from Jones Street.

Arcanum
346 Whitaker Street, 31401. Just a few steps north of Jones Street,
912-236-6000. *www.arcanummarket.us.* Antiques and interiors.
Stained-glass wall hangings, James Mont specialists.

The Annex
400 Whitaker Street, 31401, 912-447-4600. Fashionable resort wear.

One Fish Two Fish

401 Whitaker Street, 31401, 912-447-4600. *www.onefishstore.com.*
Gifts, bedding, bath, jewelry, furniture, entertaining, upholstery,
local books and art, fashionable apparel.

La Paperie

409 Whitaker Street, 31401, 912-443-9349. *www.lapaperiesavannah.com.*

Fancy paper products. Drawings by Pamela Lee sold here.

Number Four Eleven

411 Whitaker Street, 31401, 912-443-0065. *www.numberfoureleven.com.*
Monogrammed luxuries, plus furniture and gifts.

Lily Bay

412-C Whitaker Street, 31401, 912-777-7621. *www.lilybaybazaar.com.*
Painted furniture and gifts.

James Hogan

412 Whitaker Street, 31401, 912-234-0374. *www.jameshogan.com.*
Clothes designed by James Hogan plus Etro, Piazza Sempione, and Max Mara.

Bottega Bellini

413 Whitaker Street, 31401, 912-231-3518. *www.bottegabellini.com.*
Handmade ceramics and gifts imported from Italy.

The Corner Door

417 Whitaker Street, 31401, 912-238-5869. *thecornerdoor@bellsouth.net.*
Antiques and accessories.

Custard Boutique

422 Whitaker Street, 31401, 912-232-4733. *www.custardboutique.com.* Women's
clothing made in the United States, with an emphasis on eco-friendly material.

Madame Chrysanthemum

101 West Taylor Street, 31401, 912-238-3355. Floral design studio and boutique.
Note cards by Dan Kaufman sold here.

Mercer Williams House Carriage Shop

430 Whitaker Street, 31401, 912-238-0208. *www.mercerhouse.com.*
Items relating to *Midnight in the Garden of Good and Evil*, Bird Girl statues,
Johnny Mercer and Emma Kelly CDs, and the *Savannah Style* cookbook.

P W Short General Store

441 Whitaker Street, 31401, 912-349-6378. *www.pwshort.com.*
Items for gardening, cooking, dining, bar ware, canning supplies, and entertaining.
Products and cookbooks by culinary historian and author John Martin Taylor under
the Hoppin' John's label.

Beyond the Historic District

Abercorn Antiques and Designs @ 37th Street

201 East 37th Street, 31401, 912-233-0064. *www.37aad.com.*
Featuring antiques from country French to American primitive.
Unusual clocks, unique lighting, estate jewelry, and vintage clothing.

Annabelle's

8409 Ferguson Avenue, 31406 (in Sandfly),
912-691-4729. *www.sweetteasavannah.com.*
Home décor, interior design, and books. Located inside is
Merry Times offering fine stationery and invitations.

Barnes and Noble

7804 Abercorn Extension in Oglethorpe Mall. 31406, 912-353-7757.
www.barnesandnoble.com. A full-service bookstore. Authors' signings.
Children's area with games and readings. Local books. Coffee bar.

Byrd Cookie Company

6700 Waters Avenue, 31406, 912-355-1716. *www.byrdcookiecompany.com.*
Many specialty and gift items, specializing in cookies.
Try the oatmeal and key lime cookies.

Canine Palace

2805 Bull Street, 31405, 912-234-3336. *www.caninepalacesavannah.com.*
Dog food, leashes, collars, beds, sweaters, furniture, finery,
and foolery for your friend Fido. Cat supplies.

CJ's Hallmark Shop

4-B Skidaway Village Walk, 31411, 912-598-8889. *www.hallmark.com.*
Recordable storybooks, nostalgic children's books, cards, gifts, and local books.
Prints and note cards by Pamela Lee sold here.

Clay Tile Murals
912-308-0063 or 912-353-9999. Custom-made for home or office. Offering beach themes (turtles, pelicans, or crabs), and designs for children's rooms (puppies, flowers, or butterflies), among others. Call for details.

Coastal Empire Trading Company
215 West Liberty Street, 31401, 912-352-2994. *www.savannahcoffee.com*. Fifty coffee varieties, including single origin, blends, and favored mixtures. Coffee pots and presses, cigars, chocolates, and olive oil. Note cards by Dan Kaufman sold here.

Cobb's Galleries
122 East 37th Street, 31401, 912-234-1582.
Art, pottery, fine silver, coins, stamps, porcelain, crystal, old jewelry, and cookbooks, located in the historic 1895 Krouskoff House.

Cottage Shop
2422 Abercorn Street, 31401, 912-233-3820. *www.cottageshopgifts.com*.
Bridal registry, china, crystal, and garden accessories.
The building dates from 1799, and the shop was established in 1946.

Curiosities Antiques and Stuff
2819 River Drive, 31404, 912-351-6009. Architectural salvage, restoration, antiques, hardware, lighting, and doors.

Diaspora Market Place
510 Martin Luther King Jr. Blvd., 31401, 912-232-2626. *www.diasporamarketpl.com*.
Woodcarvings from Africa, clothes, jewelry, straw baskets, and brass and bronze pieces, as well as furniture and musical instruments.

Dolphin and the Mermaid
7702 Waters Avenue, 31404, 912-351-9911.
Custom framing, watercolors by Rebecca Willis, work by Ray Ellis, Nancy Solana, Sharon Saseen. Art glass and metal sculptures.

East-West Gallery
2003 Bull Street (facing the city library), 31401, 912-233-8183.
Chinese and oriental imports, carved jade pendants, charms, and lacquer boxes.

Ex Libris Bookstore
228 Martin Luther King Jr. Blvd., 31401, 912-525-7550. Art supplies, magazines, greeting cards, and coffee bar—all in a preppy college bookstore atmosphere.

Fort Pulaski Gift Shop

U.S. 80 East (near Tybee), 31328, 912-786-5787. Educational items for teachers, educational toys, Civil War books, and local books. Hand-blown Jamestown glass.

Frali Gourmet

217 West Liberty Street, 31401, 912-234-4644. Homemade pastas, gourmet vegetables in jars, and ready-made dinners to take out.

Habersham Antiques

2502 Habersham Street, 31405, 912-238-5908. *www.habershamantiquesmarket.com*. Rooms full of antiques on consignment.

Islands Ace Hardware Gift Shop

318 Johnny Mercer Blvd., 31410, 912-897-1288. *www.acehardware.com*. Wind chimes, straw hats, pottery, hammocks, and birdhouses. Prints and note cards by Pamela Lee sold here.

J. D. Weed Company Antiques and Preservations

102 West Victory Drive, 31401, 912-234-8540. *www.jdweedco.com*. American antiques, furniture from colonial Virginia. Southern silver and accessories from the eighteenth and nineteenth centuries.

Kitchenware Outfitters

5500 Abercorn Street, 31405, 912-356-1117. *www.kitchenwareoutfitters.com*. Cookware, kitchen tools, and gifts. Paula Deen products. Cookbooks.

Le Chai

15 East Park Avenue, 31401, 912-713-2229. *www.lechai.com*. Wine shop specializing in the wines of Europe. Bottles stored in temperature- and humidity-controlled conditions.

Lee Smith Antiques and Design

916 East 72nd Street, 31405, 912-352-4151. *www.leesmithantiques.com*. Fine antiques and authentic reproduction furniture.

Local Color

7360 Skidaway Road, 31406 (in Sandfly), 912-349-5130. *www.localcolorsavannah.com*. Local painters, sculptors, glassblowers, jewelry makers. Custom framing. Art classes and workshops. The work of artist Jill Howell is available here.

Picker Joe's Antique Mall & Vintage Market

217 East 41st Street, 31401, 912-239-4657. *www.pickerjoes.com*.
Booths available for over seventy dealers.

Pinch of the Past Architectural Antiques

2603 Whitaker Street, 31401, 912-232-5563. *www.pinchofthepast.com*.
Many items for restoring old properties. Iron stoves, cabinets, light fixtures,
porcelain sinks, lighting, and hardware. It's a cinch you'll find it at The Pinch.

Sanders Country Store

7908 U.S. 80 (on the road to Tybee), 31410, 912-897-4861.
www.sandersgiftsandhome.com. Lighted miniature villages, scented
candles, stained-glass lamps, seashells, and jams.

Sandfly Marketplace

8511 Ferguson Avenue, 31406, 912-777-4081.
Consignment antiques, furniture, home décor, glass, pottery, and more.

Savannah Antique Mall

1650 East Victory Drive, 31404, 912-232-1918. *www.savannahantiquemall.com*.
Chandeliers, china, porcelain, silver, books, art, and fountains.

Savannah Canoe and Kayak

414 Bonaventure Road, 31404, 912-341-9502. *www.savannahcanoeandkayak.com*.
Full retail paddlesports center.

The Gator Hole (Savannah National Wildlife Refuge Gift Shop)

694 Beech Hill Lane, Hardeeville, South Carolina, 29927, 843-784-2468.
www.coastalrefuges.org. Books, hats, coffee cups, and nature toys.

Seventh Heaven Antique Mall

3104 Skidaway Road, 31404, 912-355-0835. *www.antiquesinsavannah.com*.
Victorian antiques, paintings, silver, rugs, cut glass, and collectibles.

Southern Charm

1 Resort Drive, 31421 (inside the Westin Hotel), 912-201-2000.
Souvenirs, gifts, and local books.

Trends and Traditions

5401 Waters Avenue, 31404, 912-354-5012. *www.trendsinframing.com*. A gallery with
local art, custom framing, home accessories, and Trapp candles. Local books.

Two Smart Cookies

6512 White Bluff Road, 31405, 912-353-2253. *www.twosmartcookies.com*.
Cookies, cakes, gift boxes, party trays.

Two Women and a Warehouse

2819 Bull Street, 31405, 912-351-5040. *www.twowomenandawarehouse.com.*
Painted furniture, fun home furnishings. In the words of Savannah Magazine,
"Best used furniture/thrift store." There is a second location at 13051 Abercorn
Street (Savannah Crossing II).

Tybee Lighthouse Museum Gift Shop

30 Meddin Drive, 31328, 912-786-5877. *www.tybeelighthouse.org.*
Tybee lighthouse souvenirs, books, postcards, nautical
ornaments, T-shirts, and jewelry.

Universe Trading Company

352 Martin Luther King Jr. Blvd., 31401, 912-233-1585.
Take home life-sized dinosaurs or quirky metal goats and chickens for
the garden. This shop offers jukeboxes, gnomes, metal fish, and many
surprises. A refreshing experience.

Verdery's House of Lamps and Shades

280 Eisenhower Drive, 31406, 912-691-0807 or 800-596-1425.
www.yeoletobaccoshop.com. Lamps, shades, lamp restoration, and finials.

Veronica's Closet

205 East 37th Street, 31401, 912-777-4190. This shop is a hidden treasure,
so don't miss it! Unique contemporary clothing for women.

Wiley's Book Exchange

8408 Abercorn Street, 31406, 912-349-7615.
Trade in your paperback books, CD audiobooks, DVDs, vinyl records, and graphic
novels for store credit. Offering children's books and works by best-selling authors.

Wormsloe Historic Site Gift Shop

7601 Skidaway Road, 31406, 912-353-3023. *www.gastateparks.org/wormsloe.*
Gifts for children, books on Georgia history, magnets,
postcards, and quilting and sewing kits.

Consignment and Thrift Shops

Who can resist a bargain? And why pay seventy-five dollars for a new designer blouse when that same barely worn blouse might set you back only seven dollars in a consignment store? These thrifty stores are all the rage for the savvy shopper. In today's purse-pinching economy, prices on these clothes don't sting!

Best in Show
Inside 37th and Abercorn Antiques, 201 East 37th Street, 31401, 912-233-0064. *www.humanesocietysav.org*. Higher-value collectibles, silver, crystal, and jewelry. The proceeds benefit homeless animals.

Cents and Sensibility
7360 Skidaway Road, 31406, 912-897-4961.
Fine antique linens, Oriental rugs, used designer furniture, silver, and cut glass.

Cherry Pick
402 West Broughton Street, 31401, 912-944-2888.
Gently worn dresses, slacks, blouses, shoes, and jewelry.

Civvies New & Recycled Clothing
22 East Broughton Street, 31401, 912-236-1551.
Vintage new and recycled clothing, shoes, and jewelry, to buy, sell, or trade.

Clutter Furnishings and Interiors
714 Mall Blvd., 31406, 912-354-7556.
A boutique and consignment store. Gently used furniture and accessories.

Goodwill
108 West Broughton Street, 31401, 912-233-2276. *www.goodwillsavannah.org*.
Men's and women's clothing, shoes, belts, ties, glassware, purses, and jewelry.

Hello Again
832 East DeRenne Avenue, 31405, 912-355-3344.
An upscale consignment shop with career casual and professional wear.

Jewelry Consignment Network
139 Bull Street, 31401, 912-234-0207. *www.jewelryconsignment.com*. Estate jewelry, plus new and contemporary watches from consigners around the country.

Old Savannah City Mission Bargain Center
2424 Bull Street, 31401, 912-236-7546. *www.oscm.org.*
Furniture, men and women's clothes, shoes, linens, gifts.

Threads and Things
3123 Bull Street, 31405, 912-234-5994.
Classy quality apparel and accessories.

Downtown Galleries

Welcome to the "Galleries" section of the *Savannah Guidebook*. New galleries are opened and others closed on a regular basis. If you need an updated catalogue of recent additions or deletions, check our website at *www.savannahguidebook.net*. Savannah is a city that loves art. Stroll through the Historic District to explore its neighborhood art galleries. Many galleries are found in City Market and on River Street, and here are some others within walking distance of one another in the Historic District.

− A −

Alexander Hall
668 Indian Street, 31401, 912-525-4948. *www.scad.edu*.
Art in the old 1940s Centennial Mill Flour Company building.

American Craftsman Gallery
223 West Broughton Street, 31401, 912-239-8989. *www.anamericancraftsman.com*.
Jewelry and handmade wooden items.

Art Center at City Market
204 West St. Julian Street, 31401, 912-232-7731. *www.savannahcitymarket.com/art*.
Entertainment, dining, art, and retail in the Historic District. Working artists' studios.

Arts and Craft Emporium

40 Factor's Walk, 31401, 912-238-9148. *www.artsandcraftsemporium.com*.
A unique gallery offering handmade objects from the coastal region and from across
the nation. Look for the Betty Boop statue on the stairs.

– B –

Beach Institute African American Cultural Center

502 East Harris Street, 31401, 912-234-8000.
The Ulysses Davis collection of American folk art.

The Butcher

19 East Bay Street, 31401, 912-234-6505. *www.whatisthebutcher.com*.
An art gallery as well as a tattoo studio.

– C –

City of Savannah Cultural Arts Gallery

9 West Henry Street, 31401, 912-651-6783.
Contemporary art by local and regional artists.

Compass Prints

205 West Congress Street, 31401, 912-234-3537. *www.rayellis.com*.
Ray Ellis's gallery has been on Ellis Square near City Market for twenty-five years.
Prints, Southeast landscapes, books, and note cards.

– D –

Daedalus Gallery

129 East Liberty Street, 31401, 912-233-2005. *www.daedalusgallery.com*.
William Weyman and his French wife Jacqueline Carcagno display their paintings,
which will transport you to Provence.

Diaspora Marketplace

510 Martin Luther King Jr. Blvd., 31401, 912-232-2626.
A rich and diverse selection of keepsakes from West Africa.

Downstairs Gallery

19 West Gordon Street, 31401, 912-233-0920. *www.downstairsgallery.com*.
Original oil paintings, photographs, and jewelry by local artists. Notecards by Dan
Kaufman sold here.

– F –

Friedman's Fine Art
28 West State Street, 31401, 912-234-1322. *www.friedmansfineart.com*.
They've been framing great art for a hundred years. Also offering art for sale.

– G –

Gallery 209
209 East River Street, 31401, 912-236-4583. *www.gallery209savannah.com*.
Located in a historic warehouse featuring local artists.

Gallery Espresso
234 Bull Street, 31401, 912-233-5348. *www.galleryespresso.com*. Coffee, tea, and art.

Gallery le Snoot
6 East State Street, 31401, 912-480-7460. *www.lesnoot.com*.
The gallery and Porkfellow Studio are dedicated to the creation and exhibition of
high-quality art and design.

Goldon House Gallery
220 West Bay Street, 31401, 912-238-0220. *www.vincentgolshanti.com*.
Antique Chinese furniture and fine art.

Grand Bohemian Gallery
700 Drayton Street, 31401 (inside the Mansion Hotel). *www.grandbohemiangallery.com*.
Exhibitions and artist receptions showcase paintings, sculpture, glass art, ceramics,
and jewelry.

Gutstein Gallery
201 East Broughton Street, 31401, 912-525-4735. *www.scad.edu*.
Next-door to the Jen SCAD Library.

– H –

Hamilton Hall Gallery
522 Indian Street, 31401, 912-525-4948. *www.scad.edu*. Home to SCAD exhibitions.

– I –

Indigo Sky Community Gallery
915 Waters Avenue, 31404, 912-233-7659.
Located in the old icehouse, the gallery enlivens the local neighborhood and
contributes to the cultural life of the city.

Iocovozzi Fine Art
349 Abercorn Street, 31401, 912-844-3261. *www.iocovozzifineart.com.* Everything from an eighteenth-century Goya to contemporary works.

– J –

John Tucker Fine Arts
5 West Charlton Street, 31401, 912-231-8161. *www.johntuckerfinearts.com.*
Museum-quality pieces by local artists. Landscapes, portraits, and folk art.

Julia Christian Gallery
114 West Taylor Street, 31401, 912-234-1960. *www.bobchristiandecorativeart.com.*
Decorative furnishings designed by Bob Christian. Hand-painted original designs.

– K –

Kobo Gallery
33 Barnard Street, 31401, 912-201-0304. *www.kobogallery.com.*
A group of artists in a co-op that is unique and supportive of all genres.

– L –

Liquid Sands Gallery
5 West York Street, 31401, 912-232-3600. *www.liquidsands.com.*
American-made glass and jewelry. Bright and colorful.

– M –

May Poetter Gallery
342 Bull Street, 31401, 912-525-5100. *www.scad.edu.*
A showcase for SCAD students.

– N –

Non-Fiction Gallery
1522 Bull Street, 31401, 912-662-5152. *http://nonfiction-gallery.tumblr.com.*
Innovative, thought-provoking contemporary work spanning a myriad of media.

– O –

Oglethorpe Gallery
406 East Oglethorpe Avenue, 31401, 912-272-1477. *www.oglethorpegallery.com.*
Solo exhibitions, group shows, private events, and photo shoots.

Pei Ling Chan Gallery
324 Martin Luther King Jr. Blvd., 31401, 912-525-8567. *www.scad.edu.*
A gallery and garden for the arts.

Pinnacle Gallery
320 East Liberty Street, 31401, 912-525-4950. *www.scad.edu.*
A showcase for students' art.

Ray Ellis Gallery
205 West Congress Street, 31401, 912-234-3537. *www.rayellis.com.*
Prints, books, and other gift items by Ray Ellis.

Reynolds Square Fine Art
31 Abercorn Street, 31401, 912-236-9797. *www.reynoldssquarefineart.com.*
Sculptures in bronze, paintings, wood-turnings. Across from the Lucas Theatre.

Roots Up Gallery
6 East Liberty Street, 31401, 912-677-2845. *www.rootsupgallery.com.* Southern folk
art created by legacy and contemporary artists.

- S -

Savannah Belle Boutique and Gallery
206 East Bay Street, 31401, 912-484-5803. *www.michelesnell.com.*
Local artists' paintings, drawings, sculpture, and jewelry.

Savannah Galleries
30 East Bryan Street, 31401, 912-232-1234. *www.savannahgalleries.com.* Rugs,
sideboards, and chests, estate silver.

SCAD Galleries
320 Liberty Street, 31401, 912-525-4950. *www.scad.edu/exhibitions/galleries.*
The galleries include the following:
    Alexander Hall – 668 Indian Street
    Arnold Hall – 1810 Bull Street
    Fahm Hall Gallery – 1 Fahm Street
    Gulfstream Gallery – 3116 Montgomery Street
    Gutstein Gallery – 201 East Broughton Street
    Kiah Hall – 227 Martin Luther King Jr. Blvd.
    May Poetter Gallery – 342 Bull Street

Pei Ling Chan Gallery – 322 and 324 Martin Luther King Jr. Blvd.
Pinnacle Gallery – 320 East Liberty Street

SCAD Museum of Art
601 Turner Blvd., 31401, 912-525-7191. *www.scadmoa.org.*
The college's museum, with exhibitions of drawings, painting, sculpture,
photography, and more.

S. P. A. C. E. Gallery
9 West Henry Street, 31401, 912-651-6783. *www.savannahga.gov/arts.*
Community venue for promotion of local arts. Displays of contemporary art, design,
and fine crafts.

-T-

ThincSavannah
35 Barnard Street, Suite 300, 31401, 912-544-1200. *www.thincsavannah.com.*
A collaboration of artists and other professionals who share office space.

Tiffani Taylor Gallery
11 Whitaker Street, 31401, 912-507-7860. *www.tiffaniart.com.*
Moments of beauty and inspiration in nature are transformed into rich, textured
paintings and pottery.

-V-

Village Craftsmen
223 West River Street, 31401, 912-236-7280. *www.thevillagecraftsmen.com.*
Artwork and handmade crafts from Low Country artisans.

-W-

Whitney Gallery
415 Whitaker Street, 31401, 912-495-0024.
Fine art, photography, and paintings.

Sandcrab
Painting by Kitty Strozier

Restaurants, Pubs, Cafés, Coffee Shops & Baked Goods

Savannah has a creative assortment of restaurants from cocktail-dress elegant, jeans-'n-sneakers casual, hoist-a-mug English pubs, hide-away cafes, funky-food fads, carry-outs for feeding the pigeons, feed-the-alligators at the Crab Shack and eye-opener breakfast buffets. For any last-minute changes, our website, *www.savannahguidebook.net*, will keep you posted.

Alligator Soul – 114 Barnard Street, 31401, 912- 232-7899. *www.alligatorsoul.com*. Selections ranging from eclectic fare to local southern dishes, dietary restrictions accommodated. Enjoy the romantic fireplaces.

Al Salaam Deli – 2311 Habersham Street, 31401, 912-447-0400. Middle Eastern food, casual and affordable. Locally owned. Falafel, grape leaves, gyros, kataifis.

A.Lure – 309 West Congress Street, 31401, 912- 233-2111. *www.aluresavannah.com*. Local seafood, Low Country cuisine.

Anna's – 314 West St. Julian Street, 31401, 912-236-2066. Enjoy breakfast, lunch, dinner, or a late-night snack in City Market.

Aqua Star at Westin – 1 Resort Drive, across the river, 31421, 912-201-2085. *www.aquastar@westin.com*. Live jazz with Sunday brunch. Drive over the Savannah

River Bridge for free parking, or enjoy a free ferryboat ride. Fresh local catches and Pacific specials.

Aroy Jung – 8 East Broughton Street, 31401, 912-441-0716. Asian barbecue, sushi, Thai noodle soup, curry-fried rice, and pad thai.

B and D Burgers – 13 East Broughton Street, 31401, 912-231-0986. *www.bdburgers.net*. Premium burgers and beers. Happy hour.

B and D Burgers – 209 West Congress Street, 31401, 912-238-8315. *www.bdburgers.net*.Premium burgers, premium beer, premium service.

Back in the Day Bakery – 2403 Bull Street, 31401, 912-495-9292. *www.backinthedaybakery.com*. For breakfast: tarts, jam pastry, savory ham and cheese, and biscones. For lunch: sandwiches, salads, and paninis. All fresh! Veggie fare.

Bayou Café – 14 North Abercorn Ramp, 31401, 912-233-6411. *www.bayoucafesavannah.com*. Cajun and Italian seafood. Live entertainment nightly. A fun place.

Belford's Savannah Seafood and Steaks – 315 West St. Julian Street, 31401, 912-233-2626. *www.belfordssavannah.com*. This 1902 brick building was once a wholesale food company. Sit inside, or out in the colorful courtyard.

Betty Bombers – 1108 Bull Street, 31401, 912-272-9326. Sandwich shop, burger restaurant. Chicken club, Philly cheesesteak sandwiches.

Billy's Place at McDonough's – 20 East Perry Street, 31401, 912-231-9049. *www.billysplacesavannah.com*. Tapas menu, and the cocktail "hour" extends from 4:30 p.m. to 8:00 p.m. Call about live entertainment. Wine, martinis, and full dinner menu.

B. Matthews Eatery – 325 East Bay Street, 31401, 912-233-1319. *www.bmatthewseatery.com*. Casual bistro, with full bar, in Savannah's oldest tavern. Also offers a full breakfast menu. Try the famous black-eyed-pea sandwich.

B. Tillman – 6700 Waters Avenue, 31406, 912-721-1564. *www.byrdcookiecompany.com*. Located at Byrd Cookie Company, you can get soups and salads at lunch, and more at dinner. Try the burger topped with pimento cheese and a fried green tomato.

BT Byrd's – 102 East Liberty Street, 31401, 912-349-5583. *www.byrdcookiecompany.com*. Stop in the Drayton Tower for breakfast, lunch, or dinner. Try a southern hot dog with pimento cheese and bacon, or the bourbon-and-tarragon-cured trout salad.

Bernie's Oyster House – 115 East River Street, 31401, 912-236-1827. *www.berniesoysterhouse.com.* Affordable, delicious and fun. Fresh oysters, shrimp, sandwiches, salads, and the best Bloody Mary in town. Live music on weekends.

Blowin' Smoke Cantina – 1611 Habersham Street, 31401, 912-231-2385. *www.blowinsmokebbq.com.* Sandwiches, baby back ribs, burgers, and barbecue. Delivery available.

Boar's Head – 1 Lincoln Street, 31401, 912-651-9660. *www.boarsheadgrillandtavern.com.* USDA steaks, Maine lobsters, local seafood, aged steaks and chops, and sinfully delicious desserts. Full bar. Fine wines. Serving food down on the riverfront in an old cotton warehouse since 1964, long before the whole area was restored.

Brighter Day Deli and Juice Bar – 1102 Bull Street, 31401, 912-236-4703. *www.brighterdayfoods.com.* A natural-foods store and small deli since 1978. Seating inside and out. At the south end of Forsyth Park.

Butterhead Greens Café – 1813 Bull Street, 31401, 912-201-1808. *www.butterheadgreens.com.* Environmentally sensitive. The chef uses produce from local farmers. Fresh, fast, and affordable sandwiches. Great lunches.

Cha Bella – 102 East Broad Street, 31401, 912-790-7888. *www.cha-bella.com.* Organic and seasonal fare. Outdoor patio.

Chart House – 202 West Bay Street, 31401, 912-234-6686. *www.chart-house.com.* Romantic and classy. Snapper Hemingway, shrimp fresca, roasted prime rib, fresh fish, and a full bar.

Chive Seafood Bar and Lounge – 4 West Broughton Street, 31401, 912-233-1748. The most recent restaurant and bar opened by the owners of The King and I, Tangerine Fusion, Ele's, and Fire Street Food. An upscale seafood dining experience.

Churchill's Pub and Restaurant – 13 West Bay Street, 31401, 912-232-8501. *www.thebritishpub.com.* Cheeseboards, olives, nuts, shrimp 'n grits, bangers and mash, Yorkshire pudding, Guinness. Rooftop terrace.

Cilantros's Grill and Cantina – 135 West Bay Street, 31401, 912-232-7070. Moderate prices. Niños- y niñas-friendly. Sit outside and enjoy the fountain and a cold margarita.

Circa 1875 – 48 Whitaker Street, 31401, 912-443-1875. *www.circa1875.com*. French bistro with paté, mussels, lamb shank, cassoulet, lobster, and salmon served in a nineteenth-century authentic Old World bistro setting.

CO – 10 Whitaker Street, 31401, 912-234-5375. *www.eatatco.com*. In Vietnamese, "CO" is the word for "feast." Contemporary Asian cuisine, serving dumplings, sushi, and excellent Thai curry. Signature cocktails.

Coffee Fox – 102 West Broughton Street, 31401, 912-401-0399. *www.thecoffeefox.com*. A craft coffeehouse serving locally roasted coffee.

Collins Quarter – 151 Bull Street, 31401, 912-777-4147. *www.thecollinsquarter.com*. A farm-to-table neighborhood café. Open for coffee, breakie, or lunch.

Corleone's – 44 Martin Luther King Jr. Blvd., 31401, 912-232-2720. *www.corleones.tv*. Italian menu, family-friendly, children's menu, veggie and gluten-free meals, martinis, and Amanti wine bar.

Cotton Exchange Tavern – 201 East River Street, 31401, 912-232-7088. *www.savannahmenu.com/cottonexchange*. Formerly a cotton warehouse. Watch the ships slide by in the river. Seafood, steaks, and buckets of oysters in season.

Crystal Beer Parlor

Crystal Beer Parlor – 301 West Jones Street, 31401, 912-349-1000. *www.crystalbeerparlor.com*. A local Savannah tradition since 1933. Good down-home cooking. All-beef burgers, hand-cut fries, crab stew. The walls are decorated with historic newspaper clippings and photos.

Department 7 East – 7 East Broughton Street, 31401, 912-232-0215. Try a Cracklin' Cuban with pickled okra or a Redneck Reuben with spicy collard greens, field pea hummus, and pulled pork and bacon. Meta Adler and Michele Jamison will serve you in the building that was once Meta's great-grandfather's department store.

DeSoto Grille & Lion's Den Pub – 15 East Liberty Street, 31401, 912-443-2000. *www.desotohilton.com*. Located in the lobby of the Hilton, with complimentary valet parking for restaurant/pub patrons. NFL happy hour and appetizer specials.

Distillery – 416 West Liberty Street, 31401, 912-236-1772. *www.distillerysavannah.com*. Craft beers, sweetgrass dairy cheese plate, pecan-encrusted catfish, and grilled asparagus. Crab cake sandwich.

The District Café and Eatery – 202 East Broughton Street, 31401, 912-443-0909. Butternut squash bisque, ham, apple and brie panini, and roasted cheese with chicken and avocado sandwich.

Driftaway Café – 7400 Skidaway Road in Sandfly, 31406, 912-303-0999. Casual coastal cuisine, including steaks, ribs, grouper sandwiches, turkey Reubens.

Dub's, a Public House – 225 West River Street, 31401, 912-200-3652. *www.dubspubsavannah.com*. Enjoy good food while you take in any sports event on one of the fifteen TVs. Sample craft beer and enjoy live music.

Elizabeth's on 37th Street – 105 East 37th Street, 31401, 912-236-5547. www.elizabethon37th.net. The elegance of this 1900s mansion sets the perfect tone for a southern coastal menu with house-grown herbs and edible flowers. Founded in 1981 by award-winning chef Elizabeth Terry and her husband Michael, this restaurant continues a tradition of excellence.

Ele's Fine Fusion – 7815 U.S. 80, 31410, 912-898-2221. *www.elesavannah.com*. Sushi rolls, Thai dishes, crunchy tempura, specialty martinis, sake. Pleasing ambience.

Fiddler's Crab House – 131 West River Street, 31401, 912-644-7172. *www.liveoakstore.com/fiddlersriverstreet*. Local seafood, including crab cakes, shellfish platters. Balcony seating overlooks the Savannah River.

Fire Street Food – 13 East Perry Street Lane, 31401, 912-234-7776. *www.firestreetfood.com*. Beer and wine, sushi burgers, wings, fried fish sandwiches.

Firefly Café – 321 Habersham Street, 31401, 912-234-1971. *www.fireflycafega.com.* Neighborhood charm on Troup Square. An emphasis on healthy dining, with pet-friendly outdoor seating. Saturday and Sunday brunch.

5 Spot – 4430 Habersham Street, 31405, 912-777-3021. *www.5spotsavannah.com.* A neighborhood kitchen and bar.

The Florence – 1 West Victory Drive, 31405, 912-234-5522. *www.theflorencesavannah.com.* Italian dishes with Tybee Island shrimp.

Flying Monk Noodle Restaurant – 5 West Broughton Street, 31401, 912-232-8888. *www.flywiththemonk.com.* Noodles with chicken, beef, or shrimp. Rice with chicken or pork.

45 Bistro – 123 East Broughton Street, 31401, 912-234-3111. *www.45bistro.com.* Built in 1852 and renovated in 1999, this restaurant offers private events and public dining. Can host groups of up to two hundred, or just two. Adjacent to the Marshall House Hotel.

Frali Gourmet – 217 West Liberty Street, 31401, 912-234-4644. Homemade pastas, gourmet vegetables in a jar, ready-made dinners to take out.

Funky Brunch Café – 304 East Broughton Street, 31401, 912-234-3050. *www.thefunkybrunchcafe.com.* Breakfast and lunch. Make your own pancakes at the table.

Gallery Espresso – 234 Bull Street, 31401, 912-233-5348. *www.galleryespresso.com.* European coffees and teas. Baked goods and desserts. Comfy chairs. Pet-friendly. Cyclists' favorite. Wall-art from local artists. Light fare.

Garibaldi's Café – 315 West Congress Street, 31401, 912-232-7118. *www.garibaldisavannah.com.*A local favorite for Italian food. Festive and romantic. Housed in the 1871 Germania Fire House in City Market.

Goose Feathers Café – 39 Barnard Street, 31401, 912-233-4683. *www.goosefeatherscafe.com.* Family-friendly café and bakery. Breakfast, sandwiches, soups, salads, and coffee. Try the Whoopie Pie.

Green Truck Pub – 2430 Habersham Street, 31401, 912-234-5885. *www.greentruckpub.com.* "Whole farm" burgers come with fried egg. Also on the menu: pimento cheeseburgers, veggie burgers. Beer choices.

The Grey – 109 Martin Luther King Jr. Blvd., 31401, 912-662-5999. *www.thegreyrestaurant.com.* Great food in the old Greyhound Bus Station in the Historic District.

Gryphon Tea Room – 337 Bull Street, 31401, 912-525-5880. Housed in a turn-of-the-century pharmacy, and offering tea scones, mango curry chicken sandwiches, and quiche, among other treats.

Henry's – 28 Drayton Street, 31401, 912-232-6628. *www.facebook.com/henrys28*. Early breakfast, lunch, plus a soup and salad bar. Easy on the pocketbook.

Huey's New Orleans Café – 115 East River Street, 31401, 912-234-7385. *www.hueysontheriver.com*. Authentic New Orleans Creole and Cajun cuisine and other southern dishes. Enjoy Mardi Gras on River Street.

J. Christopher's – 122 East Liberty Street, 31401, 912-236-7494. *www.jchristophers.com*. Housed in a converted gas station/garage. Bright and airy, with artwork on the walls. Great breakfast, full lunch menu.

Jazz'd Tapas Bar – 52 Barnard Street, 31401, 912-236-7777. *www.jazzdtapasbar.com*. A below-street-level gathering place for a specialty martini or eclectic Americanized tapas. Live entertainment six nights a week.

Jepson Café – 207 West York Street, 31401, 912-790-8833. *www.telfair.org/cafe*. Located on the second floor of the Jepson Center, the café serves up a light, refreshing menu.

Joe's Crab Shack – 504 East River Street. 31401, 912-232-1830. *www.joescrabshack.com*. Enjoy a bucket of shrimp, crab dip, or crispy calamari while sitting on the deck watching the ships come up the Savannah River.

Johnny Harris, a Savannah institution

This image taken from a placemat used at Johnny Harris's back in the day.

Johnny Harris – 1651 East Victory Drive, 31404, 912-354-7810. *www.johnnyharris.com*. A Savannah tradition. World-famous barbecue sauce. Steaks, seafood, and chicken. Dine with locals. Established 1924. The publisher of this Guidebook has been a regular customer since 1944, when there were carhops and even a small zoo out back. He still stops by for a pulled pork sandwich on every trip to Savannah.

Kayak Kafé – 1 East Broughton Street, 31401, 912-233-6044. *www.kayakkafe.net*. Healthy choices, fresh salads, seafood, and tacos. Popular with locals.

La Berry Yogurt – 225 West Broughton Street, 31401, 912-233-1900. *www.laberryfrozenyogurt.com*. Friendly service and delicious frozen yogurt flavors.

Lady and Sons – 102 West Congress Street, 31401, 912-233-2600. *www.ladyandsons.com*. Family atmosphere, southern cooking. Try the crab stew, fried green tomatoes, and pecan pie. Buffet and entrées. Gluten-free items. You'll love Paula Deen's cooking! Visit the Paula Deen gift shop.

Leoci's Trattoria – 606 Abercorn Street, 31401, 912-335-7027. *www.leocis.com*. Romantic and casual, offering beer and wine, along with artistically presented meals.

Leopold's Ice Cream – 212 East Broughton Street, 31401, 912-234-4442. *www.leopoldsicecream.com*. This is "the top of the charts" for ice cream. Old family recipes. Try the tutti-frutti or root beer floats. Lunch menu. Owned and operated by Hollywood movie producer Stratton Leopold and his wife, Mary. Decorated with movie posters, and the producer himself may be scooping your favorite flavor. Founded in 1919 by three immigrant brothers from Greece.

Leopold's Ice Cream – Original Location – Not an operating store

Liberty Street Grill (formerly the Brasserie 529) – 529 East Liberty Street, 31401, 912-235-2907. *www.libertystreetgrill.com*. A casual, relaxed neighborly atmosphere.

Local 11 Ten – 1110 Bull Street, 31401, 912-790-9000. *www.local11ten.com*. A block south of Forsyth Park. A stylish revamp of a midcentury bank. Local seasonal ingredients used in southern dishes. The rooftop deck "perch" is open in fine weather.

Love's Seafood

Love's Seafood – 6817 Basin Road, 31419 (U.S. Highway 17 South), 912-925-3616. *www.savannahepass.com/loves*. It's a good ten miles south of downtown Savannah on the Ogeechee River, but nowhere else can you get such delicious fresh-fried catfish. Operated by the Love family since 1949, the fresh seafood keeps the locals and the tourists coming.

Lulu's Chocolate Bar – 42 Martin Luther King Jr. Blvd., 31401, 866-461-8681. *www.luluschocolatebar.net*. The best desserts in the universe. Drinks, martinis, live music. A perfect end to the evening. Yum!

Ma Randy's – 530 Martin Luther King Jr. Blvd., 31401, 912-335-8843. Great soul food.

Mabel's Cupcake Emporium – 151 West Bryan Street, 31401, 912-341-8014. The vanilla cupcake is to die for.

Maxwell's – 109 Jefferson Street, 31401, 912-349-5878. *www.maxwellssavannah.com*. Wine bar with steaks, crab cakes, and poached pear salad.

McDonough's – 21 East McDonough Street, 31401, 912-233-6136. Good drinks and karaoke. Full service bar and restaurant.

Mellow Mushroom – 11 West Liberty Street, 31401, 912-495-0705. *www.mellowmushroom.com*. Pizza, hoagies, calzones, and salads.

The Melting Pot – 232 East Broughton Street, 31401, 912-349-5676. Four-course dining, or fondue cheese paired with that perfect glass of wine.

Molly MacPherson's Scottish Pub and Grill – 311 West Congress Street, 31401, 912-239-9600. *www.macphersonspub.com*. Shepherd's pie, potato scones, and a huge selection of single malt whiskies. Thursdays are open-mic night.

Moon River Brewing Company – 21 West Bay Street, 31401, 912-447-0943. *www.moonriverbrewing.com*. Great beers in a comfortable relaxed setting, with a variety of fresh foods. Grass-fed beef burgers.

Mrs. Wilkes Dining Room – 107 West Jones Street, 31401, 912-232-5997. *www.mrswilkes.com*. A Savannah tradition, offering platters of fried chicken, cornbread, sweet potato soufflé, black-eyed peas, and okra gumbo. The menu changes daily. Boardinghouse-style dining since 1943. Cash or checks.

Mrs. Wilkes Dining Room

Left photo: The line outside is worth the wait! *Right photo:* Boardinghouse-style dishes are great for sharing.

Noble Fare – 321 Jefferson Street, 31401, 912-443-3210. *www.noblefare.com*. Contemporary French cuisine. Clam soup, ahi tuna, scallops, steaks, duck.

Olympia Café – 5 East River Street, 31401, 912-233-3131. *www.olympiacafe.net*. Enjoy authentic Greek and Mediterranean food along with beautiful views of the river. We've never had a bad experience here.

One-eyed Lizzie's – 417 East River Street, 31401, 912-341-8897. Seafood, steaks, crab cakes, chicken fingers, fried shrimp, burritos.

The Olde Pink House – 23 Abercorn Street, 31401, 912-232-4286. *www.plantersinnsavannah.com/the-olde-pink-house*. Visitors and locals patronize this eighteenth-century mansion in the Historic District for new American fare. It has long enjoyed a haunted reputation! In cold weather you might want to sit by the cozy fireplace.

The Olde Pink House

Outback Steakhouse – 7 Drayton Street, 31401, 912-232-1611. *www.outback.com.* Delicious steaks, seafood, salads, and more.

Pacci – 601 East Bay Street, 31401, 912-233-6002. *www.paccisavannah.com.* An Italian kitchen and bar inside the Brice Hotel.

Panera Bread – 1 West Broughton Street, 31401, 912-236-0275. *www.panerabread.com.* Great sandwiches on fresh-baked bread.

Papa's Bar-B-Que and Seafood – 119-A Charlotte Road, 31410, 912-897-0236. *www.papasbar-b-que.com.* Making hungry people happy since 1972, on Whitemarsh Island.

Papillote – 218 West Broughton Street, 31401, 912-232-1881. *www.papillote-savannah.com.* Sit outside on the sidewalk of Broughton Street, and pretend you are in Paris. Smoked salmon and asparagus quiche, truffles, the soup du jour, and macarons, all prepared by a chef trained at the finest restaurants in Europe. Take out or eat in.

Pearl's Saltwater Grille – 7000 Laroche Avenue, 31406, 912-352-8221. *www.opentable.com/pearls-saltwater-grille.* Seafood, steaks, full menu. Offering delightful views of the creeks and marshes.

Persepolis – 41 Whitaker Street, 31401, 912-443-0414. Ethnic food, Persian, Iranian.

The Pirates' House – 20 East Broad Street, 31401, 912-233-5757. *www.thepirateshouse.com.* Family dining, in addition to a rousing good time and a

"The Nationally Famous Pirates' House"
Built in 1754 20 East Broad – Trustees' Garden, Savannah, Georgia

bounty of delicious food. Once an inn for seafarers in 1753, a Savannah "must not miss." Two of the fifteen dining rooms that make up the restaurant are in the Herb House, considered perhaps the oldest house in Georgia. Gift shop.

Public's Kitchen and Bar – 1 West Liberty Street, 31401, 912-200-4045. *www.thepublickitchen.com.* Modern American cuisine. Lump crabmeat, Eggs Benedict, cheese board, spinach salad.

Rancho Alegre Cuban Restaurant – 402 Martin Luther King Jr. Blvd., 31401, 912-292-1656. *www.ranchoalegrecuban.com.* Savor steaming plates of traditional Cuban food with up to twenty-three different features, plus everyday specials.

River House Seafood – 125 West River Street, 31401, 912-234-1900. *www.savannahriverhouse.com.* An 1820s cotton warehouse with atmosphere. Sit riverside, and enjoy local seafood. Try the chocolate cheesecake.

River Street Oyster Bar – 411 East River Street, 31401, 912-232-1565. Bring the family. Local seafood, raw oyster bar, happy hour, land lovers' choices.

River Street Riverboat Company – 9 East River Street, 31401, 800-786-6404. *www.savannahriverboat.com.* The *Savannah River Queen* and the *Georgia Queen* offer supper and entertainment. Sunday brunch and Saturday luncheon cruises available on this premier cruise line.

Rocks on the River – 102 West Bay Street, 31401, 912-721-3800. *www.bohemianhotelsavannah.com.* On top of the Bohemian Hotel on River Street, offering food and entertainment. Pizza oven, wine and beer, a cozy fire pit, and a tapas-style menu, along with drinks and martini choices. View of the Savannah River.

Ruan Thai Cuisine – 17 West Broughton Street, 31401, 912-231-6667. *www.myruanthai.com.* Authentic Thai restaurant. Tradition with a tasteful touch.

Russo's Seafood Restaurant – 209 East 40th Street, 31401, 912-341-8848. *www.russosseafood.com.* Locally owned. Order at the counter. Seafood comes from the proprietor's fish market next door.

Ruth's Chris Steak House – 111 West Bay Street, 31401, 912-721-4800. *www.ruthschris.com.* Happy hour, wines, cocktails, steaks, seafood, varied menu. Kim Polote's Jazz Trio usually performs on Fridays.

Sakura Japanese – 116 East Broughton Street, 31401, 912-234-9300. The sushi here is inexpensive but good. Try the green onion fry bread.

Sapphire Grill – 110 West Congress Street, 31401, 912-443-9962. *www.sapphiregrill.com.* In City Market, offering coastal cuisine and a full bar. Classy.

Savannah Coffee Roasters – 215 West Liberty Street, 31401, 912-352-2994. *www.savannahcoffeeroasters.com*. Offering a wide variety of special coffees, breads, and pastries served in-house or as takeout.

Savannah Rum Runners Bakery and Café – 324 West Bolton Street, 31401, 912-355-4177. *www.savannahrumrunners.com*. Sandwiches, salads, and soup du jour. Rum cakes, iced shortbread cookies.

Seasons Café – 10 Barnard Street, 31401, 912-349-6230. *www.seasonscafejapan.com*. Fast casual Japanese cuisine.

Sentient Bean – 13 East Park Avenue, 31401, 912-232-4447. *www.sentientbean.com*. Organic, fair trade, homemade food, drinks, art, and entertainment.

Seven Hundred Drayton – 700 Drayton Street, 31401, 912-721-5002. *www.mansiononforsythpark.com*. Located in an 1880s-era mansion on Forsyth Park. Offering eclectic specialties, a wine list, and the Grand Bohemian gallery. Fresh seafood and regionally inspired delicacies.

17 Hundred 90 Inn and Restaurant – 307 East President Street, 31401, 912-236-7122. *www.17hundred90.com*. Named for the year the building was constructed. Captures the authentic flavor of an eighteenth-century port hotel and restaurant.

Shrimp Factory – 313 East River Street, 31401, 912-236-4229. *www.theshrimpfactory.com*. Local seafood dishes, soups, salads, and desserts in a friendly setting, where you can watch the ships come and go. Lunch until 4:00 p.m. Dinner menu available after 4:00 p.m. The old cotton warehouse still has the original heart-pine beams and floors. The stones and the Savannah gray bricks have been there since the building's construction in 1826.

Sisters of the New South – 2605 Skidaway Road, 31404, 912-335-2761. *www.thesistersofthenewsouth.com*. Fried chicken, fish, shrimp, ox tails, gumbo, collard greens, fried okra, corn, butterbeans, squash, and yams.

Six Pence Pub – 245 Bull Street, 31401, 912-233-3151. *www.sixpencepub.com*. A British pub, offering Guinness, bangers and mash, shepherd's pie, and crème brulée, near Chippewa Square.

Skyler's – 225 East Bay Street, 31401, 912-232-3955. *www.skylersrestaurant.com*. The decor features brick interior walls and Windsor chairs. Enjoy Asian, European, and American cooking, including crab cakes, shrimp cocktails, and Vietnamese spring rolls.

Sly's Sliders and Fries – 1710 Abercorn Street, 31401, 912-239-4219. Comfort food, burgers, hot dogs, and fries.

Soho South Café – 12 West Liberty Street, 31401, 912-233-1633. *www.sohosouthcafe.com*. Where food is an art. Voted best business lunch. Sunday brunch.

Spanky's – 317 East River Street, 31401, 912-236-3009. *www.liveoakstore.com/spankys*. Home of the original chicken fingers. Great bar food, hand-battered spuds.

Spudnik – 416 West Broughton Street, 31401, 912-232-1986. From classic to exotic, Spudnik has plenty of baked potatoes. You might go just to see the new floor tiling made up of eighty thousand pennies.

Starbucks – 1 East Broughton Street, 31401, 912-447-6742. *www.starbucks.com*. Coffee or hot chocolate, as well as bakery items.

Sweet Melissa's – 103 West Congress Street, 31401, 912-443-1622. Jamaican jerk chicken, late-night pizza.

Sweet Potatoes – 6825 Waters Avenue, 31406, 912-352-3434. *www.sweetpotatoeskitchen.com*. Fried chicken, cheese grits, corn pudding, banana pudding, and the sweet potato of the day.

Tequila's Town Mexican Restaurant – 109 Whitaker Street, 31401, 912-236-3222. *www.tequilastown.com*. Simple, traditional Mexican food with diverse influences. Burritos, carnitas, seafood, grilled steak, and their unique Molcajete, a lava rock filled with grilled meats and special sauce and cheese.

Tondee's Tavern – 7 East Bay Street, 31401, 912-341-7427. *www.tondees.com*. Fresh local seafood in an 1850s bank building. Baby back ribs, quality steaks, crab-stuffed flounder. The eponymous tavern of Revolutionary War legend stood on the corner of Barnard and Broughton Streets, and a plaque marks the spot.

Top Deck – 125 West River Street, Rooftop, 31401 (Above the Cotton Sail Hotel), 912-436-6828. *www.topdeckbar.com*. Top Deck's prime location above the Cotton Sail Hotel offers exceptional views of the Savannah River and bridge and historic Bay Street. Craft cocktails, local brews, charcuterie and cheese board, pork and chicken sandwiches, shrimp and crab spring rolls, flatbreads and sliders.

Toucan Café – 531 Stephenson Avenue, 31405, 912-352-2233. *www.toucancafe.com*. A popular restaurant on the south side. Southern/Greek cuisine.

Tubby's Tank House – 115 East River Street, 31401, 912-233-0770. A view of the Savannah River. Grouper fingers, fresh seafood. Outdoor diners are cooled with a misting system. An additional location at Thunderbolt.

22 Square Restaurant and Bar – 14 Barnard Street, 31401, 912-233-2116. *www.savannah.andaz.hyatt.com/en/hotel/dining/22SquareRestaurant.html.* Inside the Andaz Hotel. Local food, farm to table.

Vic's on the River – 26 East Bay Street, 31401, 912-721-1000. *www.vicsontheriver.com.* Happy hour. Outdoor deck. This 1859 building once housed a cotton warehouse and a shipping company. Enter from Bay Street or take the lift up from River Street.

Vinnie Van Go-go's – 317 West Bryan Street, 31401, 912-233-6394. *www.vinnievangogo.com.* Thin hearty crust pizza. Will deliver in the downtown area.

Wall's Barbecue – 515 East York Street Lane, 31401, 912-232-9754. *www.wallsbarbecue.com.* Pulled pork, chicken, deviled crab, fried fish. Limited seating.

Wasabi's Fusion – 113 Martin Luther King Jr. Blvd., 31401, 912-233-8899. *www.sushisavannah.com.* Authentic sushi bar and open kitchen.

Whistle Stop Café – 303 Martin Luther King Jr. Blvd., 31401, 912-651-3656. *www.chsgeorgia.org/whistlestop-cafe.html.* Located next to the Savannah Visitor Center, this is the best place for a hot cup of coffee, peach cobbler, or fried green tomatoes. Dine in an authentic Central of Georgia railcar.

Wicked Cupcakes – 38 Whitaker Street, 31401, 912-298-0040. *www.wickedcakesofsavannah.com.* Great variety of cakes and cupcakes.

Wild Wing Café – 27 Barnard Street, 31401, 912-790-9464. *www.windwingcafe.com.* Hot wings, cold beer. Live entertainment daily, sit inside or out.

Wiley's Championship BBQ – 4700 U.S. 80, 31410, 912-201-3259. *www.wileyschampionshipbbq.com.* Wiley and Janet McCrary have brought their fabulous barbecue from Atlanta to Savannah, and they continue to win awards for the best-tasting BBQ anywhere around.

Windows Chop House – 2 West Bay Street (in the Hyatt Hotel), 31401, 912-238-1234. *www.windowsworldsavannah.com.* Overlooks the Savannah River. Full menu.

Wright Square Café – 21 West York Street, 31401, 912-238-1150. *www.wrightsquarecafe.com.* A casual European café where you'll savor the aromas of baking bread, coffee beans, herbs, and fruits. Fine chocolates.

The Wyld Dock Bar – 2740 Livingston Avenue, 31406, 912-692-1219. *www.thewylddockbar.com.* Enjoy a tapas style dinner sitting outside on a dock overlooking the Herb River.

Zunzi's – 108 East York Street, 31401, 912-443-9555. *www.zunzis.com.*
A tiny café with outdoor tables offering Swiss, Italian, South African, and Dutch takeout dishes.

Zunzi's 2 – 9 Drayton Street, 31401, 912-443-1554. *www.zunzis.com.*
The same good food as found at the Zunzi's located just a few blocks down the street, but this one opens at 4:00 p.m. to catch the evening crowd. This location has been a lunch spot under other names for many years, and it still has the same bar that was used in Grand Central Terminal before being shipped to Savannah over a hundred years ago.

Postcard showing the Old Hotel DeSoto,
demolished in 1968

Lodging in the
Historic District

Welcome to the "Lodging" chapter of the *Savannah Guidebook*. Savannah's picturesque Historic District has been a center for commerce for three centuries, and remains so today. Keep in mind that new hotels open and others close on a regular basis. Changes will be noted on our website, *www.savannahguidebook.net*.

Hotels

Andaz Savannah – 14 Barnard Street, 31401, 912-233-2116 or 888-591-1234. *www.savannah.andaz.hyatt.com*. A boutique Hyatt hotel in the heart of the Historic District on Ellis Square. Offering a relaxed urban vibe and southern sophistication.

B Historic Savannah Hotel – 320 Montgomery Street, 31401, 912-921-5300 or 954-641-9006. *www.bhistoricsavannah.com*. Offering Internet, pool, suites, and a fitness center.

Best Western Plus – 412 West Bay Street, 31401, 912-233-1011 or 800-780-7234. *www.promenadesavannah.com.* Walk to River Street, restaurants, museums, and squares.

Bohemian Hotel – 102 West Bay Street, 31401, 912-721-3800 or 801-468-4032. *www.bohemianhotelsavannah.com.* A spectacular rooftop bar with live music, overlooking River Street. View of the impressive Savannah River bridge.

Brice on Washington Square – 601 East Bay Street, 31401, 912-238-1200 or 877-482-7423. *www.bricehotel.com.* Southern charm with contemporary style in the old Coca-Cola bottling plant. Formerly the Mulberry Inn.

Comfort Suites – 630 West Bay Street, 31401, 912-629-2001 or 800-4choice. *www.meetsavannah.com/promo1.* Welcoming staff, nice rooms, reasonable rates.

Cotton Sail Hotel – 126 West Bay Street, 31401, 912-200-3700. Situated on the top three floors of a 150-year-old brick-and-timber-framed building, now a boutique hotel overlooking the Savannah River. Rooftop lounge and bar. Located in the old Ryan Building next to the Bohemian Hotel.

Courtyard Savannah – 415 West Liberty Street, 31401, 912-790-8287 or 800-321-2211. *www.courtyard.com/savdt.* A new hotel near City Market and River Street.

DeSoto Hilton – 15 East Liberty Street, 31401, 912-232-9000 or 800-hiltons. *www.desotohilton.com.* Modern and spacious. Near Madison Square, the Green Meldrim House, and E. Shaver's Bookseller.

Double Tree by Hilton – 411 West Bay Street, 31401, 912-790-7000 or 888-370-0998. *www.doubletree.com.* An easy walk to west end of River Street. Near antique malls and City Market.

East Bay Inn – 225 East Bay Street, 31401, 912-238-1225 or 800-500-1225. *www.EastBayInn.com.* Some rooms are pet-friendly. Skyler's restaurant on site.

Embassy Suites – 605 West Oglethorpe Avenue, 31401, 912-721-6900 or 866-319-5034. Two-room suites and a contemporary atrium area.

Hampton Inn and Suites – 603 West Oglethorpe Avenue, 31401, 912-721-1600 or 800-426-7866. *www.hamptonsavannah.com.* Near the Visitor Center, Roundhouse Railroad Museum, and Tricentennial Park.

Hampton Inn – 201 East Bay Street, 31401, 912-231-9700 or 800-Hampton. *www.hotelsavannah.com.* A short walk to River Street, restaurants, and shopping.

Hilton Garden Inn – 321 West Bay Street, 31401, 912-721-5000 or 800-445-8667. Near River Street and antique malls.

Holiday Inn Savannah Historic District – 15 Martin Luther King Jr. Blvd., 31401, 912-790-1000 or 800-368-7764. *www.fourpoints.com/historicsavannah.* An easy walk to City Market, restaurants, River Street, and shopping.

Holiday Inn Express – 199 East Bay Street, 31401, 912-231-9000 or 888-465-4329. *www.savannahlodging.com.* An easy walk to River Street and shopping.

Hotel Indigo – 201 West Bay Street, 31401. *www.ihg.com.* Under renovation – opening March 2016 as an upscale boutique hotel with 252 rooms in the historic Guckenheimer building (1851). Near City Market and River Street.

Hyatt Regency – 2 West Bay Street, 31401, 912-238-1234 or 800-233-1234. *www.savannah.hyatt.com.* Elevators to River Street. Next-door to City Hall.

The Mansion – 700 Drayton Street, 31401, 912-238-5158 or 888-711-5114. *www.mansiononforsythpark.com.* Overlooking Forsyth Park, where guests can enjoy jogging, picnics, and outdoor concerts.

Marshall House – 123 East Broughton Street, 31401 912-644-7896 or 800-589-6304. *www.marshallhouse.com.* Check out the interesting shops on Broughton Street. Good restaurants and nightlife nearby.

Olde Harbour Inn – 508 East Factor's Walk, 31401, 912-234-4100 or 800-553-6533. *www.oldeharbourinn.com.* Faces the Savannah River. Twenty-four suites. Once a cotton warehouse. Pets welcome.

Planters Inn – 29 Abercorn Street, 31401, 912-232-5678 or 800-554-1187. *www.plantersinnsavannah.com.* On Reynolds Square. An easy walk to River Street and nearby art galleries.

Quality Inn – 300 West Bay Street, 31401, 912-236-6321 or 844-800-5293. *www.qualityinnhistoricsavannah.com.* Close to River Street, art galleries, and shopping.

Residence Inn – 500 West Charlton Street, 31401, 912-233-9996 or 800-331-3131. *www.marriott.com/savdv.* Near the historic Roundhouse Railroad Museum, the Visitor Center, and Tricentennial Park.

River Street Inn – 115 East River Street, 31401, 912-234-6400 or 800-253-4229. *www.riverstreetinn.com.* In a restored 1800s cotton warehouse. Just a short walk to the Ships of the Sea Maritime Museum, the First African Baptist Church, and the Telfair Museum of Art and the Jepson Center.

Savannah Marriott Riverfront – 100 General McIntosh Blvd., 31401, 912-233-7722 or 800-285-4100. *www.marriott.com/SAVRF.* At the east end of River Street. Hosts conventions, weddings, and meetings.

Springhill Suites by Marriott – 150 Montgomery Street, 31401, 912-629-5300 or 888-682-1233. *www.marriott.com.* An easy walk to sites and attractions in the Historic District. Free breakfast.

Staybridge Suites – 301 East Bay Street, 31401, 912-721-9000 or 866-251-2776. *www.staybridge.com.* Pet-friendly, free hot breakfast, laundry, fitness center.

Studio Homes at Ellis Square – 120 West Bryan Street, 31401, 912-233-6820 or 800-424-6423. Convenient to shopping, City Market, and museums.

Westin Savannah Harbour Golf Resort – 1 Resort Drive, 31421, 912-201-2090 or 800-782-9488. *www.westinsavannah.com.* A new hotel across the Savannah River. Drive over the new bridge or catch a ferryboat. Gift shop.

Bed and Breakfast Inns

As with hotels, new inns open and others close regularly. For the latest information, check our website at *www.savannahguidebook.net.*

109 West Liberty Street – 31401, 912-232-6633. *www.109west.net.* The William A. Thomas House (1871) rents as one property or can be divided into three separate units. Ideal for family reunions.

Amethyst Inn at Sarah's Garden – 402 East Gaston Street, 31401, 912-234-7716. *www.amethystinnsavannah.com.* Family- and pet-friendly

Amethyst Inn at Sarah's Garden
Courtesy of the artist, Jill Howell

Catherine Ward House Inn

Courtesy of the artist, Jill Howell

Azalea Inn and Gardens – 217 East Huntingdon Street, 31401, 912-236-6080 or 800-582-3823. *www.azaleainn.com.* Casual elegance, parking, full breakfast.

Ballastone Inn – 14 East Oglethorpe Avenue, 31401, 912-236-1484 or 800-822-4553. *www.ballastone.com.* A comfortable inn next to the Juliette Low Birthplace. Beer and wine bar.

Catherine Ward House Inn – 118 East Waldburg Street, 31401, 912-234-8564 or 800-327-4270. *www.catherinewardhouseinn.com.* Located in the Victorian District. In a quiet neighborhood close to Forsyth Park.

Dresser Palmer House – 211 East Gaston Street, 31401, 912-238-3294 or 800-671-0716. *www.dresserpalmerhouse.com.* An elegant inn near Forsyth Park. Ideal for weddings.

Eliza Thompson House – 5 West Jones Street, 31401, 912-236-3620 or 800-348-9378. *www.elizathompsonhouse.com.* A beautifully restored townhouse on a charming brick street near Mrs. Wilkes Dining Room.

Foley House Inn – 14 West Hull Street, 31401, 912-232-6622 or 800-647-3708. *www.foleyinn.com.* In the heart of the Historic District on Chippewa Square. Fireplaces, antiques, Oriental rugs.

Forsyth Park Inn – 102 West Hall Street, 31401, 912-233-6800. *www.forsythparkinn.com.* An imposing 1896 Queen Anne Victorian mansion overlooking Forsyth Park.

Galloway House – 107 East 35th Street, 31401, 912-658-4419. *www.thegallowayhouse.com.* Featuring a lovely garden and a breezy sitting porch.

Gastonian – 220 East Gaston Street, 31401, 912-232-2869 or 800-322-6603. *www.gastonian.com.* Casual elegance. Rooms and suites. Antiques, Persian rugs. Walk to Forsyth Park.

Kehoe House
Courtesy of the artist, Jill Howell

Green Palm Inn – 548 East President Street, 31401, 912-447-8901 or 888-606-9510. *www.greenpalminn.com.* A small gingerbread classic near Greene Square. Fodor's guide gives it a "thumbs up."

Hamilton Turner Inn – 330 Abercorn Street, 31401, 912-233-1833 or 888-448-8849. *www.hamilton-turnerinn.com.* An imposing mansion on Lafayette Square near the Cathedral of Saint John the Baptist.

Inn at McDonough's – 19 East McDonough Street, 31401, 912-233-6136. Luxury rooms on Chippewa Square next to the Savannah Theatre. The historic Colonial Park Cemetery is just one block away.

Joan's on Jones – 17 West Jones Street, 31401, 912-234-3863 or 888-989-9806. *www.joansonjones.com.* On a quaint brick street near the famous Mrs. Wilkes Dining Room. Cozy and elegant.

Kehoe House – 123 Habersham Street, 31401, 912-232-1020 or 800-820-1020. *www.kehoehouse.com.* An imposing red brick Victorian mansion on Columbia Square.

McMillan Inn – 304 East Huntingdon Street, 31401, 912-201-2128. *www.mcmillaninn.com.* An 1885 Italianate Revival inn in an old neighborhood. Hot breakfast. Walk to restaurants, shops, and Forsyth Park.

The Olde Savannah Inn – 217 East Gaston Street, 31401, 912-247-8254. *www.theoldesavannahinn.com.* A luxury bed and breakfast inn. Walk to Forsyth Park for outdoor concerts, jogging, and café.

Park Avenue Manor – 107 West Park Avenue, 31401, 912-233-0352. *www.parkavenuemanor.com.* An 1889 Victorian inn near a yoga center, health food store, and Forsyth Park, where you can enjoy jogging and concerts.

Presidents' Quarters – 225 East President Street, 31401, 912-233-1600 or 800-233-1776. *www.presidentsquarters.com.* On Oglethorpe Square next to the Owens-Thomas House museum.

Roussell's Garden Bed and Breakfast – 208 East Henry Street, 31401, 912-239-1415. *www.roussellsgarden.com.* An 1888 Queen Anne–style home. Lots of warm hospitality.

Sanctuary Place Inn – 202 West Duffy Street, 31401, 912-224-7072. *www.sanctuaryplacesavannah.com.* Two stunning church lofts, c. 1889. Two cottages, a courtyard, and free wifi. A Victorian house is also available.

Savannah Bed and Breakfast Inn – 117 West Gordon Street, 31401, 912-238-0518 or 888-238-0518. *www.savannahbnb.com.* Enjoy the feeling of a private home in a gracious inn. The Mercer House is nearby. Courtyard garden.

17 Hundred 90 Inn – 307 East President Street, 31401, 912-236-7122 or 800-487-1790. *www.17hundred90.com.* Near the Owens-Thomas House Museum on Oglethorpe Square. An easy walk to River Street.

Spanish Moss Inn – 425 East Bay Street, 31401, 912-655-9366. *www.bedandbreakfast.com.* King-size beds, heart of pine floors, and four paired wood-burning fireplaces.

The Stephen Williams House – 128 West Liberty Street, 31401, 912-495-0032. *www.thestephenwilliamshouse.com.* A tastefully restored inn near Orleans Square and the Jepson Center for the Arts.

Whitaker-Huntingdon Inn – 601 Whitaker Street, 31401, 912-232-8911. *www.whinn.com.* This circa-1831 home overlooks thirty-two green acres of Forsyth Park and its historic fountain. Heart-pine floors, twelve-foot ceilings, and modern amenities.

The Zeigler House Inn – 121 West Jones Street, 31401, 912-233-5307 or 866-233-5307. *www.zeiglerhouseinn.com.* Located on brick-cobbled Jones Street, under a canopy of live oaks. Nineteenth-century charm. All suites have kitchenettes.

Golf Courses

The following public golf courses are within an easy drive of the Historic District.

 **Bacon Park Golf Course, Live Oak Course** – 1 Shorty Cooper Drive, 31406, 912-354-2625. N32° 00. 387´ W081° 04. 900´ Eight miles from the Historic District. Nine holes, putting/chipping greens, driving range.

Bacon Park Golf Course, Cypress Course – 1 Shorty Cooper Drive, 31406, 912-354-2625. N32° 00. 387´ W081° 04. 900´
Eight miles from the Historic District. Nine holes, putting/chipping greens, driving range.

Bacon Park Golf Course, Magnolia Course – 1 Shorty Cooper Drive, 31406, 912-354-2625. N32° 00. 387´ W081° 04. 900´
Eight miles from the Historic District. Nine holes, putting/chipping greens, driving range.

The Club at Savannah Harbor, Savannah Harbor Course – 2 Resort Drive, 31421, 912-201-2240. N32° 05. 200´ W081° 04. 960´
Three miles from the Historic District, across the Savannah River. Eighteen holes, putting/chipping greens, driving range.

Crosswinds Golf Club, Crosswinds Course – 232 James B. Blackburn Drive, 31408, 912-966-1909. N32° 08. 104´ W081° 13. 918´
Eighteen miles from the Historic District. Near the Savannah–Hilton Head International Airport. Eighteen holes, putting/chipping greens, driving range.

Crosswinds Golf Club, Par 3 Course – 232 James B. Blackburn Drive, 31408, 912-966-1909. N32° 08. 104´ W081° 13. 918´
Eighteen miles from the Historic District. Near the Savannah–Hilton Head International Airport. Nine holes, putting/chipping greens, driving range.

Henderson Golf Club, Henderson Memorial Course – 1 Al Henderson Drive, 31419, 912-920-4653. N32° 00. 283´ W081° 16. 081´
Fourteen miles from the Historic District. Eighteen holes, putting/chipping greens, driving range.

Hunter Golf Course, Hunter Course – 1546 South Perimeter Road, Building 8205, 31409, 912-315-9115. N32° 00. 104´ W081° 08. 003´
Seven miles from the Historic District. Enter only at the Montgomery Street gate. Eighteen holes, putting/chipping greens, driving range.

Mary Calder Golf Club, Mary Calder Course – West Lathrop Avenue, 31402, 912-238-7100. N32° 05. 787´ W081° 07. 954´
Five miles from the Historic District. Nine holes, putting green, driving range.

Southbridge Golf Club, Southbridge Course – 415 Southbridge Blvd., 31405, 912-651-5455. N32° 04. 001´ W081° 13. 575´
Seven miles from the Historic District. Off I-16, Exit 160 south. Eighteen holes, putting/chipping greens, driving range.

Wilmington Island Club, Wilmington Island Course – 501 Wilmington Island Road, 31410, 912-897-1612. N32° 00. 203´ W080° 59. 652´
Seven miles from the Historic District. Eighteen holes, putting/chipping greens, driving range.

Fun Activities for Youngsters

Bamboo Farm and Coastal Gardens – 2 Canebrake Road, 31419, 912- 921-5460. *www.bamboocaes.uga.edu*. Pets on leashes are allowed. Pick fruit in season, and enjoy plant sales and other special events.

Captain Mike's Dolphin Tour – 1 U.S. 80, 31328, 912-786-5848. *www.tybeedolphins.com*. See shrimp boats and watch bottle-nosed dolphins at play. Go past the Cockspur Island Lighthouse.

Dolphin Magic – 313 East River Street, 31401, 912-897-4990. *www.dolphin-magic.com*. Depart from River Street. You'll see historic sites en route to the dolphin playground.

Forsyth Park – At the south end of the Historic District. The wooded arboretum at the north end of the park features a central fountain, and leads down to acres of green grass, benches, playground equipment, and tennis courts. Take a picnic, and feed the pigeons. Great for rugby, Frisbee, sunbathing, and dog walking.

Fun Zone – 1040 Highway 80, Pooler, Georgia 31322. A quarter-mile east of I-95, at Exit 102, 912-330-9860. *www.poolerfunzone.com*. Go-kart racing, miniature golf, a large arcade, paintball, kiddy land, and refreshments.

Jepson Center for the Arts, ArtZeum – 207 West York Street, 31401, 912-790-8800. *www.telfair.org*. Exciting hands-on activities in a learning gallery designed to inspire creative approaches to art.

Lake Mayer Park – Montgomery Crossroads at Sallie Mood Drive, 31406, 912-652-6780. Boat rental, with a ramp and dock, along with fishing, picnic benches, tennis courts, and a track. Take bread to feed the ducks. Jogging track with fitness course.

National Museum of the Mighty Eighth Air Force – 175 Bourne Avenue, Pooler, Georgia, 31322, 912-748-8888. *www.mightyeighth.org*. Powerful exhibits of the units, men, and machines of the United States Eighth Air Force. Moving and memorable. Well worth the easy drive.

North Island Surf and Kayak – Old U.S. 80 on Lazaretto Creek, Tybee Island, 31328, 912-786-4000. *www.northislandkayak.com*. See dolphin, otter, osprey, and wading birds. Paddle to Cockspur beacon. Guides available.

Oatland Island Wildlife Center – 711 Sandtown Road, 31410, 912-898-3980. *www.oatlandisland.org*. Here you can explore trails through the woods and boardwalks over the marshes. Bobcats, eagles, alligators, bison, and wolves in their natural habitats. Check the website for events. Sheep-to-shawl, cane grinding, and more. Bring bug spray.

Puppet People – 3119 Furber Avenue, 31404, 912-355-3366. *www.puppetpeople.com*. Most popular party place in town! Puppet shows, corporate events. Puppet-making workshops for all ages.

Roundhouse Railroad Museum – 601 West Harris Street, 31401, 912-651-6823. *www.chsgeorgia.org/roundhouse*. Antebellum railroad repair buildings. Scheduled train rides, railcar, handcar, baggage car tours. All aboard! Children's awesome museum in same complex.

Savannah Children's Museum – 655 Louisville Road, 31401, 912-651-4292. *www.savannahchildrensmuseum.org*. Featuring an outdoor hands-on museum called Exploration Station, as well as a spiral slide, a life-size maze, and much more. Built in and around the ruins of Central of Georgia Railway buildings.

Savannah Children's Theatre – 2106 East Victory Drive, 31404, 912-238-9015. *www.savannahchildrenstheater.org*. Featuring rotating plays by young actors.

Savannah Movie Tours – 912-234-3440. *www.savannahmovietours.com*. Savannah is a popular movie town. From a comfortable air-conditioned bus, you'll see where scenes from Forrest Gump, Something to Talk About, Glory, Midnight in the Garden of Good and Evil, and other movies were filmed.

Savannah National Wildlife Refuge – U.S. Highway 17, South Carolina, 29927, 843-784-2468. Six miles from the Historic District. *www.fws.gov/savannah/*.

Open Monday–Saturday, 9:00 a.m.–4:30 p.m. Twenty-nine thousand acres of freshwater marshes, tidal rivers, creeks, and bottomland hardwoods. You're likely to spot teal, pintails, wood ducks, geese, wading birds, bald eagles, wood storks, and great horned owls. **Alligators often bask on the banks and the roads. Do not get out of the car or let your dog out. Alligators are unpredictable, dangerous, and fast. Do not feed them!**

Savannah Safari Walking Adventure – 912-353-9999. *www.savannahsafari.com.* Explore an artistic jungle in the Historic District as you look for dolphin downspouts, iron birds, clay lions and lizards, and other surprises. Girl Scouts can earn official badges! Safari books are available at the Girl Scout Birthplace Gift Shop, 10 East Oglethorpe Avenue, 31401, 912-233-4501, or Girl Scout First Headquarters, 330 Drayton Street, 31401, 912-232-8200. Follow the easy map in the Safari books.

Lion in front of Andrew Low House found on the Savannah Safari

Ships of the Sea Maritime Museum – 41 Martin Luther King Jr. Blvd., 31401. 912-232-1511. *www.swhipsofthesea.org.* A stunning garden, and a beautiful collection of models of historic ships, including the *Ann*, the *Wanderer*, the *Titanic*, and more. Workshops offered.

Skidaway Island State Park – 51 Diamond Causeway, 31411, 912-598-2300. *www.gastateparks.org/skidawayisland.* Great for hiking and biking. Fun programs, including a sandpiper trail hike, a bird walk, crafts, and more.

Tybee Island – U.S. 80 East, sixteen miles from the Historic District. Clean sandy beaches. Buy a bucket, spade, and kite at T. S. Chu's store. Doggies are not allowed on the beaches, but do not leave them in the car. Cars can heat up to deadly temperatures fast! Visit the Marine Science Center near the pier with its collection of sea creatures and information about the sea turtle project, 912-786-5917. *www.tybeemarinescience.org.*

Tybee Light Station and Museum – 30 Meddin Drive, 31328, 912-786-5801. *www.tybeelighthouse.org.* Climb the 178 steps to the top of the oldest and tallest lighthouse in Georgia. Egad! Oh my gosh! What a view!

Uncle Ted's Walking Tours – 912-921-4455. *www.awalkthroughsavannah. bravehost.com.* Themed tours include A Child's View of Savannah, Savannah History, Spirits After Dark, a Johnny Mercer stroll, and more!

Savannah and Connor Jelks in foaming waves at Tybee

University of Georgia's Marine Education Center and Aquarium – 30 Ocean Science Circle, 31411, 912-598-2496. *www.uga.edu/aquarium.* Nature trails, a saltwater aquarium, and picnic tables on a high bluff. Touch tank.

Horse and Carriage Tours

Carriage Tours of Savannah – 912-236-6756. *www.carriagetoursofsavannah.com.*

Historic Savannah Carriage Tours – 912-443-9333. *www.savannahcarriage.com.* Follow the horse's tail, and the guide's tale of ghosts, ghouls, and goblins in attics and graveyards. Learn about the fascinating story of Savannah from 1733 up to the present.

Annual Events

Welcome to Savannah! Oh my! Where are our manners? What would you like to drink and what would you like to do? There's a-plenty to choose from!

Savannah has been named Condé Nast's most polite and hospitable city. Many exciting events throughout the year offer tourists and locals alike an opportunity to experience this hospitality firsthand.

The Indian mico (chief) Tomochichi welcomed James Oglethorpe and his passengers from the ship *Ann* with barbecued wild hogs and deer around a campfire. President George Washington was greeted with festivities in Johnson Square. James Monroe took a cruise on the SS *Savannah* in 1819 and attended a party in the elegant Scarbrough House on West Broad Street. President William Taft kept a parade waiting while he ate venison and waffles at the home of Juliette Gordon Low in 1909.

This chapter contains a month-by-month list of some of Savannah's annual events. Check websites for specific dates and further information.

January

First Tuesday Tour at City Hall
Residents and visitors can get a free behind-the-scenes look at Savannah City Hall and view special exhibits highlighting chapters of Savannah's history. Reservations required at *www.savannahga.gov/firsttuesdaytours*, or call Luciana Spracher at 912-651-6411 or e-mail her at *Lspracher@savannahga.gov*.

The Tybee Polar Bear Plunge
Invigorate both body and soul at the south end of the island with a cleansing and frigid plunge into the ocean. Yikes! Burrrrr! Every January 1 at noon. 912-663-1099. *www.tybeepolarplunge.com*.

Martin Luther King Jr. Day Celebration
Honor the life of this civil rights pioneer with a parade and festivities. Marching bands of youngsters make this a lively occasion. 912-234-5502. *www.mlksavannah.com*.

Savannah Low Country Home and Garden Show
Gardening seminars, kitchen and bath trends, pools and spas, hardscapes. *www.savannahhomeandgardenshow.com*.

Savannah Tire Hockey Classic
A collegiate hockey tournament. 912-644-6414. *www.savannahhockeyclassic.com*.

Super Museum Sunday
Many museums and historic sites in the city and throughout coastal Georgia are open, with no admission fee. 912-651-2125. *www.georgiahistory.com*.

Telluride Film Festival
Films at the SCAD Theatre educate, inspire, and motivate audiences about issues that matter, cultures worth exploring, environments worth preserving, adventures worth pursuing, and conversations worth having. 912-525-5050. *www.mountainfilm.org*.

February

First Tuesday Tour at City Hall
Residents and visitors can get a free behind-the-scenes look at Savannah City Hall and view special exhibits highlighting chapters of Savannah's history. Reservations required at *www.savannahga.gov/firsttuesdaytours*, or call Luciana Spracher at 912-651-6411 or e-mail her at *Lspracher@savannahga.gov*.

Art and Oysters
A ticketed event at the Pin Point Heritage Center, 9924 Pin Point Road. The featured artist in 2014 was Jonathan Green. Enjoy the featured art and artist, in addition to music and Gullah Geechee cooking. Oysters cooked outside, along with a taste of oxtails, deviled crab, and red rice. 912-667-9176.

Black Heritage Festival
Performing and visual arts, ethnic cuisine, crafts, and family fun. 912-691-6847. *www.savannahblackheritagefestival.com*.

Critz Tybee Run Fest
A 5K, 10K, half-marathon, and 2.8-mile beach run, plus a one-mile kiddie run. If you run them all, you will have run a full marathon, 26.2 miles. Tybee Island, 31328. *www.critztybeerun.com*.

Georgia History Festival
Educational programs for kindergarten through twelfth grade. Celebrating the founding of the Georgia colony in 1733, history comes to life with a parade and the two-day Colonial Faire and Muster at the Wormsloe State Historic Site. 912-651-2125. *www.georgiahistory.com*.

Historic Savannah Foundation's Race for Preservation
A 5K/10K run, beginning and ending in Forsyth Park. 912-233-7787. *www.myHSF.org*.

Savannah Book Festival
A world-class literary event centered on Telfair Square, with author presentations in churches, on the squares, and at the Telfair Museum. 912-525-5050. *www.savannahbookfestival.org*.

Savannah Irish Festival
A weekend of traditional Irish music and dancing to celebrate the arts and culture of Ireland and Irish Americans. 912-232-3448. *www.savannahirish.org*.

Telfair Ball and Art Auction
An elegant event on the social scene. Fine food, cocktails, and dancing to benefit the Telfair Museum. 121 Barnard Street, 31401, 912-790-8844. *www.telfair.org/events.*

March

First Saturday on the River
Featuring food vendors, strolling musicians, and artists displaying their work in tents. 912-234-0295. *www.riverstreetsavannah.com.*

First Tuesday Tour at City Hall
Residents and visitors can get a free behind-the-scenes look at Savannah City Hall and view special exhibits highlighting chapters of Savannah's history. Reservations required at *www.savannahga.gov/firsttuesdaytours,* or call Luciana Spracher at 912-651-6411 or e-mail her at *Lspracher@savannahga.gov.*

Bamboo Farm Spring Garden Festival
Educational talks, children's activities, plant vendors, arts and crafts. 2 Canebrake Road, 31419, 912-921-5460. *www.coastalgeorgiabg.org.*

Fort McAllister's Confederate Fort Occupation
Confederate soldiers demonstrate their daily duties and fire muskets and cannons. Join the candle lantern walk at 7:00 p.m. 912-727-2339. *www.gastateparks.org/fortmcallister.*

March of Dimes Shamrock Run
A 5K race and fitness walk. Easy kiddie run. 912-354-5900. *www.marchofdimes.com.*

Oatland Island Sheep to Shawl Festival
Watch sheep-shearing, carding, spinning, dyeing, and weaving a garment. Crafts, games, hayrides, and more. 711 Sandtown Road, 31410, 912-395-1212. *www.oatlandisland.org.*

St. Patrick's Day Parade
The day begins with mass at the Cathedral of St. John the Baptist, then a breakfast of eggs and green grits. Celebrations begin two weeks prior to the parade, including the Investiture of the Grand Marshal, the greening of the fountain in Forsyth Park, Tara Feis, the Celtic Cross Mass and Ceremony, and the Sergeant William Jasper Green Ceremony. 912-233-4804. *www.savannahsaintpatricksday.com.*

Tybee Island St. Patrick's Day Parade
Usually held on a Saturday near St. Patrick's Day (March 17), the Tybee St. Patrick's Day parade begins at City Hall and continues to the south end of Butler Avenue. Floats are decorated in green, and marchers celebrate in family-friendly Tybee style.

Savannah Music Festival
This two-week-long festival is the largest musical arts event in Georgia and one of the most distinctive cross-genre music festivals in the world. Artists and audiences are united in Savannah for classical music, jazz, dance, film, narrative programs, and musicals. 912-234-3378. *www.savannahmusicfestival.org.*

Savannah Tour of Homes and Gardens
Sponsored by Christ Church and the Historic Savannah Foundation. Visit fine homes and enjoy seminars, evening events, excellent food, and warm hospitality. 912-234-8054. *www.savannahtourofhomes.org.*

Tara Feis Irish Festival
An outdoor celebration of Irish culture, featuring stage performances, dancing, music, crafts, and food in Emmet Park. 912-651-6417. *www.savannahga.gov/arts.*

April

First Saturday on the River
Featuring food vendors, strolling musicians, and artists displaying their work in tents. 912-234-0295. *www.riverstreetsavannah.com.*

First Tuesday Tour at City Hall
Residents and visitors can get a free behind-the-scenes look at Savannah City Hall and view special exhibits highlighting chapters of Savannah's history. Reservations required at *www.savannahga.gov/firsttuesdaytours*, or call Luciana Spracher at 912-651-6411 or e-mail her at *Lspracher@savannahga.gov.*

Fine Arts on the River
Fine art, music, beverages, and live performances at this delightful al fresco event. 912-234-0295. *www.riverstreetsavannah.com.*

Liberty Mutual Legends of Golf PGA Championship Tour
Attracts many all-time top players teeing off at the Westin Savannah Harbor Resort. 912-236-1333. *www.lmlog.com.*

NOGS Tour of Hidden Gardens

This popular event features admission to private walled gardens. Visit hidden sanctuaries shaded by ancient oaks. 912-961-4805. *www.gardenclubofsavannah.org.*

Savannah College of Art and Design International Festival

Ethnic cuisine, dance, music, art, and a global fashion show in Forsyth Park. 912-525-5231. *www.scad.edu.*

Tybee Wine Festival

Enjoy fine wines and delicious food to benefit the restoration of the Tybee Post Theater. Help turn Tybee's old 1930s movie theater into an operating performing arts and cultural center. 912-663-1099.

May

First Saturday on the River

Featuring food vendors, strolling musicians, and artists displaying their work in tents. 912-234-0295. *www.riverstreetsavannah.com.*

First Tuesday Tour at City Hall

Residents and visitors can get a free behind-the-scenes look at Savannah City Hall and view special exhibits highlighting chapters of Savannah's history. Reservations required at *www.savannahga.gov/firsttuesdaytours,* or call Luciana Spracher at 912-651-6411 or e-mail her at *Lspracher@savannahga.gov.*

Historic Savannah Foundation May Day Festival for Preservation

Check the website for information about this highly worthwhile event. 912-233-7787. *www.myhsf.org.*

Massie May Festival

Children welcome spring with a queen and her court and colorful dances, such as Dancing Around the Maypole. 207 East Gordon Street (in Calhoun Square), 31401, 912-395-5070. *www.massieschool.com.*

Memorial Day Program at Fort McAllister

Learn all about Confederate soldiers—their diet, living conditions, clothing, and medicines, plus musket and cannon firings. 912-727-2339. *www.gastateparks.org/fortmcallister.*

Memorial Day Program at Wormsloe State Historic Site
This event commemorates the War of Jenkins' Ear, Georgia's first war, which took place between 1739 and 1748. 912-353-3023. *www.gastateparks.org/wormsloe*.

Savannah Challenge Tennis Tournament
Exciting matches in a tournament with professionally ranked players. 910 Franklin Creek Road, 31411 (at the Landings Club), 912-598-3500. *www.savannahchallenger.com*.

Savannah Scottish Games
Celebrate Celtic heritage with the sounds, tastes, and visual images that Highlanders would have experienced as early as A.D. 100. Watch youthful dancers and competitors. 912-233-6017. *www.savannahscottishgames.com*.

SCAD Sand Arts Festival
Imaginative sand sculptures and sand castle creations using shells, seaweed, and objects found on the beach at the north end of Tybee. 912-525-5231. *www.scad.edu*.

Tybee Beach Bum Parade
Riders on floats are armed with water-shooting gizmos. Spectators return fire with buckets of water, squirt guns, and hoses. A bad hair day for everyone! 912-786-5444. *www.tybeevisit.com*.

June

First Saturday on the River
Featuring food vendors, strolling musicians, and artists displaying their work in tents. 912-234-0295. *www.riverstreetsavannah.com*.

First Tuesday Tour at City Hall
Residents and visitors can get a free behind-the-scenes look at Savannah City Hall and view special exhibits highlighting chapters of Savannah's history. Reservations required at *www.savannahga.gov/firsttuesdaytours*, or call Luciana Spracher at 912-651-6411 or e-mail her at *Lspracher@savannahga.gov*.

Savannah Asian Festival
Arts and crafts, live musicals, martial arts, ethnic cuisine, and dances of Korea, Vietnam, Indonesia, Polynesia, and Thailand. 912-651-6417. *www.savannahga.gov/cityweb/culturalaffairsweb.nsf*.

July

First Saturday on the River
Featuring food vendors, strolling musicians, and artists displaying their work in tents. 912-234-0295. *www.riverstreetsavannah.com.*

First Tuesday Tour at City Hall
Residents and visitors can get a free behind-the-scenes look at Savannah City Hall and view special exhibits highlighting chapters of Savannah's history. Reservations required at *www.savannahga.gov/firsttuesdaytours*, or call Luciana Spracher at 912-651-6411 or e-mail her at *Lspracher@savannahga.gov.*

July 3 Fireworks Spectacular at Tybee
Starting at dusk, fireworks are set off at the pier, but will be visible from anywhere on the island. 912-786-5444.

July 4 Fireworks Spectacular on River Street
Starting at dusk, fireworks are synchronized with music simulcast live on the radio. 912-234-0295. *www.riverstreetsavannah.com.*

July 4 at Fort McAllister
Celebrate our nation's birthday with Civil War troops firing salutes for all who died in the cause of freedom. Special games. 912-727-2339. *www.gastateparks.org.*

August

First Saturday on the River
Featuring food vendors, strolling musicians, and artists displaying their work in tents. 912-234-0295. *www.riverstreetsavannah.com.*

First Tuesday Tour at City Hall
Residents and visitors can get a free behind-the-scenes look at Savannah City Hall and view special exhibits highlighting chapters of Savannah's history. Reservations required at *www.savannahga.gov/firsttuesdaytours*, or call Luciana Spracher at 912-651-6411 or e-mail her at *Lspracher@savannahga.gov.*

The Declaration of Independence
The document is read aloud, just as it was after it arrived in Savannah on August 10, 1776. Join in the commemorative festivities held at Wormsloe Historic Site during the Georgia's First Fourth program. 912-353-3023. *www.gastateparks.org/wormsloe.*

Old Fort Jackson Auction and Low Country Boil
Sponsored by the Coastal Heritage Society. Watch the sun set, and enjoy live music, good food, cannon firings, fireworks, and an auction. 912-232-3945. www.chsgeorgia.org.

Savannah Craft Brew Festival
Hosted by the Westin Hotel. Enjoy beers from around the world, an oyster roast, and fireworks. 912-644-6452. www.savannahcraftbrewfest.com.

Savannah Riverkeepers Annual Paddlefest –
Join the Riverkeepers at the Paddlefest or at the Roast on the River to benefit the endangered Savannah River. 912-228-5158. www.savannahriverkeeper.org.

Savannah Voice Festival
A two-week-long festival of concerts, films, classes, and workshops with over one hundred vocalists from all over the country. 855-766-7372. www.savannahvoicefestival.org.

September

First Saturday on the River
Featuring food vendors, strolling musicians, and artists displaying their work in tents. 912-234-0295. www.riverstreetsavannah.com.

First Tuesday Tour at City Hall
Residents and visitors can get a free behind-the-scenes look at Savannah City Hall and view special exhibits highlighting chapters of Savannah's history. Reservations required at www.savannahga.gov/firsttuesdaytours, or call Luciana Spracher at 912-651-6411 or e-mail her at Lspracher@savannahga.gov.

Gray's Reef Ocean Film Festival
Celebrate the beauty and bounty of the oceans and learn about ways to protect them. Sponsored by NOAA Gray's Reef National Marine Sanctuary. Three days of films and talks with the filmmakers. www.graysreef.noaa.gov.

Labor Day at Fort McAllister
See Civil War soldiers at their chores, from blacksmithing and cooking to woodworking. Live music, food, and games. 912-727-2339. www.fireworks.gastateparks.org/fortmcallister.

Ogeechee Riverkeeper Rivers Rock
Music, delicious food, and craft beer, a silent auction and raffle, all for the benefit of the Ogeechee River. 124 Savannah Avenue, Suite 2-B, Statesboro, Georgia, 30459, 866-942-6222. *www.ogeecheeriverkeeper.org.*

Pin Point Seafood Festival
Sponsored by the Sweetfield of Eden Baptist Church at Pin Point. Enjoy steamed crab, shrimp, and fish while learning about the history of Pin Point. Seafood served by residents of Pin Point, many of whom are descendants of slaves. Proceeds benefit the Greenbriar Children's Center. 9992 Pin Point Road, 912-355-9072.

Savannah Jazz Festival
A free top-notch week-long jazz festival with an impressive lineup of musicians. 912-232-2222. *www.savannahjazzfestival.org.*

Tools and Skills That Built a Colony at Wormsloe State Historic Site
Actors show how Georgia's first colony was built. 912-353-3023. *www.gastateparks.org/wormsloe.*

October

First Saturday on the River
Featuring food vendors, strolling musicians, and artists displaying their work in tents. 912-234-0295. *www.riverstreetsavannah.com.*

First Tuesday Tour at City Hall
Residents and visitors can get a free behind-the-scenes look at Savannah City Hall and view special exhibits highlighting chapters of Savannah's history. Reservations required at *www.savannahga.gov/firsttuesdaytours,* or call Luciana Spracher at 912-651-6411 or e-mail her at *Lspracher@savannahga.gov.*

Battlefield Memorial March
The Coastal Heritage Society reenacts the Battle of Savannah on October 9 at 7:00 a.m. and honors the soldiers who fought here and those killed or wounded in battle. A series of four lectures at the Savannah History Museum make up the annual Revolutionary Perspectives Lecture Series. 912-651-6840. *www.chsgeorgia.org.*

Candle Lantern Tour of Fort McAllister
Stroll these historic grounds and watch soldiers at their nightly duties. You'd better stay with your guide, or you might be captured as a spy. 912-727-2339. *www.gastateparks.org/fortmcallister.*

Coastal Empire Fair
A petting zoo, stunts, rides, hay bales, pumpkins, sugarcane, and candied apples. 912-354-3542. *www.coastalempire.com.*

Day on the Island
Sponsored by the Isle of Hope United Methodist Church every two years. House tours, an art market, and lunch. 912-355-8527. *www.iohumc.com.*

Flannery O'Connor Fall Lecture Series
Check the website for information about lectures and readings from the works of this important novelist and short story writer. 207 East Charlton Street, 31401, 912-233-6014. *www.flanneryoconnorhome.org.*

Historic Savannah Foundation Fall Gala
Held in a venue chosen for its preservation and historic relevance. Cocktail parties, fine dining, silent auction, dancing, and an "After Glow" party. 912-233-7789. *www.myhsf.org.*

Oktoberfest on the River
Wiener dog races, bratwurst, accordion polka music. An oom-pah good time. *www.riverstreetsavannah.com.*

Picnic in the Park
The City of Savannah sponsors Peter Shannon and the Savannah Philharmonic Orchestra with a free outdoor concert at Forsyth Park. Listeners enjoy classical and popular music. Prizes are awarded for the most spectacular picnic spread. 912-651-6417. *www.savannahga.gov.*

Savannah Film Festival
Films from around the world by professional and emerging student filmmakers. Panel discussions unveil the art of filmmaking. 912-525-5050. *www.scad.edu/experience/filmfest.*

Savannah Folk Music Festival
Top folk musicians perform in a variety of music styles and genres in a free three-day event. 912-786-6953. *www.savannahfolk.org.*

Savannah Food Day Festival
Build your awareness of healthy and sustainable foods. Featuring vendors, exhibitors, and workshops. 912-440-4345. *www.wellfedsavannah.com/foodday.*

Savannah Greek Festival
Greek food, dancing, church tours, a market, and live music. Hellenic Community Center, 14 West Anderson Street, 912-236-8256. *www.savannahgreekfest.com.*

Savannah's Yellow Fever Epidemic of 1820

Live presentations every Friday and Saturday evening in October at the Isaiah Davenport House. Not for the faint of heart. This story is based on real events. 912-236-8097. *www.davenporthousemuseum.org.*

The Shalom Y'all Jewish Food Festival

Try Jewish cuisine in Forsyth Park. Family entertainment with music, dance, and magic and puppet shows. 912-233-1547. *www.mickveisrael.org.*

St. Vincent's Academy Annual Tour of Homes and Tea

Self-guided tours of the 1845 convent and private homes. Tea on the grounds of the convent. 912-236-5505. *www.svatourofhomes.com.*

Tybee Island Pirate Fest

Swashbucklers in a parade with entertainment, costume contests, children's games, and the Thieves Market with treasures, grog, and grub. 912-786-5393. *www.tybeepiratefest.com.*

November

First Tuesday Tour at City Hall

Residents and visitors can get a free behind-the-scenes look at Savannah City Hall and view special exhibits highlighting chapters of Savannah's history. Reservations required at *www.savannahga.gov/firsttuesdaytours*, or call Luciana Spracher at 912-651-6411 or e-mail her at *Lspracher@savannahga.gov.*

Boat Parade of Lights –

Sailboats and yachts in festive holiday decorations parade up the Savannah River. Fireworks. Bring the family. 912-201-2000. *www.westinsavannah.com/events.*

Children's Book Festival

Hail the joy of reading and storytelling with major authors and illustrators. Many coastal authors, arts and crafts, and an international tent. 912-652-3600. *www.liveoakpl.org/SCBF.*

Johnny Mercer's Birthday

Every November, on a day close to Johnny Mercer's birthday (November 18), David Oppenheim gives a multimedia presentation called Up Close and Personal, focusing on the life of Johnny Mercer, his songs, and his music. Free. Southwest Chatham Public Library, 14097 Abercorn Street, 31419, 912-925-8305. *www.livoakpl.org.*

Oatland Cane Grinding and Harvest Festival –
Old-timey hearth cooking, cane syrup, apple butter, blacksmithing, spinning, and more. 711 Sandtown Road, 31410, 912-395-1212. *www.oatlandisland.org.*

Rock 'n Roll Savannah Marathon
Enjoy a run through Savannah's historic district and beyond with the Rock 'n Roll Marathon or Half Marathon. Enjoy the music of a different rock band at every mile along the route. 912-644-6414. *www.runrocknroll.competitor.com./savannah.*

Savannah Food and Wine Festival
A week-long celebration of wine and food in Savannah's historic district and festive riverfront. From the Connoisseur Wine Dinners to A Taste of Savannah in Ellis Square, participants will enjoy a variety of culinary treats. 912-232-1223. *www.savannahfoodandwinefest.com.*

Savannah Seafood Festival
Family fun, fishing, shrimp boat and champ boat races, along with live music and performers. 912-234-0295. *www.riverstreetsavannah.com.*

SMA Angels Charity Ball
This gala event benefits spinal muscular atrophy. 912-727-4762. *www.smaangels.org.*

St. John's Church Holly Days Bazaar –
A fund-raiser for charity, featuring a white elephant sale, a treasure room, book sale, and more. 1 West Macon Street, 31401, 912-232-1251. *www.stjohnssav.org.*

Telfair Art Show
An open-air show with paintings, pottery, prints, sculpture, photography, furniture, and much more. 121 Barnard Street, 31401, 912-790-8800. *www.telfair.org.*

Veterans Day Parade
Every November the city honors World War II veterans with a parade that begins in Forsyth Park and continues around the squares and down Broughton Street.

December

First Saturday on the River
Featuring food vendors, strolling musicians, and artists displaying their work in tents. 912-234-0295. *www.riverstreetsavannah.com.*

First Tuesday Tour at City Hall
Residents and visitors can get a free behind-the-scenes look at Savannah City Hall and view special exhibits highlighting chapters of Savannah's history. Reservations required at *www.savannahga.gov/firsttuesdaytours,* or call Luciana Spracher at 912-651-6411 or e-mail her at *Lspracher@savannahga.gov.*

Christmas on the River and Lighted Holiday Parade
Featuring live holiday entertainment, a children's play area, and the arrival of St. Nick in a colorful parade. 912-234-0295. *www.riverstreetsavannah.com.*

City Market Holiday Open House
Holiday lights in the courtyard, along with carolers and Christmas treats. Jefferson at West St. Julian Street. *www.savannahcitymarket.com.*

Colonial Christmas at Wormsloe State Historic Site
A reenactment of the holiday festivities of the early colonists. Includes carols, treats, and burning the Yule log. 912-353-3023. *www.gastateparks.org/wormsloe.*

Enmark Savannah River Bridge Run
Run, walk, crawl, or creep. It's not only about running. Creative runners can dress up absurdly for cash prizes. Benefits the J. C. Lewis Cancer Research Pavilion. 912-644-6414 or 912-355-3527. *www.savannahriverbridgerun.com.*

Fort McAllister Winter Muster, Battle and Candle Lantern Tour
Watch Confederate troops prepare for a short bloody battle. Visitors view the destruction of war firsthand. 912-727-2339. *www.gastateparks.org/fortmcallister.*

Historic Savannah Foundation Luminary Fun Night with Santa
Enjoy a walk along the enchanting luminary trail, sing carols on hayrides, and have some hot chocolate. Held at Skidaway Island State Park. *www.gastateparks.org/events.*

Holiday Tour of Homes
Broughton Street is ablaze with lights. The squares are decorated with holiday ribbons. Afternoon and evening house tours. (Savannah Downtown Neighborhood Association) 912-236-8362. *www.dnaholidaytour.com.*

Rockin' New Year's Eve

Check the website for activities ranging from cruises and fireworks to theater, dinners, and more, as you get ready to usher in the New Year. *www.keytosavannah.com/event/rockin-new-years-eve.*

Savannah Santa Train

Guests in pajamas ride a #50 steam engine decked out for Christmas. Meet Santa. Admission fee. 912-651-6823. *www.southernmamas.com.*

Savannah Harbor Festival of Lights

Cross the bridge to Hutchinson Island to drive through the beautiful festival of lights near the Westin Hotel. Nativity scene, live animals, rides, bonfires, and over eighty brightly lit holiday scenes. *www.savannahharborfoundation.com/festival-of-lights*

Savannah's Victorian Tea

Enjoy a cup of tea in the formal living room of an old home. Downtown Garden Club ladies wear authentic Victorian dresses for this popular occasion. *www.savannahvictoriantea.com.*

Tree of Light Ceremony

Held in Forsyth Park and sponsored by Hospice Savannah, this candlelit ceremony honors our loved ones who have passed on. *www.hospicesavannah.org.*

A Few Old Savannah Recipes

Red Rice

Yields 6 to 8 servings

½ cup diced green peppers	2 8-oz. cans tomato sauce
½ cup olive oil	2 8-oz. cans of water
¾ cup diced onions	½ teaspoon salt
10 strips cooked-to-crispy bacon	2 cups white or brown rice

Sauté onion and pepper in oil. Add crumbled bacon. Mix in tomato sauce, water, salt, and sugar. When boiling, add rice; stir. Bring to a full boil. Cover and simmer on low heat for 15 minutes. Remove lid and stir rice with a fork. Place a piece of brown kitchen paper over the skillet, so moisture won't condense on lid and drip onto rice. Cover skillet again with lid over the paper. Cook on lowest heat for 15 minutes or until moisture is absorbed.

Susan Mason's Crab Cakes

Yields 8 servings

½ cup mayonnaise (use Hellmann's)

1 red bell pepper, finely chopped

2 green onions (scallions), with white and tender green parts finely chopped

2 tablespoons Dijon mustard

2 teaspoons Old Bay Seasoning

1/8 teaspoon cayenne pepper

1 dash Worcestershire sauce

2 large egg yolks

2 pounds jumbo lump crabmeat

6 cups fresh bread crumbs

Vegetable oil for frying

Mix together bell pepper, green onions, mustard, Old Bay, cayenne, Worcestershire, and egg yolks. Gently stir in crabmeat. Put bread crumbs on cookie sheet. Mold the crab cake with one hand and pat with bread crumbs with the other. Form into 8 crab cakes, 3 inches wide and ½ inch thick. Each cake will need ¾ cup of bread crumbs. Heat 4 cups of oil in a 12-inch-wide skillet over medium-high heat. Add a single layer of crab cakes and fry in oil. Turn three or four times until crispy on the outside, about five minutes on each side. Drain on paper towels. Serve hot!

Corn Pudding

Yields 8 servings

8 ears of corn

1 pint milk

2 beaten eggs

1 tablespoon butter

½ cup chopped bell pepper

½ cup chopped mushrooms

½ cup shredded cheddar cheese

Cut corn off 8 ears. Mix with all other ingredients. Sprinkle cheese on top. Bake 45 minutes at 350° or until brown around the edges and not wobbly in the center.

Hoppin' John

Yields 12 servings

2 cups dried black-eyed peas

1 cup chopped celery

1 cup chopped onion

¾ cup chopped ham or hog jowl

½ cup chopped bell pepper

1 cup rice (not instant)

Soak peas overnight in water. Drain. Put ingredients in stainless steel Dutch oven. Cover with water and simmer with lid on for 2–3 hours. Drain and collect 2 cups of the liquid. Pour into peas. Stir in rice. Cover and cook until rice is done. This dish will bring good luck for the new year.

Shrimp 'n Grits

Yields 6 servings

1 pound local shrimp, cooked and deveined

1 cup yellow stone-ground grits

3 tablespoons butter

1 cup sliced scallions

1 cup shredded cheese—your choice

5 slices bacon, cooked and crumbled

2 tablespoons chopped parsley

Salt and pepper to taste

Blanch shrimp—do not cook all the way, or shrimp will get tough. Cook grits according to directions on bag. Brown scallions in butter. Add all ingredients to cooked grits. Sprinkle cheese on top. Bake at 375° for 30 minutes.

Syllabub

Yields 4 servings

¼ cup sweet white wine

½ cup sugar

zest and juice of ½ lemon

1 cup heavy whipping cream

Combine wine, sugar, lemon juice, and lemon zest. Beat cream until it starts to thicken. Add wine mix. Whisk until fluffy with peaks. Serve over berries in season. Garnish with crushed amaretti.

Prepare the chaise longue for a nap with sweet dreams!

Fabled Chatham Artillery Punch as Brewed by Ken

Chatham Artillery Punch was first devised in Savannah during Colonial times and brewed in ice-filled horse watering buckets. Tradition has it that when President Monroe was in Savannah in 1819 for the sailing of the first steamship across the Atlantic, he was entertained on a river trip and made the acquaintance of Chatham Artillery Punch. Many a later celebrity has tested their ability to imbibe the suave and deceitful brew. Its taste is mild, but it conquers like a cyclone.

Concoct in a two and a half gallon glass container

8 cups green tea (Erewhon Yama Moto)

1 pound brown sugar (Dixie Crystals – whose home is Savannah!)

1 pint maraschino cherries

Juice of 7 lemons

Juice of 7 oranges

3 liters Catawba or Rhine wine (Rosegarden)

1 liter St. Croix Rum (Mt. Gay Repined, Eclipse, or Barbados or Cruzan VI)

1 liter brandy (Paul Masson/Hennessy)

1 liter rye whiskey (Old Overholt straight Rye)

1 liter gin (Gordon's)

1 pint Benedictine

Mix, stir, then let stand for twenty-four hours, or up to one year. Stir often. Serve with caution! *Upon assessing the ingredients, the less adventurous may wish to dilute the brew with 25 percent champagne. Call Ken if you need the antidote!*

Trunks and Bloomers

Savannah's Famous Flowering Foliage

Drawings by Lynda Potter

Flowering Plants

Azalea (*Rhododendron*)—An evergreen shrub that bursts into color in spring and summer. There are many varieties and sizes, in shades of pink, red, and white.

Camellia (*Camellia japonica*)—Featuring rich, glossy green leaves on an evergreen shrub that can become a tree. It blooms in fall and winter in myriad shades of red, pink, and white.

Spanish Moss (*Tillandsia usneoides*)
Featuring slender, gray tendrils that shroud trees and fences. It's actually a member of the pineapple family. It has no roots, but absorbs water from the humid air; home to red bugs (chiggers).

Trees

Crape Myrtle (*Lagerstroemia indica*)
A lovely ornamental tree, summer blooming in white, pink, red lavender.

Dogwood (*Cornus florida*)
A deciduous flowering tree that grows wild in the woods and showers white blossoms in spring.

Chinese Tallow (*Sapium sebiferun*)
A fast-growing deciduous tree with leaves shaped like Chinese lanterns and "popcorn" seed pods prized by flower arrangers.

Live Oak
(*Quercus virginiana*)
The state tree
of Georgia. This hardy slow-grower abounds
along Savannah's streets and in the squares.

Magnolia (*Magnolia grandiflora*)
Featuring fragrant creamy-white blossoms
from spring into summer, and lustrous green
leaves year-round. Its attractive fruit cones produce
bright red berries.

Vines

Japanese and Chinese Wisteria (*floribunda and sinensis*)
Hardy vines that produce fragrant lavender and white
clusters in springtime.

**Carolina Jessamine
(*Gelsemium sempervirens*)**
A native vine with
sweet-smelling
yellow flowers
that appear in
early spring.

Public Safety
and Emergency Care

We hope that you won't need these services while you are in our fine city, but if you do, here is a handy reference of the hospitals, urgent and dental care facilities and pharmacies as well as local veterinarians, locksmiths and news radio.

Emergency Services

Emergency (Fire, Police, Ambulance) 911

Crime Stoppers/Silent Witness 912-234-2020

Emergency Preparedness 800-237-3239

Missing Persons 912-652-6500

Coast Guard Search and Rescue (www.gocoastguard.com) 912-786-5106

Hospitals

Candler Hospital – 5353 Reynolds Street, 31405. 912-819-6000. *www.sjchs.org.*

Memorial University Medical Center – 4700 Waters Avenue, 31405. 912-350-8000. *www.memorialhealth.com.*

St. Josephs Hospital – 11705 Mercy Blvd., 31419. 912-819-4100. *www.sjchs.org.*

Urgent Walk-in Care

Urgent Care 24/7 – 912-234-2273. *www.urgentcare247.com.* Check the website for new locations. Adults and children. **Open 24 hours daily.**

- **Historic District** | 210 Fahm Street, Savannah, 31401.
- **Midtown** | 1202 East DeRenne Avenue, Savannah, 31406.
- **Pooler** | 9 Mill Creek Circle, Suite A-1, Pooler, 31322.
- **Tybee Island** | 602 1st Street, Suite A, Tybee Island, 31328.
- **Whitemarsh Island** | 4753 Highway 80 East, Ste 300, Savannah, 31410.

Southern Urgent Care – 4717 Highway 80 East, Suite H, Savannah (Whitemarsh Island, Midway between Tybee and downtown Savannah), 31410. 912-898-2227. *www.southernuc.com.* Master Card, Visa, Discover Card, American Express, personal check, cash, and most insurance coverage. **Open Monday–Friday, 8 a.m.–8 p.m.; Saturday and Sunday, 9 a.m.–5 p.m.**

St. Joseph/Candler Immediate Med – 361 Commercial Drive at Eisenhower, 31406. 912-355-6221. **Monday–Friday, 9 a.m.–8 p.m.; Saturday, 9 a.m.–5 p.m.; Sunday, Noon - 5 p.m.** *www.yourimmediatecarecenters.com.*

Nearby Pharmacies

CVS – 119 Bull Street, 31401. 912-232-1129. **Pharmacy hours Monday–Saturday, 8 a.m.–8 p.m.; Sunday, 10 a.m.–6 p.m.** *www.cvs.com.*

Walgreens – 700 East DeRenne Avenue, 31405. 912-354-4853. **Open 24 hours daily.** Fifteen minute drive from historic district. Drive-through pharmacy. *www.walgreens.com.*

Dental Service

Emergency Dental Service – 310 Eisenhower Drive, 31406. 912-351-0615. Tuesday-Friday, 11:30 a.m.–7:30 p.m.; Saturday 10 a.m.–2 p.m. **Emergency help anytime 24/7/365 with a phone call.** Mobile unit. *www.emergencydentalservice.com.*

Veterinary Care

Savannah Animal Care – 510 West Bryan Street, 31401. 912-335-1200. Located in the historic district. **Monday–Friday, 8 a.m.–6 p.m.** Appointments other times upon request.

Forsyth Park Animal Hospital – 513 Whitaker Street, 31401. 912-349-3953. Located in the historic district. **Monday–Friday, 8 a.m.–5 p.m.**

Central Animal Hospital – 2417 Bull Street, 31401. 912-234-4772. **Monday–Friday, 8 a.m.–6 p.m.; Saturday, 8 a.m.–1 p.m.** *www.centralanimalhospitalsav.com.*

Savannah Veterinary Emergency Clinic – 335 Stephenson Avenue, 31405. 912-355-6113. Five miles from Historic District. **Monday–Friday, 6 p.m.–8 a.m.; Saturday, Noon to Monday at 8 a.m.** *www.savannahemergencyvet.com.*

Locksmiths

Pop-a-Lock – 912-234-0810 (Downtown) or 912-925-0041 (Southside).

Georgia Keys Locksmiths – 912-335-1055

Bradley Lock and Key – 912-232-2148

Local Radio – 24 hours

News Radio WTKS – 1290 AM/ 97.7 FM. 912-964-7794 or 912-947-1290.

Artists and Photographers

Vivian Austin grew up in the Midwest but always had a love for the Southeast and the Coast. She moved to Savannah in 2002 and immediately discovered Tybee Island. She began to pursue photography as an art form and, in particular, loves taking photographs of the ocean, the beach, and the wildlife found there.

Susie Grantham Chisholm was born and raised in Savannah, where she grew up in a home that valued artistic expression. Her father was an architect and her mother had a degree in interior design, and Susie's natural artistic talent was encouraged and cultivated with private art instruction during her childhood. After a career in graphic design, Susie turned to sculpture and embraced the challenges of working in three dimensions.

In addition to Savannah, her public commissions can be seen in Summerville, South Carolina; Columbus, Georgia; Azel, Texas; Hilton Head Island, South Carolina; Ridgeland, South Carolina; Valley Forge, Pennsylvania; Aiken, South Carolina; Boston, Massachusetts; and Benson Park Sculpture Garden, Loveland, Colorado. She is an elected member of the National Sculpture Society. *www.susiechisholm.com*

Daniel L. Grantham Jr. is a lifelong Savannahian. For over forty years he has worked as a graphic designer and photographer for clients throughout the country. His photos have been published in numerous national publications, including Time-Life Books, the *New York Times*, *Newsweek*,

Time, and several popular music magazines. A sampling of his graphic design work and photography can be found at *www.DanielGrantham.com.*

Robb Helfrick lives in Atlanta and specializes in location photography for editorial and corporate clients. His photographs have appeared in *Atlanta* magazine, *Town & Country, Sky, Hemispheres, National Geographic Traveler, National Parks,* and *Travel Holiday* magazine, as well as in many books and calendars. He is a recipient of the Leonard Foote Memorial Award for Excellent in Conservation Photography.

Jill J. Howell is from Eastman, Georgia. She graduated summa cum laude from the Savannah College of Art and Design in 2009. Her ink wash drawings depict southern architecture and landscaping, as well as nautical maps of the Eastern Seaboard. She is currently working on a Madison, Georgia, collection and accepts private commissions. She teaches drawing at the Local Color Gallery in Sandfly. Her portraits of dogs and cats capture the uniqueness of these beloved family pets. *www.jilljhowell.com.*

Jonas N. Jordan, our cover photographer, graduated from North Georgia Technical College in 1974 with a degree in photography. He was employed at Fitz/Symm Photography in Augusta, Georgia, before returning to Savannah in 1977 to pursue a freelance photojournalism career. We are honored to use his image of the Cathedral of Saint John the Baptist on our cover. Jonas stood on the top of Drayton Towers to capture this stunning image.

Dan Kaufman began his lifelong vocation as an artist exhibiting his take on Jackson Pollock in the Bowers Museum in 1965, and continuing as an architectural photographer whose work would hang alongside that of Julius Shulman in the Chinese-American Museum in 2011.

Today Dan has brought his passion for architectural photography and the history of Savannah as a founding American city to his current work at *VintageSavannah.com* and *StudioKaufman. com.* His twenty-first-century vintage photos and greeting cards are available at the Downstairs Gallery.

Pamela Lee moved to Savannah in 1975. She is intrigued with the architectural elements of this city—the beauty of the tree canopy and the waterfront scenery. Her focus on detail distinguishes her highly recognizable style. Her drawings have enhanced cookbooks and guidebooks and have been reproduced on canvas bags for several house museums. Her architectural renderings appear in two Tour of Homes booklets for the Savannah Homebuilders' Association. Her prints and note cards are available at many local fine gift shops and house museums. *pamelaleeart@gmail.com.*

Jean Lim earned a BFA in interior design and an MFA in furniture design from the Savannah College of Art and Design in Savannah. Since then, Jean has worked in Australia, Asia, the United States, and Africa designing and building theater sets, illustrating for publications, and preserving antiques and historic buildings. She currently lectures with the Built Environment faculty at Uganda Martyrs University.

Billy Nelson, sculptor, was commissioned by the Hispanic Society at Armstrong State University to create a bronze portrait bust of Hernando DeSoto, as shown on page 113 of this volume.

Haywood Nichols, a sculptor and native Savannahian, lives in the house where he grew up. His work has been featured in many art exhibitions in Savannah and elsewhere, as well as in private collections throughout the country. He has worked in wood, stone, wax, and other materials. Many of his recent pieces have been cast in bronze.

Jeri Nokes, a Georgia native, is a freelance lifestyle and travel photographer who studied at the Savannah College of Art and Design. She spends her free time adventuring and traveling the world, documenting her journey along the way. To her, photography is a window to a world that positively captures time and space and veils the negative side of people and places. She hopes her photographs will inspire people to view the world in the same beautiful light in which she sees it. *www.snapsavannah.com*

Augusta Oelschig (1918–2000) was born in Savannah and graduated from the first class of Armstrong Junior College. She received a BFA degree with an education minor from the University of Georgia in 1939 and did graduate study at Auburn University, Mexico City College, and the New School for Social Research in New York City. Oelschig studied with Emma Wilkins, Lamar Dodd, Henry Lee MacFee, Alexander Brook, and Justino Fernandez, as well as with Diego Rivera and José Clemente Orozco in Mexico City.

She studied most recently with Dr. Horace Kallen and William Scharf of New York City. Oelschig's training encompassed approaches and techniques inspired by the Old Masters and by modern art movements, from traditional Postimpressionism through more contemporary influences.

Lynda K. Potter reveals her love for flowers in our chapter "Trunks and Bloomers." Her drawings offer Abstract Impressionist perspectives on realistic subject matter. Lynda's work is in many corporate collections and has been published on magazine covers and in the book *How to Succeed as an Artist in Your Hometown*. She is a member of Signature Gallery in City Market in Savannah.

Matthew Propst grew up in Hickory, North Carolina. He has a BA in English from the University of North Carolina at Greensboro, and an MFA in visual arts from the Vermont College of Fine Arts. He moved to Savannah to enjoy the huge arts community, and he currently enjoys living downtown. His work is frequently featured in *The South* magazine and represented in several southeast galleries. His best-known book, *Savannah Cemeteries*, is a beautiful souvenir for those who have visited Savannah and a great way to see and learn about Savannah's final resting places for those who have yet to make the journey.

Dr. Preston Russell is a retired physician, painter, historian, and writer. He lives with his wife in Savannah's Historic District. He is the author of *The Low Country: From Savannah to Charleston*, a beautiful book containing eighty-five of his paintings known for capturing the spirit of the region. He is the author of several other books, and his paintings have been displayed in regional art shows as well as in private homes and museums through the United States and Europe.

Charles St. Arnaud (1939–2014) is the author of *Bonaventure Cemetery: Savannah, Georgia*, featuring his color photographs and commentary on this historic cemetery. Born in Aurora, Illinois, Charles received a bachelor's degree from the University of Nebraska and a master's degree from the University of Richmond. He retired from the army in 1991 with the rank of brigadier general, after a distinguished career and thirty-two years of active service. After his retirement, he and his wife, Carol, settled in Savannah, where he served on the boards for CASA, the BSA, the Better Business Bureau, Justice for Children, and the Bonaventure Historical Society.

Kitty Strozier (1948–2006) was a talented artist and painter. She lived almost all of her life on Tybee Island, Georgia. She could often be seen walking her pet iguana, Lizzie Jonell, on the beach at Tybee, attracting the attention of other beach strollers, who always enjoyed engaging her in conversation.

Herbert Yai-Sun Woo (1930–1998) was one of Savannah's foremost artists. He grew up near Isle of Hope with six brothers and three sisters. There the children grew vegetables, milked the cow, and gathered eggs. Young Herbert practiced sketching and studied dimensions and light patterns. Seldom thinking of the money he could make, he often made gifts of his artwork. He felt God had given him his talent, and he was pleased to share it. His work hangs in offices, restaurants, and private homes.

About the Authors

Polly Wylly Cooper coauthored *The Visitor's Guide to Savannah* with the late Emmeline King Cooper; *Tybee Days: One Hundred Years on Georgia's Playground Island* with Ellen Lyle Taber; and *Sand Between Our Toes*, also with Ellen Taber. She is also the author of *Isle of Hope, Wormsloe and Bethesda*. She and Laura Lawton wrote *Savannah Movie Memories*, a scintillating synopsis of Savannah cinematography. With Ted Eldridge, she coauthored *Savannah Then and Now*. Her *Savannah Safari Walking Adventure* is a fun-filled badge-status activity for Girl Scouts.

After living in England, Scotland, and Illinois, she and her British husband, Tim, now live near the Skidaway River at Isle of Hope, one of Savannah's oldest and most well-preserved communities. She plays accordion with the World-famous Crabettes, Savannah's infamous "senior-ish" musicians.

Laura Connerat Lawton was born in Savannah and lives at White Bluff, where her family has lived for five generations. She attended the Charles Ellis School, the Pape School, and Savannah Country Day School, and graduated from Oldfields School in Glencoe, Maryland. She graduated from Sweet Briar College with a degree in physics, and she has a master's degree in science education from the University of North Carolina at Chapel Hill. She lectured for many years at the planetarium at the Savannah Science Museum and taught science and special education at Windsor Forest High School. She is the author with Polly Cooper of *Savannah Movie Memories* and of the *Discover Savannah* CD-ROM with her cousin Angela Lain. She is the author of *Legendary Locals of Savannah*. She is the mother of two children and the grandmother of five, and enjoys visits to Virginia to spend time with them. She enjoys playing the clarinet with the World-famous Crabettes.

Amir Jamal Touré, J.D., is from Savannah and Hilton Head, South Carolina. His relatives have lived in the area since 1814. He is a graduate of the Walter F. George School of Law at Mercer University in Macon, Georgia. He is the resident scholar for Geechee Kunda, the Gullah Geechee Cultural Center and Museum in Riceboro, Georgia, and is known as a *djeli*, a living historian who can comment on the lives of African people at home and in the diaspora (people far from their homelands.) He brings life to the African spirit in his tour company Day Clean. He was appointed to the Gullah Geechee Culture Heritage Corridor Commission by the U.S. Department of the Interior, and he serves as an adjunct professor at Savannah State University.

Index